REAL POWER TO THE PEOPLE

A Novel Approach to Electoral Reform in British Columbia

R. B. Herath

To: Lakshaman Samarasinghe

With the compliments of the author

R.B.

604-597-1920
info@rbherath.com

University Press of America,® Inc.
Lanham · Boulder · New York · Toronto · Plymouth, UK

www.rbherath.com

Copyright © 2007 by
R. B. Herath

University Press of America,® Inc.
4501 Forbes Boulevard
Suite 200
Lanham, Maryland 20706
UPA Acquisitions Department (301) 459-3366

Estover Road
Plymouth PL6 7PY
United Kingdom

Library of Congress Control Number: 2006938322
ISBN-13: 978-0-7618-3685-8 (paperback : alk. paper)
ISBN-10: 0-7618-3685-3 (paperback : alk. paper)

♾™ The paper used in this publication meets the minimum
requirements of American National Standard for Information
Sciences—Permanence of Paper for Printed Library Materials,
ANSI Z39.48—1984

This book is dedicated to the youth of British Columbia and other democracies around the world.

CONTENTS

LIST OF FIGURES AND TABLES

Figures

Tables

PREFACE AND ACKNOWLEDGEMENTS

British Columbia, Canada, adopted a novel approach to electoral reform in 2004/05. In this approach, the government of British Columbia (BC) gave its people the power to take control over an electoral reform process and make a final decision, bypassing the BC Legislature. The process involved a Citizens' Assembly on Electoral Reform and a binding referendum. The Citizens' Assembly first studied the different electoral systems used in democracies throughout the world and recommended a new electoral system for BC. Later, all adult British Columbians were asked to vote on the recommended electoral system at the referendum. This was the first time a democracy has entrusted its citizens with the power to make a final decision on electoral reform anywhere in the world; it was a unique experiment in the practice of democracy.

In the traditional approach to electoral reform in democracies, a select legislative committee or a special commission first recommends an electoral change and the legislature makes a final decision on the recommended change. At the time BC opted for the new approach, several other provinces of Canada were busy with their own programs for electoral reform using the traditional approach. These Canadian provinces include New Brunswick, Quebec, Ontario and Prince Edward Island. Democracies outside Canada also use the same traditional approach.

Because of its uniqueness, BC's novel approach has gathered attention from other jurisdictions around the world. There are indications that many of them will adopt the novel approach. The Netherlands has already established a Citizens' Assembly on Electoral Reform. Ontario has decided to commence one this fall. California has a growing movement trying to start one in the near future. Meanwhile, British Columbia is poised for a second referendum on the recommendations of its Citizens' Assembly in May 2009.

The main focus of the electoral reform exercise in BC was to look at how citizens' votes are translated into seats in the legislature, and to recommend an electoral system that best reflects voters' wishes in choosing winning candidates at elections. According to the mandate given to the BC Citizens' Assembly, any new electoral system it would recommend for the purpose of translating votes into seats should be consistent with both the Constitution of Canada and the Westminster parliamentary system.

The Citizens' Assembly created to perform this special task and how it accomplished its mission was an amazing human experience. The Assembly consisted of 160 nonpartisan ordinary British Columbians with one man and one woman from each of the 79 existing provincial electoral districts (constituencies) of British Columbia and two from the aboriginal community of the province. All these members were selected by random draw from a pool of registered voters that reflected the gender, age and geographical make-up of British Columbians. Among the members selected, there were tradespersons, office workers, technologists, professionals and specialists, business owners and operators, caregivers, fundraisers, students and retirees. The retirees included a former Assistant Deputy Minister, banker, RCMP officer and a clergyman. Only two of those selected had some practical experience in politics before. One of them had once run as a candidate at a local municipal election. The other was the author, who once cofounded and led a nonviolent, democratic political party in Sri Lanka. In the Assembly discussions, each of the 160 members was expected to represent the interests of all British Columbians, disregarding the electoral districts or the communities they came from. The Assembly Chair, Dr. Jack Blaney, was an additional Assembly member, the 161st. He is a former President of the Simon Fraser University, British Columbia.

The BC Citizens' Assembly process lasted for 11 months, from January to November 2004. It had three main phases: Learning Phase, Public Hearing Phase, and Deliberation Phase. During the Learning Phase, the Assembly members learnt about the different electoral systems that exist in modern democracies and how they function and contribute to the operations of their governing systems. The Assembly members did this with the help of a textbook and a series of presentations by a number of world-renowned political scientists. During the Public Hearing Phase, the Assembly members listened to their fellow British Columbians to understand their electoral concerns and preferences. During this phase, the Assembly members also read written submissions made by the public to the Assembly. During the Deliberation Phase, the Assembly members first reviewed what they learnt during the Learning Phase and what they read and heard during the Public Hearing Phase. Then, they chose two new electoral systems as superior to the existing system and recommended one of them to the public for a final decision.

The referendum on the electoral system finally recommended by the Citizens' Assembly was held on May 17, 2005, along with the 38th general election of the province. At the referendum, British Columbians were asked to state whether they would prefer to retain their existing electoral system or change it to the one recommended by the Citizens' assembly. The level of support required to accept the new electoral system proposed by the Citizens' Assembly was twofold: majority support in more than 48 existing electoral districts and 60% support province-wide. The results of the referendum showed that the new electoral system recommended by the Citizens' assembly had majority support in 77 of the 79 electoral districts and 57.69% support province-wide. Thus, the public support for the newly recommended electoral system vastly exceeded the requirement on one count and missed slightly on the other.

The new Government and the Opposition in BC agree that the referendum results showed strong public support for electoral reform in general. At the same time, those who favoured the recommended new electoral system expressed their concern that there was not enough information available to the public to adequately understand it by the time of the referendum. In response to this new situation, the government has arranged a second referendum on the same basis as before, but with public funding for active information campaigns, to be held in May 2009. The Opposition welcomes the idea of having a second referendum, but would like to see both the electoral systems considered by the Citizens' Assembly as superior to the existing system included in it as possible alternatives. The nongovernmental and voluntary organizations, journalists and the members of the general public that played leading roles in the first referendum have come forward with their own ideas and suggestions for the second referendum. All these have brought back the issues of electoral reform in BC to the forefront of its political agenda.

This book gives a detailed account of the new approach to electoral reform in BC, from the time of the inception of the idea of having a citizens' assembly to the aftermath of the first referendum. The specific details given in the book include the historic context of the new approach to electoral reform, strengths and weaknesses of the process used to implement it, lessons to be drawn from its first time application, and its applicability in other democracies. The book also describes the different electoral systems that exist in modern democracies. Further, the book shows the reader how 160 ordinary British Columbians performed an extraordinary task, making history in the democratic world. The book is written primarily for the lay reader, who may or may not have read books on democracy or electoral systems before. However, readers in both academic and non-academic environments can benefit from it.

This book is unique due to four main reasons. First, it would be the timeliest publication on the subject. Second, the author was directly involved with the novel approach as a Citizens' Assembly member and had past experience in the political field. This helped him to look at the issues under consideration from both academic and practical perspectives. It also helped him to include in the book firsthand information about the reform process. Third, the book presents to the reader the entire electoral reform process in just one reading. Fourth, the book speaks about a number of lessons that can be drawn from this first time experience in democracy and its worldwide applicability.

There are many people I should thank for helping me to write this book. First, let me thank the members and the staff of the Citizens' Assembly on Electoral Reform in BC with whom I had one-on-one discussions on the Assembly process and its accomplishments. I held some of these discussions while the Assembly was still sitting, and the others after the Assembly process came to an end. These discussions helped me to see the Citizens' Assembly approach to electoral reform in BC with many eyes. It was some of these Assembly members who first encouraged me to write a book like this. I also like to thank all the others who helped me and were not directly involved in the BC Citizens' Assembly: local library staff, colleagues at work, friends and family.

Help came from all these wonderful people in a number of ways. Some provided useful information that was not freely available. Some made suggestions for the contents of the book. Some helped to clear computer glitches that slowed me down in preparing its manuscript. Several read and commented on what I was writing, two on a regular basis. The support I got from all of those who helped to write the book became a source of inspiration and extra energy I needed to work on it while still doing my regular day job. I find difficult to mention here the names of all the people who helped, as the list is quite long.

I must, however, mention the names of few people from whom I received special help in completing the manuscript of the book. Bill Holden, a social studies educator, edited the first draft of the manuscript. He holds a B. A. (Honours) degree in History with Political Science minor from the University of Guelph and a B. Ed. Degree in Secondary Social Studies from the Memorial University of Newfoundland. He is currently pursuing an M. A. degree course in Adult Education at the University of British Columbia. He and I spent many evenings together discussing in vivid detail what I had written in my first draft. Then, Professor Ken Carty, Professor of Political Science of the University of British Columbia, read and made comments on the second draft of the manuscript; he was also the Chief Research Officer of the BC Citizens' Assembly. Meanwhile, Neil Turner, a friend and former colleague at work, read and commented on what I was writing from the reader's perspective on a regular basis. I had the benefit of the comments from all of them in further improving the manuscript. Carlee Bilokrely of Surrey public library was ever ready to assist me in my search for library material. Saman Kodituwakku, Joshua Chan, Shelly Gurtata and Byron Green spent considerable time during weekends in preparing the graphs, charts, tables and diagrams for the book. My wife, Hemamala, gave her fullest cooperation and assistance in completing the book, just as in my previous book projects. Our daughters were an additional source of encouragement and assistance.

I sincerely thank all those who helped me to write this book. At the same time, I must say that although all these considerate people contributed to the book in numerous ways, I alone am responsible for the views expressed in it.

R. B. Herath
Surrey, British Columbia
October 2006

ACRONYMS

AV	Alternative Vote
BC	British Columbia
BQ	Block Québécois
CCF	Cooperative Commonwealth Federation
CPC	Conservative Party of Canada
DM	District Magnitude
ECCO	Electoral Change Coalition
FPTP	First-past-the-post
IRA	Irish Republican Party
LP	Liberal Party
LR	Local representation
MLA	Member of the Legislative Assembly
MMM	Mixed Member Majoritarian
MMP	Mixed Member Proportional
MP	Member of Parliament
NDP	New Democratic Party
NOTA	None of the above
NZ	New Zealand
PIRA	Provincial Irish Republican Party
PR	Proportional representation
SBC	Statutes of British Columbia
SFU	Simon Fraser University
SMP	Single Member Plurality
SOCRED	Social Credit (Party)
STV	Single Transferable Vote
UBC	University of British Columbia
UK	United Kingdom
USA	United States of America

CHAPTER 1
INTRODUCTION

1.1   Democracy and Electoral Reform

This book is about a novel approach to the practice of democracy. This approach was first used in British Columbia (BC), Canada, in 2004/05 to select an electoral system that would best reflect the views of British Columbians.

It is important for the reader to have a fair understanding of what democracy means and the historic context of electoral reforms in Canada and British Columbia to fully appreciate the significance of the novel approach. The author devotes this introductory chapter mostly for that purpose.

Historically, democracy is one of the most abused and misconstrued ideas. Latin American military dictatorships were called democracies. Russia run by a few strongmen during its communist era was called a democracy. The United States of America (USA) was called a democracy at the time it still had millions of slaves. Today, many nations where millions of people never exercise their right to vote are being called democracies. Thus the meaning of the word democracy is seemingly up for interpretation. Perhaps, one needs to explore the origin of the word democracy to understand its basic meaning. The word democracy comes from two Greek words: demos, meaning "people" and kratein, meaning "to rule." This implies that the basic meaning of democracy is government by the people. The direct application of this concept requires the participation of all the citizens of a nation in its decision-making process. This is occasionally put to practice in some modern democracies by having citizen-sponsored ballot initiatives, binding referenda and the right to recall elected officials. As the application of direct participatory measures is not always possible, modern democracies commonly use a representative model of democracy. In this model, the people regularly elect a manageable number of officials to make decisions on their behalf for a specified term.

In their decision-making process, the elected officials vote on public policy issues either according to their own conscience or the wishes of the majority of the electorate. They decide which way to vote depending on a number of factors, including their own values, the nature of the specific issues in question, expectations of the electorate and the political culture of the society. Some argue that the elected officials in a representative model should act in the interests of their electors, but not necessarily as their proxies. Those who make this argument also say that the elected officials must have authority to exercise initiative in the face of new challenges. The precepts behind this imply that the electorate vote for people who are more informed on issues than they are, and are more capable of making informed decisions.

There is long history for this way of thinking on the role of elected officials in the representative model of democracy. For example, Edmund Burke (1729–1797), an Anglo-Irish statesman, author, and political philosopher, who served for many years in the British House of Commons, was one of those who spoke against the notion that elected officials should act narrowly as mere advocates for the interests of their electors. An illustration of similar thinking among elected officials in Canada is the abolishment of capital punishment in the 1970s. At the time, opinion polls showed that most Canadians were against the abolition. The Members of Parliament (MPs) in the House of Commons ignored the popular opinion and passed a bill, abolishing the death penalty. In the 25 years since the law was enacted public opinion has harmonized with the legal reality. In this case the elected officials worked against popular sentiment to enact laws, which they collectively felt were in the country's best interest. This way of making decisions by elected officials has come in conflict with the expectation that they should consider the views of their electors. Such expectation is particularly common in democracies with recall provisions, as in BC, or where elected officials have strong links with their constituencies, as in the USA. When elected officials act according to the wishes of their electors, it brings the general public into the decision-making process in an effective manner.

For the purpose of this book, democracy means government with the involvement of adult citizens in the decision-making apparatus of a society. This requires public consultation in policy and the regular exercise of the franchise to elect legislators. The larger the degree of public consultation and the demographically wider the franchise, one would conclude that the higher the level of democracy within the society.

The practice of democracy began in the Athens City-State in 508 B.C. One of the biggest obstacles it faced from the beginning was the impracticability in getting all the adult citizens in the society directly involved in making its governing decisions. For this, the Athenians created a ruling council of five hundred, which included representatives from all the ten tribal groups that lived there at the time. All male citizens over the age of thirty could serve on the council. The council members were appointed by rotation for a term of one year, and no one could serve more than two terms in a lifetime. The concept of governance in a democracy through a body of a manageable number of people's representatives has remained valid ever since. The system of choosing representatives for such governing bodies, however, has since changed and finally taken the shape of elections as we see today some time in the seventeenth century.

Elections are now a common feature in all modern democracies, despite the organizational and structural differences that exist among their governing systems. These differences among democracies have evolved in the process of development of their individual governing systems. The primary factors that have influenced the shaping of a governing system in a democracy include its own history, demography, geography, and cultural and religious diversity. The United Kingdom (UK) has developed a representative, multiparty, unitary governing system. In this governing system, the largest group of representatives in the legislature (Parliament/ House of Commons) that agrees on a common political platform forms the "Government." Such a group can consist of members of a single political party or a coalition of two or more different political parties. In this system of government, both the legislative and executive powers lie in the hands of the legislators. At the same time, all the governing powers of the country are centrally vested; the entire country is one political unit.

In the system of government developed in the USA, the people elect their representatives on party basis, just like in the UK. The representatives, however, do not have the responsibility to form the executive branch of the government. They are responsible for only legislative functions. Americans form their executive branch separately by electing a President and a Vice President through an "Electoral College." The President appoints members of his/her cabinet from among competent men and women in the country. These cabinet members are responsible to the people through President. All the governing powers of the USA are not centrally vested; it has a federal system of government, with a number of political units called States. The USA is formed and run as a federation of these States. Each State elects a Governor as its Chief Executive and members of its own legislature on party basis. The State Governors elected by their respective jurisdictions keep control of local affairs, while the central government led by President handles the affairs common to all the States, which together form the USA. This federal-state relationship developed over time, and was one of the most contentious elements of the early American Republic.

Canada is another democracy having a federal system of government. The federal (central) government is responsible for matters, such as national security, citizenship, foreign policy, currency and postal services, which affect all Canadians. There are 13 provincial or territorial governments at the regional level, and they are responsible for matters, such as education, health care, child welfare, and highways that affect people locally. In some areas, the central government and the regional governments have common responsibility. These common responsibility areas include agriculture, justice, protection of human rights and the environment. Canada is still a constitutional monarchy. The Queen of Canada is its official Head of State; the monarch is the constitutional head of the executive. At elections, people vote on party lines to elect their representatives to the Canadian House of Commons, Provincial Legislatures and the Territorial Assemblies.

Other democracies in the world have developed their own governing systems. Their structural organizations have many features found in the governing systems discussed above. All democracies in the world have a dominant, common feature of electing officials to their legislative and executive bodies, with rare exceptions.

Over the years, people living in democratic countries have made numerous changes to their political systems in search of "more democracy;" more participation has been the prescribed solution to the problems of democracy. Most of the changes implemented in democratic countries have primarily focused on electoral reform. These changes address the issues of franchise (right to vote) and the way in which public desires are reflected in elections. All democracies have extended the right to vote at elections to increasing numbers of their citizens, and finally universal franchise has become the norm. Other significant electoral changes have focused on a variety of electoral issues: the size of electoral constituencies and their borders, ballot design, ballot counting procedures, scrutinizing procedures, safety of citizens voting, eliminating (limiting) the influence of bribes and coercion, and the way of transferring votes-to-seats in the legislature. These changes have shaped and reshaped the way the legislatures and executives of democracies are organized.

1.2   Electoral History of Canada

The history of electoral reforms in any democracy is unique and shows the landmarks in the path of democracy it has chosen. Table 1.1 below lists some of the major electoral reforms that took place in Canada since the formation of its first Legislative Assembly in 1758.

A review of the details given in table 1.1 shows that Canada has implemented electoral changes in three main areas: franchise, provincial representation, and general improvements to the way elections were conducted. Franchise was first limited to male property owners among loyal British subjects 21 years of age or older. The aboriginal people were required to abandon all rights they possessed as members of a band to qualify for federal voting. After Confederation, the eligibility to vote at federal elections was based on the laws of individual provinces. Ontario, Quebec, Nova Scotia and New Brunswick were the only four provinces that formed the Confederation. Their individual rules for voting were not significantly different to those that prevailed at federal level. The *Wartime Elections Act* and the *Military Voters Act* (1917) extended the right to vote in federal elections to all British subjects, male or female, who were active or retired members of the armed forces. This applied to Native Canadians and persons under 21 years of age as well. In addition, the same legislation temporarily granted franchise to civilian men who were not landowners, but had a son or grandson in the armed forces. The same rule applied to women with a father, mother, husband, son, daughter, brother, or sister who had served in the Canadian armed forces.

In 1918, the federal government extended franchise to all women 21 years of age or older. In the general election that followed in 1921, Agnes Macphail became the first woman to secure a seat in the Canadian House of Commons. Meanwhile, in 1920 the federal government had taken full control over the right

Table 1.1: Landmarks in electoral reform in Canada

	Year	What took place
1.	1758	Canadians voted for their first legislative assembly (held in Nova Scotia). Only the Protestant males who owned land and were 21 years of age or older could vote or run for election.
2	1806	Limits placed on how long elected assemblies could stay in power, requiring regular elections.
3	1867	Held the first general election after 1867 Confederation (four provinces only). There were 181 seats, 65 of them for Quebec. Seats of other provinces prorated on the basis of Quebec's per seat population. Eligibility to vote was based on laws of individual provinces.
4	1874	Introduced secret ballots and the practice of holding general elections throughout the country (with some exceptions) on the same day.
5	1915	Extended franchise at federal level to military personnel on active service, and introduced the "Sensational Clause," which guaranteed that no province would have fewer seats in the House of Commons than it had in the Canadian Senate.
6	1917	Extended franchise to cover all British subjects (females included), retired military personnel, civilian men who did not own land but had a son or grandson in the military, and women with an immediate family member in the military.
7	1918	Franchise at federal level was extended to all women of 21 years or more.
8	1919	Allowed women to run for federal elections. Agnes Macphail became the first woman elected (1921).
9	1920	Enacted the Dominion Elections Act, vesting in the federal government the control over the right to vote in federal elections. It also allowed the racial and religious exclusions that already existed in the provinces.
10	1934	Revised the Dominion Elections Act. This revision specifically disenfranchised the Doukhobor religious group in BC, and allowed the continuation of the disenfranchisement of other groups.
11	1946	Increased the number of seats in the House of Commons to 225 (now 9 provinces and two territories in Confederation). Assigned seats among provinces and territories based on total population, without any direct link to Quebec's seats.
12	1960	Extended franchise at federal level to Native Canadians

Table 1.1 (Continued)

	Year	What took place
13	1970	Reduced the voting and candidacy age from 21 to 18. Political parties secured the right to have their names listed on the ballot paper.
14	1974	Passed laws to control election expenses and to make public sources of revenues of parties and candidates.
15	1976	The number of seats in Quebec (now 75) once again became a basis for determining the numbers of seats for other provinces and territories. Introduced special rules in favour of provinces and territories with smaller populations. As a result, the number of seats in the House of Commons increased to 282.
16	1982	Enacted the *Canadian Charter of Rights and Freedoms*. This entrenched in the Constitution the right of all citizens to vote and run for election.
17	1985	Enacted the *Representation Act* of 1985. This required three of the 282 seats to be allocated to the three northern Territories, one for each. The 279 remaining seats were divided amongst the other provinces, based on population and the "Sensational Clause." Also introduced the "Grandfather Clause," stipulating that no province would have fewer seats than what it held in 1976.
18	1992	Improved access to the electoral system for persons of disabilities.
19	1993	Made arrangements to facilitate voting by special ballot for those Canadians who cannot go to their regular or advance polling stations.

Source: Elections Canada (2001) and Elections Canada (2002)

to vote at federal elections. For the next fifty years there were no significant changes to franchise at federal level, except for the enfranchisement of Native Canadians in 1960, until the lowering of voting and candidacy age from 21 to 18 in 1970. Twelve years later, in 1982, the issue of franchise was finally settled with the Canadian Charter of Rights and Freedoms, entrenching the right of all citizens to vote and run for election in the Canadian Constitution.

On the issue of provincial representation, Canada has implemented a series of changes to the level of representation of its provinces in the House of Commons and electoral district boundaries at federal level. The basic principles used in determining a provincial representation formula and electoral district boundaries at the time of Confederation were two-fold: equal representation in the House of Commons and a fair distribution of power for each region of the country in the daily workings of the new federation. Accordingly, each of the four founding provinces was allocated a number of seats in the House of Commons in proportion to its share of the total population, based on the population of Quebec; Quebec had been guaranteed 65 seats in the House of Commons by the Canadian Constitution. This resulted in Ontario having 82 seats, Quebec 65, Nova Scotia 19, and New Brunswick 15, totaling to 181seats.

Some provision had been made at a later stage to recalculate the number of seats for every province after each 10-year census. Meanwhile, the population per seat in Quebec (population of Quebec divided by 65) was used as the electoral quota for determining the specific number of seats for each of the other provinces. The government had also introduced a special measure in 1915 called the "Sensational Clause," to ensure that no province would have fewer seats in the House of Commons than it had in the Canadian Senate.

The provincial representation formula based on the population of Quebec changed in 1946. By then, Confederation had grown to nine provinces and two territories, and the total number of seats in the House of Commons was 225. The new rules divided the 225 seats among the provinces and territories based on their share of Canada's total population; the average population in Quebec was not to be used as a basis anymore. This new provincial representation formula remained in effect for the next thirty years, until the enactment of the *Representation Act* in 1976. This new legislation addressed the concerns over continuing loss of seats by some provinces in seat readjustment exercises, and came up with a three-fold criterion for determining the number of seats for the provinces and territories. First, Quebec was used as a basis for the calculation of the numbers of seats for other provinces or territories, as before 1946. This time, Quebec was entitled to 75 seats, instead of 65. Second, the number of Quebec seats would grow by four in each subsequent seats readjustment. This was intended to slow down the growth of the average population of an electoral district or riding. Third, only the large provinces of population more than 2.5 million were required to allocate seats in strict proportion to Quebec, while the small (population less than 1.5 million) and intermediate (population between 1.5 million and 2.5 million) provinces could enjoy more favourable rules. With the application of these rules, which constituted the "amalgam formula," the total number of seats in the House of Commons rose to 282. Despite its intent, 1972 was the only time this new formula was used. There were serious concerns, especially after the 1981 census, that the amalgam formula would increase the number of seats in the House of Commons by substantial amounts with future population increases.

The next significant change to the representation formula came with the *Representation Act* of 1985, which still remains valid. According to the new representation formula, three of the 282 seats are allocated to the Northwest Territories, Yukon Territory, and Nunavut, one for each. The remaining 279 seats are for the provinces. The electoral quota for the provincial representation is obtained by dividing the total population of the ten provinces by 279. The number of seats for each province is determined by dividing the total population of the province by this electoral quota. Some adjustments have been made to the seat numbers, based on the "Sensational Clause" (1915) and "Grandfather Clause" (1985). The Sensational Clause guarantees that no province would have fewer seats in the House of Commons than it has in the Canadian Senate, while the Grandfather Clause guarantees that no province would have fewer seats than in 1976.

Each change to the number of seats in the House of Commons called for the readjustment of electoral district boundaries. The primary factors that have been considered in such readjustments include the geographic, cultural, demographic, and economic diversity within local communities. For choosing district representatives at elections, Canada has always used the first-past-the-post (FPTP) voting system, where the candidate who gets the highest number of votes, not necessarily more than 50% of the votes cast or registered, in an electoral district wins a seat.

The improvements made to the way federal elections were held include the introduction of secret ballots, limiting the term of elected assemblies, and providing more opportunities to vote for those who had special needs. The items numbered 2, 4, 17 and 18 in Table 1.1 briefly describe these improvements. At the same time, there also have been attempts to change the federal voting system to one of proportional representation (PR), but so far without success. The latest proposal for a federal PR system tabled in the House of Commons in September 2003 was defeated 144–76. The discussions around this topic have not gone away.

Meanwhile, the sudden collapse of the 2004 minority government of Prime Minister Paul Martin resulted from a non-confidence motion in the House of Commons on the night of November 28, 2005, lead to a new wave of calls for changing the voting system at federal level. These calls, which were far-reaching and widespread throughout Canada, brought back the issue of electoral reform to the political agenda of every federal political party at the general election that followed in January 2006. At this election, the governing Liberal Party (lead by Prime Minister Paul Martin) did not make any specific proposals to change the existing voting system that elects Members of Parliament for the House of Commons. The Liberal Party, however, proposed to reform the senate structure allowing some provinces more senators and more free votes in the House of Commons. The main opposition party, The Conservative Party of

Canada (CPC), proposed to consider changes to the existing federal voting system, including proportional representation, single transferable ballot and fixed election dates. The CPC also proposed that any electoral reform would be confirmed by referendum. The CPC further proposed to allow more free votes in the House of Commons, limit individual donations to political parties to $1,000.00, introduce an open bidding process for government advertising and public opinion research, and more. The New Democratic Party (NDP) proposed to replace the existing FPTP federal voting system with one that combines individual constituency-based Members of Parliament with proportional representation. The NDP also proposed a number of other changes that include fixed election dates, by-elections for MPs who change their party affiliations, tighter rules for regulating lobbyists and their fees and expenditures, merit-based appointments instead of ones based on political connections, and more. The Bloc Québécois (BQ) proposed to hold a referendum on proportional representation, adding that their ultimate goal was sovereignty for Québec through constitutional reform. The Green Party of Canada also called for change in the federal voting system.

The results of the January 2006 general election were somewhat similar to those of the 2004 election. The new government formed by the CPC after the 2006 election is also a minority government. In addition, a number of shortcomings inherent in the existing FPTP system became much more evident after the 2006 election. One such shortcoming is the votes-to-seats disproportionality among political parties. For example, at this general election the Bloc Québécois secured 51 seats with 10.5 percent of the popular vote, while the NDP could win only 29 seats with 17.5 percent of the popular vote. At the same time, the Green Party polled 4.5 percent of the popular vote, but failed to win any seats. The results of the 2006 election also showed that the leading CPC received only 2.07 times the number of votes cast for the NDP, but secured 4.28 times the number of seats they won (29). All these have now poised Canada for electoral reform more than ever before.

1.3 Electoral History of British Columbia

The electoral history of British Columbia since it became a province and entered Confederation in 1871 is much more eventful. Table 1.2 below lists the most significant changes made in British Columbia in these areas since 1871. The first general election of the province took place from October through December 1871. It was conducted by a show of hands on nomination day. There were also open poll books on the polling day. At this election, forty-six candidates contested for 25 seats in 12 electoral districts. No one belonged to any political party; there were no organized political parties at the time. The minimum voting and candidacy age was twenty-one. Only British subjects who met certain property and residence requirements were allowed to vote. The total number of registered voters was less than three thousand. There have been many changes to the electoral system in British Columbia since. The notable areas of such changes

Table 1.2: Historic landmarks in electoral reform in BC

	Year	What took place
1	1871	First general election for BC Legislative Assembly. Voting by a show of hands. 46 candidates contested for 25 seats in 12 ridings. Only British subjects 21 yrs. or older who met property & residence requirements voted.
2	1873	Introduced secret ballot, and disqualified federal MPs to sit as provincial MLAs.
3	1874	Disenfranchised Native Canadians and Chinese.
4	1875	Introduced absentee voting.
5	1876	Removed property qualification for voting.
6	1878	Prohibited schoolteachers from voting or campaigning at elections.
7	1883	Removed the prohibition against schoolteachers.
8	1885	Increased the numbers of seats and ridings to 27 and 13, respectively.
9	1890	Increased the numbers of seats and ridings to 33 & 18, respectively, and introduced an election deposit of $200.00.
10	1893	Disqualified those residing in Provincial Homes from voting.
11	1895	Disenfranchised the Japanese living in BC.
12	1898	Increased the numbers of seats and ridings to 38 and 29, respectively.
13	1899	Disenfranchised provincial civil servants.
14	1900	Withdrew the disenfranchisement of provincial civil servants.
15	1902	Increased the numbers of seats and ridings to 42 and 34, respectively.
16	1904	Declared the polling day as a public holiday, giving the voters 4 clear hours to vote.
17	1906	Reduced election deposit to $100.00.
18	1907	Disenfranchised Hindus (East Indians).
19	1915	Increased the numbers of seats and ridings to 47 and 39, respectively.
20	1916	Increased the term of the Legislative Assembly to 5 years, and allowed the clergy to run for elections.
21	1917	Extended franchise to women. Mary Ellen Smith was the first woman elected (1918 Vancouver by-election).
22	1920	Eliminated election deposit.
23	1923	Increased the numbers of seats and ridings to 48 and 40, respectively.

24	1931	Disenfranchised Doukhobor religious group.
25	1940	Banned public opinion polls ("straw votes") and candidature in more than one riding. Also Party on ballot.
26	1945	Allowed members of prohibited groups to vote if they served in World War I or II.
27	1947	Removed Chinese and Hindus prohibition, required proficiency in English or French, recognized Canadian citizenship as qualification to vote in addition to being a British subject, and introduced advance voting.
28	1948	Enfranchised Mennonites and Hutterites.
29	1949	Removed prohibition against Native Canadians and Japanese. Frank Calder was the first Native Canadian (Nishga) to get elected (1949).
30	1952	Used Alternative Vote (Majority) system, dropped voting age to 19, and removed Doukhobor prohibition.
31	1953	Reinstated FPTP system after the 1953 election.
32	1955	Increased the numbers of seats and ridings to 52 and 42, respectively.
33	1956	A Chinese Canadian (Douglas Jung, Vancouver) won a seat for the first time.
34	1966	Increased the numbers of seats and ridings to 55 and 48, respectively.
35	1974	Introduced a requirement for candidates to file a statement of financial and business interests.
36	1978	Increased the numbers of seats and ridings to 57 and 50, respectively.
37	1979	Enabled Blind voters to mark their own ballots by means of templates.
38	1982	Removed prohibition against public opinion polls and the need for proficiency in English or French to qualify for voting. The Charter of Rights and Freedoms removed prohibitions of all remaining groups.
39	1985	Dropped "British subject" from voter qualification, and increased seats and ridings to 69 and 52, respectively.
40	1986	An Indo–Canadian (Moe Sihota) won a seat for the first time. Also introduced out-of-province absentee voting.
41	1990	Abolished multimember districts and increased the numbers of both seats and ridings to 75.
42	1991	Voters approved a referendum to recall MLAs and bring citizen initiatives before the Legislature or to province-wide referendum. Also a woman (Rita Johnson) became premier for the first time.
43	1992	Reduced voting and candidacy age to 18.
44	2000	An Indo–Canadian (Ujjal Dosanjh) became Premier for the first time. Increased numbers of both seats and ridings to 79.
45	2001	Enacted Constitution Amendment Act (SBC 2001 c.36), introducing fixed election dates.

Source: Elections British Columbia (1988) and Elections British Columbia (2002)

include franchise, voting and candidacy age, the number of seats in the legislature, electoral district boundaries, ballot structure, election deposit, electoral
formula (how votes are turned into seats), and opinion polls.

Table 1.2 shows that on the issue of franchise, the provincial government
has passed legislation to disenfranchise different groups of people at different
times: Native Canadians and Chinese (1874), Schoolteachers (1878), Japanese
(1895), provincial civil servants (1899), East Indians/Hindus (1907), and Douk-
hobors (1931). The disenfranchisement of the provincial civil servants was removed after one year in 1990. The government removed the prohibition imposed
on some of the other groups later; Chinese and East Indians/Hindus in 1947,
Mennonites and Hutterites in 1948, and Native Canadians and Japanese in 1949.

Women received franchise in 1917. Finally, the *Charter of Rights and
Freedoms* of 1982 removed the prohibition against all other groups that still remained disenfranchised. The voting and candidacy age in British Columbia
dropped from 21 to 19 in 1952 and from 19 to 18 in 1992.

Table 1.3: Changes in Electoral districts and seats in the BC Legislature

Year	Districts	Seats
1871	12	25
1882	13	25
1885	13	27
1890	18	33
1894	25	33
1898	29	38
1902	34	42
1915	39	47
1924	40	48
1932	39	47
1941	41	48
1956	42	52
1966	48	55
1978	50	57
1985	52	69
1990	75	75
2000	79	79

Source: Elections British Columbia (1988) and Elections British Columbia
(2002)

Meanwhile, British Columbia has increased its number of electoral districts
13 times between 1871 and 2005, as shown in Table 1.3 above. The same table
shows that the number of seats in the legislature has increased 12 times during
the same period.

Table 1.3 also shows that the number of elected representatives in an electoral district (district magnitude) has not been consistent. In 1882, 1894, and 1941 the number of electoral districts increased while the number of seats remained the same. In 1885, the number of seats increased by two (from 25 to 27), while the number of districts remained the same. In 1932, both the numbers of electoral districts and seats decreased by one each; districts from 40 to 39 and seats from 48 to 47. All the changes to the number of electoral districts were associated with the necessary boundary adjustments. *The Electoral Districts Amendment Act* of 2000 confirms the boundaries of the current 79 electoral districts.

The ballot structure of BC elections went through a number of changes since 1871. One major change was the introduction of secret ballot in 1873. Another significant change came in 1940 with the requirement to state the political party or interest of candidates on ballot.

In 1890, the government introduced an election deposit of $200.00. This was later reduced to $100.00 in 1906, and completely eliminated in 1920.

In the provincial election held in 1952, British Columbia used the Majoritarian electoral system (described later in this book) in place of its traditional FPTP system for electing its members of the Legislature. The government conducted the next general election held in 1953 under the same new electoral system. After the 1953 election, however, the government reverted to the traditional FPTP system.

Changes were made to opinion polls on two occasions. The BC government first banned public opinion polls in 1940, and later repealed the prohibition in 1982. Other significant electoral changes that took place in British Columbia include the introduction of absentee voting (1875), advance polling (1947), special regulations requiring candidates for public office to file a written disclosure of financial and business interest (1974), and fixed election dates (2001). The voters of British Columbia also passed a referendum in 1991 on a mechanism to recall their elected members and to bring citizens' initiatives before the legislature or to a province-wide referendum.

1.4   Conventional Approach to Electoral Reform

Generally, all democracies in the world use the same legislative process for making important decisions on electoral changes. A member of the legislature, usually a government member, would first table the proposed changes in the legislature in the form of a legislative bill for deliberation. After deliberation, the legislature would take a vote to see whether there is enough support in the legislature for the proposed changes. The constitution in place dictates the level of support required for a certain bill; some bills may require two-thirds or more support in the legislature. Once a bill is passed with the required level of support in the legislature, it becomes law in the form of a legislative Act. Finally, the legislative Act needs to be formally proclaimed before its implementation in accordance with the constitution.

Before bringing a bill to the legislature on a major electoral change, governments generally get a recommendation from a group of people on the issues in question. For this, governments usually appoint a select legislative committee or an outside Commission. A review of electoral reforms in British Columbia shows that there was a growing trend of preference for Commissions over select legislative committees for making recommendations on electoral matters. For example, between 1871 and 1955, there have been 20 legislative committees compared to 10 Royal and Special Commissions on elections. Since 1955, however, there have been seven Special Commissions in 1965, 1975, 1978, 1982, 1984, 1989, and 1996, but no legislative committees on elections. The situation with the Canadian (federal) government in this regard is similar. In readjusting the federal electoral district boundaries, the House of Commons exclusively depended on legislative committees appointed for that purpose until the 1951 census. Then in the early 1960s, the government decided to assign this responsibility to commissions independent of the legislature and legislators. In November 1964, the Government of Canada passed legislation to this effect and followed suit ever since.

1.5   Novel Approach to Electoral Reform

In 2004, British Columbia took a novel approach to electoral reform. This time, the government of British Columbia decided not to solicit a recommendation from a select legislative committee or a special commission or to follow the traditional legislative process in pursuing electoral reform. Instead, the government decided to give power to the electorate to take full control over the electoral reform process, effectively bypassing the legislature. The process involved a "Citizens' Assembly" of a manageable number of citizens to study and make a recommendation, and a follow-up province-wide binding referendum. This is the first time citizens have been directly entrusted with the power to reshape the political process in any democracy in the world.

In the body of the book, after this introductory chapter, the author reviews the novel approach to electoral reform in British Columbia, and shares his personal experiences as a member of the Citizens Assembly. The second chapter first looks at the calls for electoral reform in British Columbia that led to the novel approach. The third chapter explains how the Citizens' Assembly was created. The fourth, fifth and sixth chapters describe the different stages (acquiring knowledge, listening to the public, and deliberation) of the Assembly process. The seventh chapter describes the efforts made by many to educate the public on the Assembly final recommendation in preparation for the follow up referendum. In the eighth chapter, the author critically examines the way in which the new approach to electoral reform was implemented in British Columbia, and comments on its major strengths and weaknesses. The ninth and last chapter lists some important lessons that can be learnt for the future from the first time application of the new approach, ponders on the scope of its applicability, and concludes the book.

CHAPTER 2
NEW CALLS FOR ELECTORAL REFORM

Chapter one included a summary of numerous electoral changes made in British Columbia since the time of its first general election in 1871. These changes have primarily centred on issues of franchise and fairness of representation in the legislature. All franchise issues have now been settled or are at least subject to judicial review with the enactment of the *Canadian Charter of Rights and Freedoms* (1982). Some issues of fairness of representation still remain unsettled. The most dominant unsettled issue of fairness of representation is the way in which votes are translated into seats in the legislature.

Elections in British Columbia were not fought on formal party lines until 1903. There were nine general elections in the province before 1903, and the candidates who stood for them campaigned for votes on their individual strengths and beliefs. The candidates of 1903 election organized themselves on party lines for the first time, and this has become the norm ever since. Independent candidates (those without any party affiliations) have continued to appear at elections even after 1903, but not in the same numbers as before.

In the elections held after 1903, the electoral system used failed to bring about a clear-cut match between the number of popular votes a party received and its corresponding number of seats in the legislature. A close review of the results of past 38 general elections in British Columbia (including 2005 general election) shows that only in 1903 and 1979 the largest percentage difference between the votes and seats a party had secured fell below 6%. In the 1903 general election, the percentages of popular votes of the first four parties were 46.43%, 37.78%, 7.96%, and 7.36%. The corresponding percentages of seats secured by the parties were 52%, 40%, 5%, and 2%, respectively. These details are graphically represented in Figure 2.1 below. In the 1979 general election, its two major parties shared 45.99% and 48.23% of popular votes and secured 46% and 54% of the seats. None of the other parties that contested these elections received more than 6% of popular votes.

In each of the remaining 36 provincial general elections of British Columbia, the smallest percentage difference between the votes and seats a party had received was greater than 6 percent. In the general elections held in 1909, 1912, 1933, 1972, and 2001, such percentage differences were high as almost 40%. The election held in 2001 resulted in the highest percentage difference

Figure 2.1: Votes-to-Seats Relationship, 1903 General
Election, British Columbia

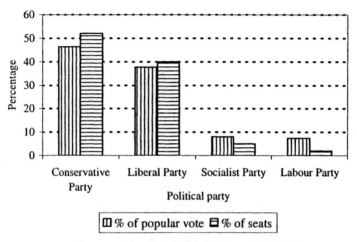

Source: Elections British Columbia (1988)

ever between the votes and seats a party received at 39.48%, with the Liberal Party securing 97% of the seats (77 of the 79) in the legislature with only 57.62% of the popular vote. At this election, the New Democratic Party, the main contender to the Liberal Party, received 21.58% of the popular vote, but could secure only 3% of the seats (2 seats) in the legislature. The Green Party received 12.41% of the popular vote, but failed to secure a single seat in the legislature.

When the disproportionality between votes and seats favours one political party, it always happens at the expense of some of the other political parties that competed with it. In consequence, the parties adversely affected by the votes-to-seats disproportionality were the ones most eager to pursue electoral reform. Over the years, however, all the major political parties in British Columbia have benefited from votes-to-seats disproportionality. For example, the Social Credit Party of British Columbia was the beneficiary of the votes-to-seats disproportionality at eight general elections held in 1952, 1956, 1960, 1963, 1966, 1969, 1975, and 1986. The Liberal Party of British Columbia became the beneficiary in seven other general elections held in 1916, 1920, 1924, 1933, 1937, 1941 and 2001, while the New Democratic Party benefited in the general elections held in 1972, 1991, and 1996. All the three parties have also faced *losses* from the votes-to-seats disproportionality. In comparison, the Liberal Party has suffered the most. The losses due to votes-to-seats disproportionality in the six general elections held in 1909, 1912, 1928, 1952, 1953 and 1956 put this party in a distinct disadvantage.

The biggest single loss as a percentage difference between votes and seats experienced by the Liberal Party was 28.21%. This occurred in the 1909 general election, when it won 33.41% of the popular vote and got only 5% of the seats (2 of 42). In the general election of 1912, the Liberal Party received 25.37% of votes but failed to win any seats. The extent of losses faced by the Social Credit Party and the New Democratic Party were of a lesser magnitude. Figure 2.2 below graphically demonstrates the Liberal Party's biggest windfall in 2001, while the Figures 2.3 and 2.4 that follow show its losses in 1909 and 1912.

Figure 2.2: Votes-to-Seats Relationship, 2001 General Election, British Columbia

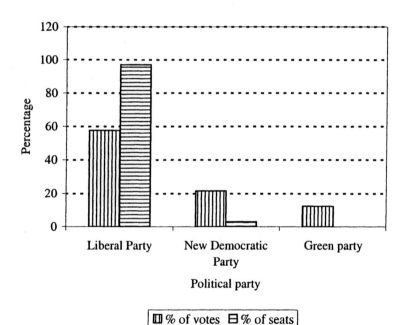

Source: Elections British Columbia (2002)

Despite the votes-to-seats disproportionality among the different political parties at elections, the party that won the highest number of popular votes has generally emerged as the winning party—with the highest number of seats in the legislature. This did not happen in the three general elections held in 1941, 1952, and 1996. In the 1941 election, the Cooperative Commonwealth Federation received the highest number of popular votes (33.36%—151,440) and secured 14 seats. The party that came second in the popular vote was the Liberal party. It received 32.94% of the popular vote (149,525), but won 21 seats, becoming the main party in the legislature. In the 1952 election, the Cooperative Commonwealth Federation won 18 seats with 34.3% (231,756, second count) of the popular vote, while the Social Credit Party won 19 seats with only 30.18% (203,932, second count) of the popular vote. In the 1996 election, the New Democratic Party outnumbered the Liberal Party by 6 seats (39 and 33 seats) with less popular votes by 2.5% (42.0% and 39.5%). All the three elections (1941, 1952, and 1996) resulted in governments formed and led by the party with the highest number of seats, not votes. The results of each of these elections did become a subject of serious discussion among the voters, politicians and academics of the province. Following each of the elections, there was general consensus on the need for electoral reform.

Figure 2.3: Votes-to-Seats Relationship, 1909 General Election, British Columbia

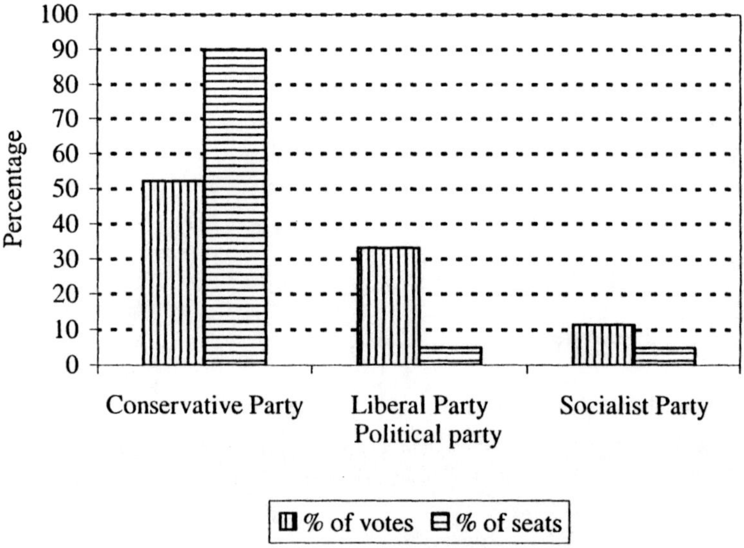

Source: Elections British Columbia (1988)

The electoral system change that occurred in 1952 (Chapter 1), however, did not correct the imbalances in the vote-to-seat transformation. With this change, the Majoritarian System (explained later in the book) was used in the two general elections held in 1952 and 1953. In the 1952 election, the Liberal Party secured only 13% (6) of the seats with 25.26% (170,674) of the popular vote. This benefited the Social Credit Party with a windfall of 40% of the seats (19 of 48) with only 30% of the popular vote. The Liberal Party faced a similar situation in 1953, with only 8% of the seats from 23.36% of the popular vote. After the 1953 general election, British Columbia abolished the Majoritarian System and reverted to the FPTP system. All elections held after 1953 have used the FPTP system.

Figure 2. 4: Votes-to-Seats Relationship, 1912 General
Election, British Columbia

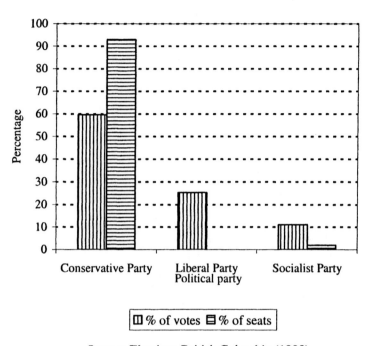

□ % of votes ⊟ % of seats

Source: Elections British Columbia (1988)

The 1996 general election results, in particular, renewed the call for electoral reform in British Columbia in an unprecedented manner. After this election, the New Democratic Party formed a majority government with 52% of the
seats (39 out of 75) secured by 39.5% of the vote. The Liberal Party that secured
44% of the seats (33 out of 75) with 42.0% of the vote became the official opposition. There were two other parties in the legislative assembly: The BC Reform
Party and The Progressive Democratic Alliance. The BC Reform Party had received 9.3% of the vote that translated into only 3% of the seats (two seats),
while the Progressive Democratic Alliance earned 5.8% of the vote that translated into 1% of the seats (one seat). Thus, while most of the parties had been affected by the votes-to-seats disproportionality, the New Democratic Party had
formed a majority government with less than 40% of the vote. The parties that
formed majority governments in similar situations in 1941 and 1952 had received still less voter support at 32.94% and 27.20%, respectively. The calls for
electoral reform after the 1996 election results were, however, much louder and
broader than ever before, as discussed later in this chapter.

The renewed calls for electoral reform after 1996 general election focused primarily on the issues of fairness in transferring votes to seats in the legislature. There was general agreement among the concerned parties that the votes-to-seats disproportionality in the existing FPTP electoral system must be corrected. At the same time, some of the concerned parties brought up ideas for a new process for doing that. By this time, there had been criticism about the process the Canadian government used in its failed attempts to change the country's constitution through the Meech Lake Accord (1991) and the Charlottetown Accord (1992). As Loenen (2004) noted, there was general agreement that this process failed primarily due to the following three reasons:

1. It tried to solve too many issues;
2. The number of people at the decision-making table was too small; Only the premiers of the provinces took part in the Meech Lake Accord decision-making, and 12 prominent Canadians (Spicer Commission) from across the country lead by Keith Spicer, the former commissioner of Official Languages, in the case of the Charlottetown Accord; and
3. Those who took part in the decision-making process came to the table representing particular interests, and were there to get something for those whom they represented.

The criticisms of the process used in Meech Lake and Charlottetown Accords had surfaced repeatedly during the subsequent discussions on electoral reform in British Columbia. In June 1991, the Canada West Foundation recommended that a Constituent Assembly of ordinary citizens with no specific political affiliations would be a more suitable mechanism for constitutional reform rather than the failed Meech Lake process. Later in 1996, the same organization published "*A Road Map to Constituent Assemblies Around the World.*" This work was designed as a teaching aid for the classroom, while having the dual purpose of generating public debate on new initiatives in participatory democracy. For example, in his teaching assignment on the Canadian Constitution at Trinity Western University, Nick Loenen, a former Social Credit MLA of the BC legislature and the author of *Citizenship and Democracy* (Dundurn Press, 1997), asked his undergraduate students to consider a Constituent Assembly of ordinary citizens for constitutional amendments in 1995–96 semesters (Loenen, 2004). In 1997, a group of advocacy groups and smaller political parties in British Columbia formed a coalition named the Electoral Change Coalition (ECCO). It was Canada's first multi-partisan electoral reform organization. It included the BC Green Party, BC Reform Party, Progressive Democratic Alliance, BC Family coalition Party, and Marxist-Leninist Party. The BC Liberal Party first joined ECCO and later withdrew from it. ECCO's main objective was to advocate an alternative voting system for British Columbia and to lobby for a referendum on electoral reform. While ECCO was making headway in their mission, Nick Loenen founded another multi-partisan citizens' organization called Fair Voting BC in mid-1998. From its inception, this organization also lobbied for a referendum on electoral reform, in particular voting system reform. In 1999, ECCO and Fair Voting BC merged together, and continued to function under the name of Fair Voting BC.

Meanwhile, after its defeat to a party with less popular support at the 1996 general election, the Liberal Party gave serious consideration for electoral reform. The Liberal Party Leader Gordon Campbell and other members conducted many discussions, exploring alternative electoral systems and a process for change. In a particular discussion he held in January 1997 with Martyn Brown, who later became his principle political advisor in 1998, Campbell had shown his strong view that the people–not politicians–should drive the electoral reform process (M. Brown, personal communication, June 14, 2005).

While the discussions on electoral reform were gathering momentum within the Liberal Party, Nick Loenen, the founder of Fair Voting BC, made a number of suggestions for their consideration. In one of his suggestions made in 1998, Nick Loenen proposed that the BC Liberal Party should commit to a two-step referendum process for electoral reform, similar to the one used by New Zealand in 1992 and 1993 (Loenen, 2004). This and other suggestions made by Nick Loenen and Fair Voting BC may have further influenced the Liberal Party and its leader on their commitment to allow the people to take control of the electoral reform process.

Then, at the BC Liberal Party Convention held in Kelowna on April 17, 1999, the Liberal Party Leader Gordon Campbell confirmed his commitment to such a course of action. At the Convention, he specifically said:

> It's time we gave the people of BC the right to determine how they want to elect their MLAs. We are going to tackle that challenge within our first term in government. An independent Citizens' Assembly will be selected, similar to how a jury is selected. That Assembly will be asked to review and publicly debate all the options for electoral reform–from the status quo, to preferential ballots, to proportional representation–you name it. It will look at how those systems have worked here and in other jurisdictions, and it will summarize the pros and cons. And at the end of the day, if the Assembly recommends changes to our electoral system, those changes will be put to the people, by way of referendum. Democracies should be designed by the people–not for the power-brokers (M. Brown, personal communication, June 14, 2004).

This was the first time the Constituent Assembly was publicly referred to as "Citizens' Assembly."

Five months later, Gordon Campbell publicly elaborated on the same commitment in the speech he made to the Union of BC Municipalities in his capacity as the Opposition Leader on September 30, 1999. In this speech he said,

> We will also give all British Columbians a say on electoral reform. A Citizens' Assembly will be selected, similar to a jury that will look at all the options for electing MLAs. Proportional representation, first-past-the-post, the preferential ballot–you name it–they'll all be debated in regional public forums. And if that Assembly recommends a change to the present system, that option will be put

to a province-wide referendum (M. Brown, personal communication, June 14, 2004).

In the fall of 1999, the initial *New Era for British Columbia* document issued by the Liberal Party of BC lead by Gordon Campbell did, among other things, reiterate the same commitment on electoral reform. This 8-page document printed on white paper in red, black and blue ink contained the following two bullets:

- Appoint a Citizens' Assembly on Electoral Reform, similar to how a jury is selected, that will be responsible for assessing all possible models for electing MLAs, including proportional representation, preferential ballots and "first past the post."

- The Assembly will hold public hearings throughout BC, and if it recommends changes to the current electoral system, that option will be put to a province-wide referendum (M. Brown, personal communication, June 14, 2004).

None of the other parties in British Columbia, including the ruling New Democratic Party, had put forward a similar suggestion for electoral reform.

When the results of the 2001 general election shifted the benefits of the votes-to-seats disproportionality to the BC Liberal Party, the BC Green Party came to the center stage of electoral reform in British Columbia. Immediately after the election, the Green Party launched a citizens' initiative under BC's *Recall and Initiative Act* to bring proportional representation to the forefront of the new Liberal Government's legislative agenda. According to the Act only a registered voter, not a political party or any other group, could apply to the chief electoral officer to initiate such a process. Adriane Carr, the Leader of the Green Party, initiated the process in her individual capacity as a registered voter in British Columbia. Eight days after the election on May 24, 2001, she first publicly announced that she would follow the process required by the *Recall and Initiative Act* to bring a proposal for proportional representation to the Liberal Government's legislative agenda. The Act requires a draft of the proposed legislation to be first submitted to the Chief Electoral Officer of the province, followed by a 60-day notice period, and a 90-day period for collecting the stipulated minimum number of province-wide signatures. At least 10 percent of the registered voters in each of the BC's provincial electoral districts are required to sign the initiative. There is also a 30-day period for the registration of the opponents to a new legislation submitted under the Act.

On March 14, 2002, the Chief Electoral Officer "accepted in principle" the proportional representation proposal submitted by Ms. Carr. The new electoral system proposed was similar to the one used in New Zealand and Germany, and was supported by many political parties, citizen groups, labour groups, businesses, and individuals. No person or organization registered as an opponent to her proposal by the set deadline of April 15, 2002. Then the signature-gathering period began on May 13, 2002. Thousands of volunteers were in the field to gather signatures in all electoral districts in the province during the next 90 days. The total number of signatures collected was 98,165, but the required number was 212,473. As a result, Ms. Carr's initiative to include her proportional representation proposal to the Liberal Government's agenda did not proceed beyond that point.

The NDP, which also failed to secure enough seats to match its popular votes at the 2001 general election, concluded in a report by the fall of 2001 some general plans to address electoral reform. Later at their Leadership and Policy Convention of November 2003, they passed a resolution in support of proportional representation (PR). This resolution did not advocate any particular PR system (Mixed Member Proportional, Single Transferable Vote, or any other). It proposed the move for proportional representation with the following undertakings:

- It would pursue proportional representation as an election platform in 2005;
- It would ensure that when the NDP returns to government they are inclusive in designing the PR system;
- It would ensure that rural representation is not excessively eroded in any new electoral system; and
- It would ensure that a fair and workable threshold for qualifying parties for seats in the legislature.

Meanwhile, the new Liberal Government headed by Premier Gordon Campbell had been extremely busy during its first year in office with other priorities. The time of convening a Citizens' Assembly on electoral reform as promised by him before the election passed unnoticed. Before the election, on March 8, 2001, he responded to a question on electoral reform by David Ingram on Shaw Cable saying, "The Citizens' Assembly will be up and running one year after we take office. If changes are recommended and accepted by the people, the election 2005 will be conducted under the new rules" (Loenen, 2004).

After benefiting from the votes-to-seats disproportionality inherent in the existing electoral system at the 2001 general election, the Liberal Party and its new government may not have had the same enthusiasm or urgency to convene a Citizens' Assembly on electoral reform. History shows that governments in similar situations both within and outside Canada had conveniently put aside any election promises they may have made to change their existing electoral systems. In 1976, Rene Levesque and his party promised proportional representation to Quebec. They did not keep this promise after winning the next election, benefiting from the votes-to-seats disproportionality of the existing electoral system to the detriment of their political opponents. Then in 1984, Jean Chrétien, the Leader of the federal Liberal Party of Canada, made a similar election promise. He said that bringing in proportional representation would be one of his first acts as prime minister. He became Prime Minister and remained in power for three consecutive terms, but did not try to keep his election promise on electoral reform. The experiences in other democracies are very much similar.

In his role as the new Premier of British Columbia, Gordon Campbell may have been under pressure by at least some of his cabinet members and party supporters not to change the existing electoral system. Premier Gordon Campbell, however, showed his continued desire and willingness to convene a Citizens' Assembly on electoral reform as promised before the 2001 election. Instead of succumbing to the opposition within his own party, he led the party, cabinet and caucus on the issue and forged ahead with his original plan to convene a Citizens' Assembly on Electoral Reform. On September 20, 2002, the new Liberal Government commissioned Gordon Gibson, one time provincial Liberal Party leader, to make a specific recommendation by December 15, 2002, on the logistics of setting up a Citizens' Assembly on Electoral Reform. The Terms of Reference for this exercise stipulated that the Citizens Assembly must be representative, randomly selected and affordable.

In his assignment, Gordon Gibson first listened to practicing politicians of different viewpoints, representatives of the First Nations, business leaders, trade union leaders, expert academics, public servants and other interested British Columbians to learn their views on the subject. The politicians he counseled include a number of MLAs from the governing Liberal Party and leaders of a number of other BC parties. The BC party leaders he counseled include Joy MacPhail (NDP), Adriane Carr (Green Party), Chris Delaney (Unity Party) and Ron Gamble (B.C. Reform Party). In the acknowledgements in his final report, Gordon Gibson comments that all these politicians were unanimously supportive of the concept of the Citizens' Assembly. The First Nations' representatives consulted include Herb George, Executive Member of the First Nations Summit, and Stewart Philip, President of the Union of B.C. Indian Chiefs.

Gordon Gibson's final report, entitled *"Report on the Constitution of the Citizens Assembly on Electoral Reform,"* that laid down a strategy for a Citizens' Assembly was submitted to Geoffrey Plant, Attorney General of British Columbia, on December 23, 2002. It was a 32-page document making specific recommendations on many aspects of the proposed Citizens' Assembly. These aspects include the Assembly's mandate, process for change, legislative requirements, size of membership, criteria and process for selecting members and the chair, remunerations to members, tripartite phasing of the assembly (education, public consultation, and deliberation), timeframe for the Assembly process, decision-making procedures, public access to Assembly meetings, and the Assembly budget.

Later, the Throne Speech of February 11, 2003, promised that the Liberal Government would proceed with the long promised Citizens' Assembly on Electoral Reform, and that the Legislature would be asked to initiate the process by resolution within weeks. The Throne Speech also indicated that should the Citizens Assembly recommend a change to the existing voting system, it would be placed before all British Columbians in a referendum in conjunction with the next BC general election on May 17, 2005. The government's intention was to create the Citizens' Assembly by an Order-in-Council passed by the legislature and signed by the Lieutenant Governor General.

The government first introduced a motion in the legislature to establish the Citizens Assembly on April 28, 2003. In introducing the motion to the legislature, Geoffrey Plant, the Attorney General of the province, tabled the Assembly's terms of reference and the duties of the Chair and nominated Dr. Jack Blaney as the Chair. The Attorney General also proposed the formation of a Special Committee of the Legislature to review the nomination of Dr. Blaney and his selections of Assembly senior staff. It was also proposed that the committee would receive interim reports from the Chair on the Assembly work.

During the discussion stage of the motion, Joy McPhail, the leader of the New Democratic Party in the Legislature, proposed an amendment to the motion to allow the Assembly to add up to four additional members ensuring representation by all communities in the province, including the First Nations. At the end, the legislature defeated the proposed amendment, and unanimously approved the original motion on April 30, 2003. On the same day, the Legislature also set up a Special Committee on the Citizens' Assembly on Electoral Reform as proposed by the Attorney General. It consisted of seven sitting Members of the Legislative Assembly (MLAs), six from the ruling Liberal Party (LP) and one from the New Democratic Party (NDP), and two staff members. The names of those who were selected to work on this committee are given in Appendix 1. The legislative process for establishing the Citizens' Assembly ended with the signing of the required Order-in-Council by the Lieutenant Governor General. This Order-in-Council was later amended in December 2003 to add two aboriginal members to the Assembly.

Following a review by the Special Committee Dr. Jack Blaney was formally appointed as the Chair of the Citizens' Assembly in mid-May 2003. He is a former president of Simon Fraser University in British Columbia, and had been instrumental in the creation of its downtown Vancouver campus and the Morris J. Wosk Centre for Dialogue where the Citizens' Assembly later met. Dr. Blaney is well known for his experience and expertise in helping groups work together. The establishment of a Citizens' Assembly office followed the formal appointment of Dr. Blaney as its Chair. Some space in a downtown Vancouver office building was found for this purpose.

The final configuration of the Citizens' Assembly as approved by the legislature and the amended Order-in-Council (December 2003) closely followed Gordon Gibson's original proposals. There were, however, three significant changes. These changes were primarily about the size of the Assembly, the extent of support needed at a province-wide referendum to ratify the recommendations made by the Citizens' Assembly, and some specific measures to ensure aboriginal representation in the Citizens Assembly. The size of the Assembly increased from 79 members to 158 to include one man and one woman from each of the existing electoral districts; two more members were later added to represent aboriginal interests. The extent of support needed to ratify Assembly recommendation also increased from 50%+1 required to pass a referendum by the existing laws to 60% of valid votes province-wide and majority support in 60% or more of the existing electoral districts.

With the above arrangements, all legislative and legal provisions had been put in place for a fresh round of electoral reform in British Columbia. There was unprecedented political will in the province to examine possible options for electoral reform. And all political parties of British Columbia both within and outside the Legislature had given their unconditional support to the proposed new Citizens' Assembly approach for reform. The government had committed public funds up to $5.5 million dollars for the implementation of the new approach. The reform process could now begin with a fully created Citizens' Assembly on Electoral Reform. We will examine in the next chapter how this was accomplished.

CHAPTER 3
CREATION OF THE CITIZENS' ASSEMBLY

3.1   Founding Documents:

The Terms of Reference of the Citizens' Assembly on Electoral Reform (Ministry of Attorney General: BC [Ministry], 2003a), Duties of the Chair of the Citizens Assembly (Ministry, 2003b) and the Terms of Reference for the Special Legislative Committee on the Citizens Assembly (Citizens' Assembly, 2004n) constituted the founding documents of the Citizens Assembly on Electoral Reform. The terms of reference of the Citizens' Assembly outlined the specific mandate of the Assembly, a process for its decision-making, and member disciplinary procedures. The same document vested in the Chair the power to decide on the procedure for the conduct of the Assembly business.

3.1.1 Assembly Mandate

The first four clauses of the Terms of Reference of the Citizens' Assembly on Electoral Reform (Ministry, 2003a) defined the mandate of the Citizens' Assembly as follows:

1. The Citizens' Assembly must assess models for electing Members of the Legislative Assembly and issue a report recommending whether the current model for these elections should be retained or another model should be adopted.
2. In carrying out the assessment described in section 1, the Citizens' Assembly must consult with British Columbians and provide British Columbians with the opportunity to make submissions to the Citizens Assembly in writing, and orally at public meetings.
3. If the Citizens' Assembly recommends under section 1 the adoption of a model for electing Members of the Legislative Assembly that is different from the current model,

      a.   The model must be consistent with both the Constitution of Canada and the Westminster parliamentary system, and

      b.   The model must be described clearly and in detail in its report.

4.   The assessment described in section 1 must

      a.   Be limited to the manner by which voters' ballots are translated into seats in the Legislative Assembly, and

      b.   Take into account the potential effect of its recommended model on the system of government in British Columbia.

The mandate of the Citizens' Assembly was clearly limited to look at how citizens' votes are translated into seats in the legislature. Any new electoral system the Citizens Assembly would recommend for the purpose of translating votes into seats should be consistent with both the Constitution of Canada and the Westminster parliamentary system. The Citizens' Assembly would make its decisions by a vote of the majority of the Assembly, and the deadline given to the Assembly for the submission of its final report to the Attorney General was December 15, 2004.

3.1.2 Duties of the Chair

The duties of the Chair covered a broad spectrum of responsibilities. These responsibilities include the supervision of a specified process for the creation of the Citizens' Assembly with the required number of members, chairing the Assembly, and all administrative functions of the Assembly (Ministry, 2003b). The process for the creation of the Assembly was designed to ensure that its members would be broadly representative of the adult population of British Columbia, particularly respecting age, gender, and geographic distribution. At the same time, some categories of people (explained later) were disqualified for Assembly membership to ensure that the Assembly work would remain as unbiased as possible.

The administrative responsibilities assigned to the Chair included the selection of the needed staff, managing the Assembly budget, and providing the members of the Assembly with the educational resources they required to carry out their duties. The Chair was also required to prepare the rules of procedure for the conduct of the Assembly business consistent with the Terms of Reference and the Duties of the Chair and present these rules for adoption by the Assembly at its first meeting.

3.2 Staff Selection

The staff selection process began in June 2003 and continued till September 2003. In all, twenty-four full and part-time staff members were recruited in five different areas: policy and procedures (1), research and education (2), media and communication (3), administration (5), and group facilitation (13). One of the special qualities required for a staff position was political objectivity; only those who did not have preference on any particular electoral system over the others were considered for these positions. The staff were also expected to meet stiff criteria in both experience and expertise to be eligible for their positions.

This enabled the Citizens' Assembly to recruit a group of twenty-four staff members of outstanding ability and recognition in their respective areas. For example, Dr. Leo Perra, Chief Operating Officer, had 35 years of experience as an educator and administrator in the post-secondary education system of British Columbia. Among his many recognitions and awards, Dr. Perra has been honoured with the *Order of British Columbia* in 2001. Professor Ken Carty who was recruited as the Chief Research Officer is one of Canada's foremost authorities on electoral systems. He is the former head of the Political Science Department of the University of British Columbia (UBC). He has published widely on the electoral recruitment, leadership and activities of political parties in Canada. Professor Sharman, Associate Research Officer, joined UBC in 2002 after a distinguished career at the University of Western Australia. While he is an expert on Australian politics, he has a longstanding interest in Canadian politics. Marilyn Jacobson, Director of Communication, has taught public relations and communications courses at both Trinity Western University and University of Victoria. Her previous experience also includes a number of years with TELUS/ BCTEL where she was responsible for executive and internal communication, issues and project management, and government relations. Cathy Stooshnov, Office Manager, had acted as an Administrator with several major commissions of inquiry in British Columbia before. She was also well experienced in all aspects of project and event management and media liaison. The thirteen Discussion Group Facilitators were postgraduate students at BC Universities interested in the Citizens Assembly process. Appendix 2 gives a complete list of the twenty-four staff members and the facilitators.

3.3   Member Selection

The selection of the members of the Citizens' Assembly began after the recruitment of the key staff members. The Terms of Reference and the Duties of the Chair had given clear guidelines for the member-selection process. These guidelines had been drafted to ensure that the Assembly would be broadly representative of the adult population of British Columbia, particularly respecting age, gender and geographical distribution. Figure 3.1 on the following page diagrammatically shows the different stages of the member-selection process.

3.3.1 First round of random selection

According to the guidelines, the starting point in the member-selection process was to randomly draw a stratified sample of names from the provincial voters'

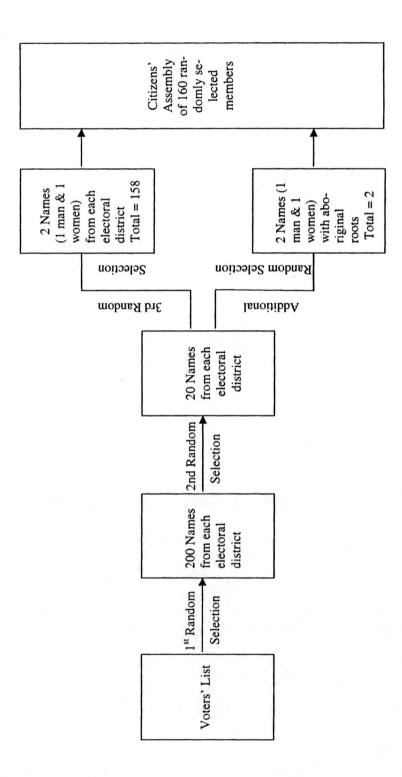

Figure 3.1: Citizens' Assembly Random Selection Process

list under the supervision of the chief electoral officer of the province, subject to his approval. The criteria for this random selection included the following:

- an equal number of names for each of the 79 provincial electoral districts;
- an equal number of men's and women's names; and
- the names drawn must reflect the age distribution of the provincial population aged 18 and over.

By the end of September 2003, such a stratified sample of names had been drawn, with 200 names from each of the 79 provincial electoral districts; the list of each electoral district had names of 100 men and 100 women, and their age distribution reflected its make-up by age. In total, there were 15,800 names from all over the province.

3.3.1.1 Letter of invitation

As the next step in the member-selection process, Dr. Blaney, the Chair of the Assembly, mailed a letter in the first week of October 2003 to each of the 15,800 chosen individuals, inviting them to participate in the Citizens' Assembly member-selection process. This letter accompanied basic information about the Citizens' Assembly, including what it would do, commitment expected from its members, member-compensation package, member-selection process, disqualifications for membership, and a reply form.

According to the information supplied, the work of the Assembly would proceed in three phases:

1. Learning phase;
2. Public hearing phase; and
3. Deliberation phase.

In the Learning phase, the members would learn about the existing electoral system in British Columbia and other electoral systems used around the world, during six weekends in the coming winter 2003/04. The public hearings would take place throughout the province in the spring of 2004 for the Assembly members to hear their fellow citizens' comments and suggestions on electoral reform. During the deliberation phase planned for five weekends in September, October and November 2004, the Assembly would decide whether the existing electoral system should be changed, and, if so, make a recommendation for a new system. The Assembly would finally report its recommendation to the Attorney General and the people of the province by December 2004. If any change was recommended, the Assembly would also frame a referendum question on the issue. The Assembly meetings would take place at the Morris J. Wosk Centre for Dialogue, a unique meeting facility in the Downtown Campus of the Simon Fraser University (SFU).

On member-commitment, it was required that all members fully committed to regular attendance, preparation and participation. In their preparation for the assembly meetings, the members were expected to read and discuss the materials provided to them and share ideas and opinions with other members. As a compensation for their efforts, the members of the Assembly would receive an honorarium of $150.00 per meeting day. Regarding the member-selection process, Dr. Blaney's letter said:

> You are one of 200 people randomly chosen by Elections BC from the voters list in your riding (electoral district). By replying to this letter, your name will be put into a pool for your electoral district. Twenty people will be randomly selected from this pool and invited to a regional information meeting. At that meeting, two people from each electoral district – one man and one woman – will be selected for membership on the Citizens' Assembly. Travel costs for the selection meeting will be covered (J. Blaney, personal communication, October 6, 2003).

Thus, the member-selection process in any electoral district would go through three stages of random selection, first drawing 200 names from its voters' list, then 20 names from those who responded to the initial invitation letters, and finally two names, a man's and a woman's, from those 20 names.

3.3.1.2   Eligibility & disqualifications for membership

The information package that accompanied Dr. Blaney's letter also laid down some ground rules for eligibility for Citizens' Assembly membership. These rules stipulated some essential requirements and disqualifications for membership. The specific requirements for membership included the following:

1. Living within the electoral district at the time of Dr. Blaney's invitation letter;
2. Living in British Columbia until the Assembly works conclude in December 2004; and
3. Ability to attend the selection meeting scheduled for his or her electoral district.
4. Ability to understand, speak, read and write the English language;
5. Ability to engage in a process of learning about electoral systems;
6. Willingness to interact with fellow members and be open to the opinions of others; and
7. Availability to attend meetings and devote the time necessary to fully engage in the Assembly process.

The disqualifications for the Citizens' Assembly membership were as follows:

1. a person who was not a Canadian citizen;

2. a person not resident in British Columbia;
3. a person under the age of 18;
4. a judge, justice or court referee;
5. a member or officer of the Parliament of Canada or of the Privy Council of Canada;
6. a member or officer of the Legislature or of the Executive Council;
7. an elected member of a local government, including a school board or a park board;
8. a candidate in the last 2 federal, provincial, municipal or regional district elections;
9. an official representative or agent of a person identified in the above clause eight;
10. an immediate family member of a sitting Member of the Legislative Assembly;
11. a current officer or official representative of a registered provincial political party;
12. a chief or band councillor elected under the Indian Act; and
13. an elected member of a Nisga'a Government as defined in the Nisga'a Final Agreement.

These eligibility rules (requirements and disqualifications) had been carefully drafted to ensure that the Assembly members finally selected would represent British Columbians, reflect their views, and be able to work together as a group as free of bias as possible. Dr. Blaney's invitation letter had requested its recipients to confirm their interest and eligibility for the Citizens' Assembly membership by completing the enclosed Reply Form by a date (in three weeks) shown on the letter. A postage paid envelope was also enclosed. Those who were either not interested or not eligible for membership did not have to return the Reply Form.

The author was pleasantly surprised and intrigued by Dr. Blaney's letter of invitation. While reading it, he felt as if he won a million dollar lottery. For him, the letter opened a new door, though not fully yet, to reenter the world of politics; it was 20 years since he left his country of origin, Sri Lanka, when his movement for democracy (a nonviolent democratic party) in that country was disarrayed by the eruption of a civil war. Later, he researched possible political solutions to the civil war through electoral reform and published a book, *Sri Lankan Ethnic Crisis: Towards a Resolution*, only a year ago. With this background, he thought that the Citizens' Assembly would be the right place at the right time for him to learn more about electoral systems and how they work in other democracies. So, he immediately returned to Dr. Blaney the reply form that accompanied his letter, expressing a great desire to be a member of the Citizens' Assembly. The author, however, knew that his chances of getting selected as an Assembly member would depend on two more random selections yet to come.

3.3.2 Second round of random selection

As required by the member-selection process, the Citizens' Assembly office placed the names of those responded to Dr. Blaney's letter of invitation confirming their interest and eligibility (Reply Form) in their respective electoral district pools. After that, 20 names were randomly selected from each of the pools for the final round of selection. The new list of candidates to be further considered for selection was now ten times shorter than the previous list, at both district and provincial levels; the number of candidates in each district has reduced from 200 to 20, while the total number representing the province has reduced from 15,800 to 1,580.

As the next step in the selection process, the office of the Citizens' Assembly sent a new letter signed by Dr. Blaney at the end of October 2004, inviting those randomly selected from the electoral district pools to their final selection meetings. These selection meetings were held regionally, facilitating the final selection of members for a number of electoral districts in one location. In this new letter of invitation, Dr. Blaney explained to the invitees that the final selection meetings were an opportunity for them to learn more about the Citizens' Assembly, ask questions, and, if still interested to be a Citizens' Assembly member, place their names into a "hat" from which the names of one man and one woman would be drawn for each electoral district. Attendance at the regional meeting was compulsory to remain eligible for final selection. Those who wished to attend their regional meetings had to return a Reply Form by a set deadline, reconfirming their interest in being a member of the Citizens' Assembly, their eligibility for membership, and their availability for the regional meeting assigned to them. The Reply Form also asked the invitees to give details of their travel, accommodation, and special needs, if any, for attending the regional meetings.

3.3.3 Final round of random selection

The staff of the Citizens' Assembly conducted the regional (final) member-selection meetings; Dr. Blaney was personally present at some of them. All the regional selection meetings began with a multimedia presentation by a senior staff member. This presentation gave a clear understanding to the participants of what they could expect as Citizens' Assembly members, including the extent of workload and compensation. The presentation was followed by a question and answer session. After the question and answer session, the participants were asked to declare, this time publicly, if they met the eligibility requirements, and were still interested in becoming a member of the Citizens Assembly. Only those who did declare that they met the eligibility requirements and were still interested could proceed to the next step in the final selection process. Their names were then placed in envelopes, one for men and one for women, belonging to their respective electoral districts. These envelopes helped to draw in public the names of one man and one woman for each electoral district.

The author attended the regional selection meeting held at Kwantlen University College, Surrey, on Tuesday, November 18, 2003. The meeting was scheduled to begin at 7:00 p.m. and last for three hours. The doors were open for registration from 6:30 p.m. As the author entered the meeting room few minutes after 6:30 p.m., he was first greeted by the Assembly staff present and directed to the registration desk. After registration, he took a seat among a dozen or so others who had registered by then. More joined afterward and the gathering began to look like a well-attended, special community event. Among attendees, there were people belonging to all ages and all the major ethnic groups living in Surrey. Some of the attendees were formally dressed up, while others were in their casual attire. In their private conversations, attendees spoke in different languages, mainly English and Punjabi. Until the meeting formally began, attendees spent their time in greeting and talking to each other, celebrating their unique experience in a political reform process.

At 7:00 p.m. the meeting was called to order, and the formal proceedings began with a multimedia presentation by Dr. Leo Perra, the Chief Operating Officer of the Citizens' Assembly. This was followed by a question and answer session, declarations of further interest and eligibility requirements, and placing names in district envelopes, as arranged. After that Cathy Stooshnov, Office Manager, drew the first name from the women's envelope of one electoral district in Surrey. As Stooshnov read the name drawn, all attendees, including the one whose name was read, cheered and applauded lustily. As the selection process continued, the attendees enjoyed the announcement of every other name selected in the same manner. The woman selected first drew a name from the men's envelope belonging to her electoral district. After that the man selected from the first electoral district drew a name from the women's envelope belonging to the second electoral district in Surrey. This process of drawing names continued until one man and one woman were selected from every electoral district in the Surrey region. This final selection process was consistently applied in all the regional selection meetings.

When the author's name was drawn from the Surrey-Newton District envelope of men, he jumped up from his chair and cried, "I am in. I am in." Soon after his selection, the author drew a name from the women's envelope of a nearby electoral district. The woman selected by this draw came running to him and thanked him profoundly as if he had picked her name by choice. By the first week of December 2003, the staff of the Citizens' Assembly had randomly selected 158 Assembly members using the random process. This, however, did not bring the Assembly member-selection process to an end due to a glaring shortcoming in aboriginal representation.

3.3.4 Aboriginal representation

A quick telephone survey of the 158 randomly selected Citizens' Assembly members showed that there was not enough aboriginal representation among the members. Only one member had claimed aboriginal roots, and she too had recently discovered her Métis roots. The aboriginal community in British Columbia, however, needed much stronger representation in the Citizens' Assembly, especially considering the ongoing efforts by nonaboriginal British Columbians to build new partnerships with that community. Dr. Blaney, the Chair of the Assembly, viewed this matter as extremely important, and asked the government to allow the Assembly to randomly select two additional members with Aboriginal ancestry. The government quickly gave its approval for this on December 10, 2003.

In selecting the two additional (aboriginal) members, the Assembly used the same selection principles as before. First, the Chair of the Assembly wrote a letter to all those who declared that they were both interested and eligible at the regional selection meetings, but whose names were not drawn in the final selection. In this letter, the Chair asked each of them to confirm whether they were Aboriginal, and, if so, whether they still remained interested in becoming a member of the Assembly. The letter also asked its recipients to respond by calling the Assembly office by December 18, 2003. Then, as the next step, the Assembly office placed the names of all those who had responded, declaring that they were both Aboriginal and still interested in becoming a member of the Citizens' Assembly, in a "hat" and drew the names of two people, a man and a woman, on December 22, 2003. With this draw, the total number of randomly selected members of the Citizens' Assembly increased from 158 to 160, consisting of 80 men and 80 women.

The Terms of Reference and the Duties of the Chair had also given specific guidelines regarding vacancies that might be created by death or resignation of the members selected. According to the guidelines, no replacements would be made until the Assembly's total membership is reduced by 25%. Replacements would then be selected by the Chair from the list of unsuccessful candidates at local selection meetings.

3.3.5 Members Selected

The randomly selected members of the Citizens' Assembly were a group of ordinary people representative of the adult population of British Columbia. Their ages ranged from 18 to 78 years, and some of them were very well educated. All the members, except for those who were still students, had worked for a living. Many members had also engaged in voluntary community work outside their normal working hours. There was not a single practicing politician or political scientist among them.

Among the members selected, there were tradespersons, office and administrative workers, technologists, professionals and specialists, business owners and operators, caregivers, fundraisers, students and retirees. The tradespersons included a carpenter, concrete worker, drywaller, farmworker, floor and window fashion worker, and a shipwright. The professionals and experts included an accountant, acupuncturist, chiropractor, physiotherapist, pharmacist, dentist, and a number of engineers, teachers, nurses, and computer experts. The businesses owned by some members include a pet care and companion business, furniture and design shop, and an auto business. The retirees included a former Assistant Deputy Minister, banker, RCMP officer and a clergyman. The membership of the Assembly also included a rancher, life skill instructor, ship captain, softball coach, stay-at-home mom, artist and writer, and a university professor.

The voluntary activities of Assembly members spread across a variety of community needs and facilities, such as health care, child and youth care, recreational centers, cultural centers, resource and energy conservation, strata councils, environmental protection, special events, and public security. Other areas of their voluntary work include elder abuse, violence against women, drug and alcohol, and First Nations issues. A number of members had played significant leadership roles in their local communities and professions. For example, one member had been a president of a local Rotary Club, while another had been the president of the BC College of Chiropractors from 2001 to 2003.

A more detailed review of the members' biodata shows that only two of the 160 randomly selected members had some practical experience in politics before. One had once run as a candidate at a local municipal election. The other was the author; in the late seventies he cofounded and led a nonviolent, democratic political party in Sri Lanka. Appendix 3 gives a complete list of the 160 randomly selected Citizens' Assembly members with some details of their individual backgrounds.

3.4   Online Resources

Meanwhile, the Assembly staff had set up two websites, one for the public and the other for the Assembly members. The public website, *www.citizensassembly.bc.ca*, was freely available to anyone who wanted to log in. The members' website, *www.myassembly.bc.ca* was, however, password protected, restricting its use to members of the Assembly and its staff. The public website had four main sections:

1. CA (Citizens' Assembly) in Action;
2. News & Events;
3. Learning Resources; and
4. Get Involved.

The pages under 'CA in Action' gave extensive information about the history of the Assembly, its purpose, the process it followed, the reports it produced, and a list of frequently asked questions and their answers. The 'News and Events' section was devoted to Assembly's latest news, events calendar, regular newsletters, media coverage, and a photo gallery. The 'Leaning Resources' section included the Assembly's learning materials, electoral maps of British Columbia, and a list of recommended reading. Finally, the section under the heading 'Get Involved' provided an opportunity for the website visitors to make online submissions to the Assembly or arrange verbal presentations at Assembly public hearings. In addition, this section listed the written submissions made by the public with an abstract for each of them. The dates and venues of the Assembly public hearings were also posted on the public website.

The members' website was similar to the public website, except for few variations. The Assembly used the members' website to post special items of interest to members and to give an opportunity for them to compare notes and chat among themselves on issues of their common interest, through an electronic *Discussion Forum*. In the *Discussion Forum*, a member could start a new topic for discussion for other members to respond, or respond to the statements made by other members on a topic already under discussion. There were also emoticons, such as smiling faces or ones in disgust, which could be conveniently used to add some fun to what the members wrote. One could even start an opinion poll to survey the views of other members on a chosen topic. Later, the reader will find how the discussions among the Assembly members through this Forum, outside the regular meetings of the Assembly, significantly influenced their final decision-making. The designers of the *Discussion Forum* were aware of current trends in online learning, and worked hard in creating what is termed an "online community."[1]

3.5   Link to the future

Being a new and unique experience in democracy, the Citizens' Assembly on Electoral Reform in British Columbia will remain a subject of discussion for many years to come. Political scientists, students of politics, politicians and voters in and outside British Columbia will like to know the successes as well as failures, if any, of this new experience in democracy. In particular, those who live outside British Columbia may be interested to know whether British Columbians were inventing a process that could work for them as well. For all this, proper recording of the Assembly process from its beginning to the end and the entire range of views of the Assembly members on issues they have discussed during the Assembly process would play an important role. The Assembly initiated two main projects to meet these ends.

One of the two projects was to make a documentary film of the Assembly from start to finish. This was done in partnership with BC's Knowledge Network. The final product of this project was an hour-long documentary film that would be aired in British Columbia, and later made available to other television networks across Canada and around the world.

The other project was initiated to evaluate the following three aspects of the Citizens' Assembly process:

1. How the different stages (educational, public hearings, and deliberation) of the Citizens' Assembly process progressed;

---

[1] Technology-based distributive learning.

2. The specific considerations of the Citizens' Assembly members during the Assembly process; and
3. The critical issues among the Assembly members during the same period.

This was done with the help of regular end-of-the-week evaluations and three main member-survey questionnaires. The regular weekend evaluations focused on how well the presentation and reading materials were prepared and presented to the Assembly and the way in which discussion groups were led. The weekend evaluations also focused on how the support services to Assembly members could be further improved. The three main member-survey-questionnaires focused on the views of the Assembly members about a range of issues. The Assembly members responded to the first questionnaire before the commencement of the Assembly process. Later, the Assembly members responded to the second questionnaires between the public hearing and deliberation phases. The third questionnaire was distributed to the Assembly members only after the Assembly process came to an end.

The research officers of the Assembly had the responsibility to complete this evaluation project. They continued to work on the project in partnership with Dr. Andre Blais of the University of Montreal, one of the world's leading survey researchers. In conducting the project, the Assembly members were assured of complete confidentiality in all their answers; for this the surveys were coded so that members' names would not appear on any form. An independent research firm, Adventure Consulting, was appointed to process the forms completed by the Assembly members. The evaluation process was planned to identify the dynamics and evolving thinking of the Assembly members as a group, and not to analyze the opinions of any one individual. The expected end products of this project were research documents (papers, books) by the research officers, telling how and what the Citizens' Assembly did during its term.

Meanwhile, Amy Lang, a graduate student of the University of Wisconsin-Madison had undertaken a Ph.D. research study on the Citizens Assembly; more students may follow suit. Such research studies will add academic findings on what the Citizens' Assembly achieved. In addition, writings of the individual Citizens' Assembly members, like this book, would tell the Assembly story to the world in their own perspectives. Such writings could unveil important discussions among members and issues that mattered to them, but not necessarily addressed in other reviews.

With its selection of members and staff, two new websites, carefully planned three-phase program of action, and recording systems for future reference, the Citizens' Assembly was ready to begin its work. Everyone involved in the Assembly process as well as other interested parties were now eagerly looking forward to its ceremonial opening.

3.6   Ceremonial Opening

The ceremonial opening of the Citizens' Assembly was scheduled for Saturday, January 10, 2004, 9:00 a.m., at the beginning of the first day of the first phase of the Assembly process. The Assembly members were expected to first register at the hotel (Delta Suite Hotel) adjacent to the Wosk Centre for Dialogue, where Assembly meetings would take place, anytime after 3:00 p.m. on the previous day (Friday), and attend a member-reception at the lower level of the Wosk Centre from 7:30 p.m. to 9:00 p.m. that evening. One hundred and fifty seven members registered on the Friday evening, and one on the next day morning just before the ceremonial opening. The Chair and the Assembly staff were present throughout the weekend. The reception in particular gave an opportunity for the members to meet and greet their fellow members and the Assembly staff.

Before the reception, the author thought that meeting and greeting such a large number of strangers of varied backgrounds at one place would be a nerve-braking exercise. It, however, turned out to be an interesting and pleasant event for everyone. The Assembly Chair Dr. Blaney took time to individually welcome every person who entered the reception hall. After entering the hall, some mingled with others and started conversations on their own. The Chair also walked around and introduced those who were waiting for company to others. All present showed their eagerness to come to know each other with their smiling faces of warmth and friendship. As time passed by, the reception that started as an event of strangers looked like a local community reception where the attendees were by no means strangers. The Assembly members who were present also particularly enjoyed the humility and friendliness of the Assembly Chair and staff members.

The Assembly members met again on Saturday morning at the lower level of the Wosk Centre for breakfast. After breakfast, they picked up their tent cards that carried their names and the assigned discussion group (room) numbers for the weekend, and climbed up the stairway to the Atrium for a historic moment in their lives. By 8:55 a.m. all the 158 members registered for the weekend had reached the Atrium and were waiting to enter the Asia Pacific Hall of the Wosk center to begin their Assembly work; two members failed to attend the ceremonial opening due to some unavoidable circumstances. The meeting hall had only two entrances, and each member was given a red or blue card indicating the particular entrance he or she should be using. While the Assembly members were crisscrossing the floor of the Atrium trying to get closer to their assigned entrance, the media personnel were busy trying to take a position for the best possible view of the events of the day. Then, a few seconds before the inaugural time, Simon Fraser University Scots Piper Sylvia DeTar came through the crowd in her colourful Highland dress and stood in front of Dr. Jack Blaney, the Chair of the Citizens' Assembly. At nine o'clock sharp she began to play and lead the members into the Asia Pacific Hall through its two entrances in the form of a dual procession. As the members entered the hall, they filled the back rows of the seats first, and then the others, one by one towards the innermost row. They all sat in their chairs together after everyone had found a seat.

At 9:10 a.m., the Chair called the Assembly to order, and after some opening remarks went into introductions, first the members, then the guests, and finally the Assembly staff, including the facilitators. Two large electronic screens of the Hall displayed their photographs as they were introduced.

Following the introductions, the Chair gave his keynote opening speech. He began the opening speech stating that it was a "rare and precious moment," (Blaney, 2004) and that the Assembly carried "the hopes and expectations of many," (Blaney 2004), quoting from two of the guests of the day. Then he talked about the uniqueness and importance of the Assembly and the work it was undertaking. Regarding the uniqueness and the importance of the Assembly, he said:

> Starting today, we have an incredible and unique opportunity, and an equally incredible and unique responsibility. To our knowledge, nowhere, at any time in a democracy, has a government asked nonelected citizens to undertake such a commitment, and then give those same citizens such potential power over an important public policy question (Blaney, 2004).

After dwelling more on the uniqueness and importance of the Assembly, he spoke about the work it had undertaken to do. Referring to the Assembly work, he stressed on the power and importance of learning and how the Assembly proposed to make its decisions through meaningful dialogue. Regarding the power and importance of learning, he said:

> Throughout history most of the really significant and beneficial initiatives had their birth in adults coming together to learn and then act, sometimes to protest, sometimes to celebrate, sometimes to invent new ways of doing things, sometimes to strengthen institutions and build better communities (Blaney, 2004).

In explaining this point further, he referred to the unprecedented increase in the adult student population in colleges and universities resulted from the influx of American and Canadian veterans into higher leaning institutions after World War II, and said:

> The huge productivity gains in North America through the 50s to 70s, and indeed the foundation of our technology transformation are very much a product of that vast and intensive investment in adult education (Blaney, 2004).

Regarding the process for decision-making through dialogue, he said:

> We are here to invent a new way to engage citizens in the practice of democracy. Of course we will challenge ideas, but will do so within the context of dialogue, where all are equal, where individuals will for some time suspend judgment, where different views are respected, and where individuals will focus on understanding different values. We will listen to understand. We will ensure that others have the same space and time to speak as we do. And our work will not be about winning, but about exploring common ground (Blaney, 2004).

In concluding his remarks on the importance of having a proper process for decision-making, he referred to a statement made many years ago by the pedagogue of education John Dewey that in a democracy how one comes to a decision is fundamentally far more important than the decision itself.

After his keynote speech, the Chair opened the floor for members' comments and questions. The author of this book was the first Assembly member to speak from the floor of the Assembly on this first day. He started his comments with a traditional greeting in his mother tongue, Sinhalese, 'Oba Samata Aayubowan,' and made a personal declaration of his appreciation of the Legislative Assembly of British Columbia for establishing the Citizens Assembly. In his declaration of appreciation, he also referred to his own experiences elsewhere, and said:

> I was born in Sri Lanka. I completed my studies in the United Kingdom, and have worked and lived in a number of countries in Asia, Europe, Africa, and North America. Wherever I lived, I took keen interest in learning and understanding the electoral and governing systems. I must say, Mr. Chairman, nowhere have I seen anything like this: an independent and nonpartisan Citizens' Assembly, with members drawn on a territorial basis that could play a vital role in shaping the electoral system of a democracy. I see this as a groundbreaking step in reshaping and uplifting democracy in British Columbia. It is a step that could lead the way in reshaping democratic institutions not only in British Columbia, but also in the rest of Canada, and other democracies of the world.

He ended his comments with the cry, 'Viva British Columbia! Viva Canada! Viva The World!' A news item in The Globe and Mail referred to the author's speech on the first day of the assembly, and said, "The first speaker at the first official gathering of the Assembly seemed to epitomize the uniqueness and diversity of this fascinating experiment in people power" ("Ordinary people," 2004). Lill Brulhart, another Assembly member, wrote to a local newspaper saying: "This articulate speech set the tone for the rest of the day" (Brulhart, 2004).

Several other members followed the author with equally heart-felt comments. With these comments from the members of the Assembly, its ceremonial opening came to an end by about 10:00 a.m. The end of the ceremonial opening was also the beginning of the Assembly's mandated tasks.

CHAPTER 4
LEARNING PHASE

4.1 Overview

The Assembly work was divided into three separate phases: Learning Phase, Public Hearings Phase and Deliberation Phase. The Learning Phase of the Citizens' Assembly took place over six alternate weekends in January through March 2004. The goal of this phase was to give an opportunity to the Assembly members to learn the different electoral systems that exist in democracies and how they function and contribute to the operations of their governing systems.

The learning sessions of the Assembly included formal presentations to the Assembly members by its research officers and a number of invited academics and experts, question and answer sessions immediately after these plenary presentations, and follow up discussions among the Assembly members in their group meetings. The presenters provided basic outline documents for each of their sessions, and recommended additional reading material when appropriate. In addition, a textbook entitled *Electoral Systems: A Comparative Introduction* authored by David M. Farrell (2001) had been distributed to all the Assembly members as a basic reference source. Professor Farrell was also among the academics and experts who were invited to make a personal presentation to the Assembly. The other academics and experts invited to make a presentation to the Assembly included Professor Elizabeth McLeay of the Victoria University of Wellington, New Zealand, Professor André Blais of the University of Montreal, Professor Lisa Young of the University of Calgary and David Baxter, a renowned demographer, futurist and economist. Trained, senior graduate students at either Simon Fraser University or the University of British Columbia, who had broad knowledge of how different electoral systems worked, facilitated the group discussions of the Assembly members. One of the main duties of the facilitators of the group discussions was to ensure that all members get a chance to fully participate in their discussions.

The learning sessions on the Assembly floor were open to the public. The Assembly members' group discussions were also open to the public. The public could attend the learning sessions or group discussions only as observers, and were not allowed to take part in any of the ongoing discussions or ask questions from the presenters or the Assembly members. At the same time, the Assembly websites, both public and Members,' were regularly updated with the learning material the Assembly members were using. This gave an opportunity to the members of the public, who were not Assembly members, to learn with them.

Many British Columbians made use of the opportunity to come and observe the proceedings of the Assembly and its discussion groups during the learning phase. There were some Members of the Legislature (MLAs) and other well-known politicians among them. Adrian Carr, the Leader of the Green party of British Columbia was present as a guest at almost all Assembly sessions. In addition, there were guests from outside British Columbia, some from other provinces and territories of Canada, and some from outside Canada. For example, the Hon. Jacques Saada, federal Minister responsible for Democratic Reform and Leader of the Government in the House of Commons of Canada, his Parliamentary Secretary Roger Gallaway, a Ministerial Assistant Anita Vandenbeld, and Press Secretary Marie-Claude Lavigne observed the proceedings of the Citizens' Assembly during the last weekend of its learning phase. During the same weekend, Matthew Mendelsohn, Deputy Minister for Democratic Renewal representing the Government of Ontario and John Gastil from the University of Washington were also present.

4.1.1 Eight initial tasks

In addition to learning, Assembly members had to complete eight special tasks during their learning phase. These tasks were as follows:

1. Agreeing on some rules for conduct;
2. Adopting guiding principles for communication;
3. Selecting best advocacy presentations;
4. Preparation for Public Hearings;
5. A June meeting in between the Learning Phase and the Deliberation Phase;
6. Computer/Website training;
7. Media and communication training; and
8. Preparation of a Preliminary Statement.

4.1.1.1 Agreeing on some rules for conduct.

One of the founding documents, *The Terms of Reference and the Duties of the Chair*, required the Chair to prepare some rules for the conduct of the business of the Assembly and present them at its first meeting. The rules had to be consistent with the duties of the chair and the terms of reference of the Citizens' Assembly. The chair presented the rules prepared by him (Recommendation #1) to the Assembly under the heading "Policies and Procedures," laying down basic ground rules for conducting Assembly business. There were sixteen rules in all. The main areas covered by these rules included a quorum of fifty percent of the membership for Assembly meetings, the need for a majority support for all formal Assembly decisions, voting by a show of hands or by electronic motion buttons, deciding-vote for the chair in the event of a tie on a resolution, a daily question period, a format for discussion groups, and public and media access to the activities of the Assembly. After some discussions, the Assembly adopted the Policies and Procedures with one amendment proposed by a member. The amendment changed the "majority" support requirement for formal decisions to "50% plus one" support in article 7 of the Policies and Procedures document. Appendix 4 gives the Policies and Procedures document as adopted by the Assembly in full.

4.1.1.2 Adopting guiding principles for communication

This task was to develop some common values to structure how Assembly members would work together. For this, the members were first asked to meet in their discussion groups (12 in all) and to identify the three most important values. The members managed to complete the tasks of adopting the Policies and Procedures proposed by the chair and members' group discussions on shared values by 12:00 noon. After reconvening at 1:30 p.m. a member from each discussion group reported to the Assembly the three main shared values his or her group considered during its discussion on the subject. The plenary discussion that followed helped to synthesize the values developed by the different groups and to arrive at a reduced number of values shared by all the members. Finally the Assembly adopted the following resolution (Recommendation #2) with nine key shared values:

> That the following shared values will guide our work together, recognizing that all the values suggested in the discussion group reports are important to some members and that this set of shared values will be adopted today and may, at any time, be reviewed and changed.
> * Respect people and their opinions
> * Open-mindedness; challenging ideas not people
> * Listening to understand
> * Commitment to the process
> * Focus on mandate; preparedness
> * Simple, clear, concise communication
> * Inclusivity: all members are equal
> * Positive attitude
> * Integrity

(Citizens' Assembly, 2004a).

4.1.1.3 Selecting best advocacy presentations

The Chair introduced a draft recommendation on advocacy presentations to the Assembly plenary sessions (Recommendation #3) during the second weekend of the learning phase. The draft recommendation suggested that the Assembly would hear some presentations from organizations and individuals in a plenary session to be held in the first weekend of the Deliberation Phase (September, 2004). This draft recommendation was heavily debated in the Assembly plenary sessions, group discussions of the Assembly members and the Discussion Forum of the Members' Website. Allowing such presentations to plenary sessions itself was a point of contention. At the same time members also expressed different views on the criteria for the selection of a few presentations from those made in writing or at public hearings. The Assembly finally adopted the recommendation with some important amendments on February 22, 2004, giving authority to a randomly selected committee of the Assembly to select a manageable number of presentations for the plenary sessions.

The committee selected consisted of six Assembly members, with two each from the Interior, Lower Mainland, and the Vancouver Island. The criteria to be used in the selection of the plenary presentations included the following:

- Quality—Clear, well thought out, and contains coherent arguments;
- Mandate—consistent with the Assembly mandate;
- Balance and Representativeness—offers a fair and balanced representation of submissions and public views, regions, interest groups and electoral systems;
- Merit—advances the Assembly's objectives with strong arguments worthy of consideration; and
- Other factors—as the committee members may determine.

The Assembly members developed these criteria with a view to selecting a minimum number of public presentations that could be of maximum benefit to their task in the upcoming deliberation phase.

4. 1.1.4 Preparation for Public Hearings:

Dr. Leo Perra, the Chief Operating Officer of the Assembly provided an overview of the Assembly public hearing process and a proposed schedule for the hearings to the Assembly for its consideration on Sunday, January 25, 2004. In the discussions that followed, Assembly members brought up a number of suggestions to improve both the hearing format and schedule. According to the final arrangements, there would be 50 public hearings spread throughout British Columbia, and four to eight Assembly members would officiate at each of them, with more members in urban sittings. The Assembly would use a random selection process to resolve conflicts if too many members indicated a preference for any particular location. Any member could attend public hearings not assigned to him or her in the capacity of a member of the public. The Assembly would also prepare a special presentation to be made at the beginning of every hearing, describing the purpose of the public hearings and the activities of the Assembly. All hearing updates were to be posted on the Assembly websites for the information of both the members and the public. Appendix 5 gives the full list of the public hearings held by the Assembly.

4.1.1.5 A June meeting in between the Learning Phase and the Deliberation Phase:

Assembly considered the need for a special plenary session of the Assembly after all the public hearings are over and before the deliberation phase. The main purpose of this special meeting was three-fold:

1. to review what the members heard at the public hearings;
2. to review written submissions submitted until then; and
3. to plan a decision-making process for the deliberation phase.

There was interest among the Assembly members to have this special meeting in a northern location, away from Vancouver. This would also help to show British Columbians that the Assembly members cared for the rural areas of the province, as geographic equity had always been a concern. The Assembly members considered two cities, Kamloops and Prince George, for this special meeting, and finally opted for Prince George as its venue. The meeting was scheduled for the weekend of June 26 and 27, 2004.

4.1.1.6 Computer/Website training:

Two optional training sessions were offered to the members of the Assembly who wished to have more training in working with computers on Friday, January 23, 2004. These training sessions gave an opportunity to those members who were not familiar with website browsing to feel comfortable in using the Assembly websites. More than 25 members made use of this training opportunity.

4.1.1.7 Media and communication training:

The media and communication staff of the Assembly, Marilyn Jacobson, Director of Communication, and Don MacLachlan, Associate Director of Communication, held an optional media training session for the Assembly members on Friday, February 6, 2004. This session gave an opportunity for the Assembly members to be familiar with the basic ground rules for and approaches to media interviews and to conduct mock interviews. More than 100 Assembly members attended this training session. Later, on Saturday, March 6, 2004, Jacobson also provided an overview of the Assembly communication strategy to raise awareness of the importance of the Assembly public hearings among the members of the public.

4.1.1.8 Preparation of a Preliminary Statement to the Province:

The members of the Assembly prepared and issued a Preliminary Statement to the Province at the end of its learning phase. The purpose of the Preliminary Statement was to summarize the work accomplished by the Assembly during its learning phase and generate interest among the public to get involved in the Assembly public hearing process. The members of the Assembly spent considerable time during the last two weekends of the learning phase in the preparation of this important document.

4.1.2 Scope of learning

What the members of the Citizens' Assembly learnt during its Learning Phase was both wide-ranging and challenging. In the plenary sessions of the Learning Phase, the Assembly members listened to fifteen presentations of learning material, eleven from the Assembly research and education staff and four from outside academics and experts. Ken Carty, Chief Research Officer, made seven of the eleven Assembly staff presentations, and Campbell Sharman, Associate Research Officer, made the rest. André Blais, David Farrell, and Elizabeth McLeay and the demographer David Baxter made their individual presentations on invitation. These academics and experts together constituted a unique and unprecedented pool of expertise and experience in electoral and related matters. Their specific areas of expertise had a multi-disciplinary appeal to the Assembly members. Each of the experts had a wealth of local, national and international experiences. All this helped the Assembly members to learn and look at electoral systems applicable to British Columbia in a broader perspective.

After each of the presentations made by the academics and experts, the Assembly members asked questions to further clarify what they heard during the presentation. There were also requests for new information, sometimes even beyond the domain of electoral reform. It appeared that many members of the Assembly had fully read its textbook, *Electoral Systems: A Comparative Introduction (*Farrell, *2001),* by about the third weekend sessions of the learning phase. The specific learning material presented to the plenary sessions of the Assembly by the academics and experts had been planned to provide adequate knowledge to its members on the following topics:

1. The place of electoral systems in democracies;
2. The nature of electoral systems in democracies;
3. Five basic families of electoral systems;
4. Assessing and choosing electoral systems;
5. The impact of electoral system reform; and
6. The demographics of British Columbia.

What follows below is a summary of the knowledge imparted to the Assembly members on these topics.

4.2   Place of electoral systems in democracies

The specific presentations that covered the above topic were as follows:

1. Politics in British Columbia—What do we want? (Professor Carty, January 10, 2004);
2. Elections, Representation and Parliaments (Professor Carty, January 11, 2005);
3. Political parties and party competition (Professor Carty, January 24, 2005); and
4. BC electoral experiments and reform initiatives and impulses (Professor Sharman, January 25, 2005).

The first of these presentations looked at the need to include a judgment on the past and a preference for the future in deciding on electoral choices, identified five recognizable features of the existing system of elections in British Columbia, and explored possible alternatives that could be considered for change. At the end, it encouraged the Assembly members first to ask themselves what kind of politics they really wanted to see in British Columbia as a starting point in the task ahead of them. This presentation helped to generate much enthusiasm and interest among the Assembly members to learn more about electoral systems in other democracies, especially in comparison with the existing electoral system in British Columbia. Thus, it set the tone for the rest of the learning phase. The second focused on what do representative assemblies made through elections really represent, how parliamentary governments work, actual and potential functions of the legislature, and the costs and benefits of coalition and minority governments. The third explained the rise of political parties, their role in parliamentary systems of government, costs and benefits of party discipline, recruitment of candidates at elections, and the nature of two-party and multi-party competitions. The fourth and last gave an account of the past experience of electoral reform and coalition and minority governments in Canada. It also discussed the contemporary Canadian electoral reform initiatives and how and why these initiatives came about. Some of the highlights of the points raised during these presentations and the follow-up group discussions are listed below:

(i) Adversarial politics versus consensual Politics

The current politics in British Columbia is based on a system like the courts, where it is assumed that the truth will come out if both prosecution and defense do their job by making their best case and trying to undermine the arguments of the other. As a result the Government and the Opposition in the legislature operate on the assumption that the best solution to any situation will appear only if they oppose the other side as vigorously as possible. Voters act as the judge and the jury, and make a decision as to which side should be supported or rejected. It is an adversarial system of politics with clear winners and losers that promote accountability, as the assumption being voters clearly know who stands for specific policies. According to the critics of the existing system, it encourages an 'our side is right about everything and the other side is wrong about everything' style of politics (a binary relationship) that forces choices into a simplistic for or against framework. This builds winning majorities rather than a broad consensus, and works best only when there are two political parties.

The systems of consensual politics act as an alternative to the current adversarial politics. Consensual political systems are designed to allow as many different opinions as possible represented in the legislature and even in government. Such systems bring about coalition politics and governments, where the distinction between the government and the opposition is not rigorously drawn, unlike in the case of adversarial politics. Any political system is likely to be neither completely adversarial nor consensual, but falls somewhere in between the two extremes.

(ii) Government dominated legislature:

In the existing system, the government dominates the legislature with the help of its majority status in the house and party discipline. Some governments can get too strong majorities in the legislature under the current system, depriving the opposition of the strength they should have to do their job effectively. Past records show that on average BC governments have been twice as large as their opposition, and more than three times larger than the opposition in one legislature out of three. A review of Canada-wide provincial elections show that governments have had over 70% of the seats in the legislature in about 40% of the cases, and over 90% of the seats in almost 10% of the cases. This translates to provincial governments having dominated by clear majorities. The provinces of New Brunswick, Prince Edward Island and British Columbia have experienced the worst-case scenarios in this regard. In the 1988 New Brunswick election, government won all the seats in the legislature. In the 1993 and 2000 elections of Prince Edward Island, the opposition won only one seat. The 1989 election of Prince Edward Island gave only two seats to the opposition, mirroring BC's 2001 predicament.

Strong party discipline, which is further discussed later in the book, can lead to 'friendly dictatorships' with the dominance of the whole system by the head of the government (premier). This can happen even with a slim majority of the government. The remedy to the dominance of the legislature by the government and potential 'friendly dictatorships' lies in the ways of avoiding a majority status in the legislature or strong party discipline, or both. Other electoral systems are less likely to produce majorities. In those situations, government becomes dependent on the votes of legislative members. In addition, legislators choose the government, and play a greater role in public decision-making. At the same time, the inter-party bargaining to build consensus on issues of public interest becomes a central theme in such systems. The minority government of Canada lead by Prime Minister Paul Martin experienced this situation. In 2005, after introducing its 2005/06 budget to the House of Commons, the Martin minority government had to amend it with enhanced financial commitments to social programs to get the support of an opposition party, the New Democratic Party of Canada. The government would have not succeeded in getting the budget approved by the legislature if not for the support it received from the New Democratic Party.

(iii) Representation based on geography:

The history of the present system of having representation based on geography goes back to the times when most of the population lived in separate communities spread across a rural society. In a typical situation, the system ties politicians to a clearly defined group of voters, gives voters an identifiable representative, and helps to defend each community's interests in the legislature. Party discipline acts in contrary to some of these expectations, especially when elected representatives vote party line against the wishes of their local constituents. The current system, even without strong party discipline, will have only limited results in the urban areas that are carved into different electoral districts, disregarding their common interests. It should be noted, unlike in the past, today voters appear to think more on party lines. There are other systems, where voters choose their representatives from or between lists of party candidates, without concerns of geographic representation.

(iv) Unpredictable votes-to-seats relationships:

As stated before, in the current FPTP electoral system in British Columbia, the candidate who gets the highest number of votes, not necessarily more than 50% of the votes cast or registered, in an electoral district wins a seat. This has often led to majority governments with less than 50% support in the electorate. Sometimes a political party could win an election and form a government with fewer popular votes than those of its main opponent, as happened in BC in 1996. It is also possible for a winning party to get an exaggerated majority, decimating the strength of the main opposition party (ies) and effectively barring small parties their share of seats in the legislature. This happened in BC in 2001. As a result, the critics of the current system argue, it mistreats unrepresented or underrepresented parties, fails to adequately represent the views of the people in the legislature, and, in the process, shuts off the interests and concerns of some people and groups from the decision-making process. Those who support the present electoral system in BC, however, argue that it has served well for over a century, facilitates a clear two-party competition, keeps out small "nuisance groups," and allows the voter to choose who should form the government.

There are other electoral systems, which can produce legislatures that mirror voters' opinions on Election Day.

(v) Simple and limited voter choice:

Under the current electoral system, political parties choose a candidate for each electoral district to represent them at a general election. The choice given to the voter is to choose one from a list of such selected candidates of different political parties and independents. Voters do not have any say as to who would be on the list. Critics argue that the choice given to the voter under the current system can be too simplistic; the voter has to simply choose among parties. There are other electoral systems that can give the voter more choices, including:

- Choice among parties;
- Choice among candidates;
- Choice among the candidates from the same party;
- Ranking a set of parties and candidates; and
- Designating an alternate person in case the elected representative dies or resigns (to avoid by-elections)

The degree of choice given to the voter will have an important effect on the way the parties and governments organize and operate.

(vi) What kind of politics do we need?

In exploring the electoral systems, the Assembly members need to first find out what kind of politics we need in British Columbia. To accomplish this they have to ask themselves what has worked well in the existing electoral system, and what they would like to change. Some of the specific questions they could ask in this regard include the following:

1. Would it be better if it were less adversarial and more consensual?
2. Are our governments too strong; do they get their own way too easily?
3. Do we need local representatives if they are just going to go to Victoria (where provincial legislature is located) and vote on party lines?
4. Do we want a more preferential counting system so that vote shares and seat shares are better balanced?
5. What kinds of choices should voters have at the poll?
6. Do we need more women and minorities in the legislature?

(vi) Some preconditions:

In a democracy, government should be responsive to the preferences of citizens, and, at the same time, be also accountable for its activities. This is possible only if the following preconditions exist:

- A constitutional framework that limits governing activities;
- Laws made only with the consent of a representative assembly;
- Key government office holders can be replaced at periodic elections; and
- Freedom of speech, assembly and association.

(vii) Representative Assemblies, elections and representation:

Any elected representative assembly is expected to represent the range of political views and interests across the community, and operate as its law making body and a source of authority for raising and spending public funds. It is also expected to act as a forum for discussing matters of public concern and to inquire into the operations of the government.

It is important that the members of representative assemblies are elected through periodic elections to meet the changing needs and aspirations of their communities. In their role, representative assemblies can amend or reject any legislation government proposes, and can even force government to resign by withdrawing their support. This shows how the legislature can be in control of the government in a democracy. This situation appears to have changed over the years, especially with the emergence of disciplined political parties in modern democracies. Today, representative assemblies appear to be central institutions of government with a monopoly of law making power. In a parliamentary system, like the one in British Columbia, the most important officers of the government, including the Premier or Prime Minister and cabinet ministers, are chosen from amongst the members of the representative assembly. This has made periodic elections to choose representatives and key government officials more important than ever before.

(viii)   Parties, parliament and majority governments:

In modern democracies political parties dominate elections, and woo voters with their party platforms that lay out some details of their main programs and policies. If a single political party manages to secure a majority of seats in the legislature, it forms government on its own. All the representatives elected from other parties form the "opposition." The party that secures most number of seats next to the governing party is generally referred to as the "official opposition," and the house leader of that party is referred to as the "leader of opposition." In British Columbia, a political party must have at least four seats in its legislature to gain 'official opposition' status. The salient features of such a representative assembly, with or without an 'official opposition,' can be summarized as follows:

1. The government can be assured of majority support in the assembly;
2. Voting in the assembly is by party blocks;
3. The business of the assembly is controlled by the governing party;
4. New legislation or changes to existing legislation can be made only with the consent of the government;
5. The ability of the assembly to scrutinize government is greatly curtailed;
6. The major function of the opposition members is reduced to airing matters of public concern; and
7. The news media and the courts become more important for political opposition.

(There are few exceptional minor variances to these features)

In summary, when majority governments exist, they control the legislature, and not the other way around.

(ix)   Parties, parliament and coalition governments:

Sometimes no party manages to win a majority of seats at a general election. In these situations, two or more parties can get together and form a government, sometimes with cabinet ministers drawn from all the parties. Such governments are referred to as coalition governments. The parties that form coalition governments enter into agreements to do so before or after an election; sometimes last minute agreements on the floor of the representative assembly result in coalition governments. The way a representative assembly works in such situations depends on the type of government it produces. Three salient characteristics of an assembly under a coalition government are listed below:

1. The coalition parties may have to compromise in the formation of policy;
2. The opposition will seek to exploit the differences between the coalition parties; and
3. There is the possibility that the coalition will collapse and the government fall.

(x)   Parties, parliament and minority governments:

When no party secures a majority of seats in the assembly and no parties come together to form a coalition government, the party with the most number of seats may form a government on its own. Such governments are called minority governments. For minority governments to survive, they need the support of elected representatives of one or more other parties in the legislature. Supporting parties generally do not share in the government or cabinet. At the same time, supporting parties reserve the right to vote against any legislation proposed by the government. This means that the supporting parties support specific legislations, but not necessarily the government in office. The main characteristics of a legislature under a minority government are listed below:

1. The government can still enjoy majority support in the legislature, with the goodwill of the supporting party(ies);
2. Voting in the legislature still by party blocks;
3. Business of the legislature is NOT controlled by the governing party;
4. Discussions over policies can now take place in the legislature;
5. Changes to legislation can be made without the consent of the government;
6. The government no longer dominates the legislative process;
7. The legislature can scrutinize government very effectively;
8. The legislature becomes the most important forum for political debates; and

9.   The activities of the legislature become the major focus for political news.

On the whole, minority governments enhance the role of the legislature, and meet the following challenges:

1.   Make it difficult for governments to act without compromise;
2.   Force governments to spend more time justifying their policies;
3.   Prelude action on unpopular policies;
4.   Increase the transparency of government activities;
5.   Transfer some lobbying activities from the public service to legislature members;
6.   Make it more likely that ministers resign for bad decisions or improper actions; and
7.   Remove the certainty of a government's continuation in office.

(xi)   The role of the members of the legislative assembly:

Under a parliamentary system of government like the one in British Columbia, the members of the legislature are elected by the people to represent them on an area basis. In some democracies only one member is elected to represent a designated area, generally referred to as a riding, constituency or electoral district. Some electoral systems are not based on single-member ridings. Instead, two or more members get elected for the same area, usually larger than a single-member riding. In either case, the elected members of the legislature represent their constituents on matters that may or may not have been discussed before the election. This is a bigger role than one of mere delegation on a pre-arranged list of things to do. At the same time, in their role as representatives, the members of the legislature perform a variety of tasks, both within and outside the legislature.

Their tasks directly related to the legislature include attending the meetings of the legislature and taking part in the discussions of its plenary sessions and committees, preparing for parliamentary debates and committee activities, voting in the legislature (generally on party line), and participating in party caucus meetings. In addition to the tasks directly related to the assembly activities, the members of the legislature also lobby government agencies on behalf of their constituents or interest groups, attend to the concerns of their constituents, and participate in community functions in their ridings. With all these and other tasks they perform, both within and outside the legislature, the members of the legislature can be seen as a linkage between local communities and the legislature.

(xii)   Political parties:

There are political parties in democracies, with few exceptions of nonparty democracy. The legislative assemblies in northern Canada are examples of the exceptions. Politicians and nonpoliticians create political parties. A close review of the political parties created by politicians shows that such parties are typically centred in the legislature, and their external activities primarily focus on vote gathering. Often parties emerge as a result of political ambitions of certain politicians. In contrast, parties created by nonpoliticians (citizens) typically arise out of groups of social activists, trade unions and other groups, who are determined to make government pay attention to their interests. The parties formed by these groups generally have more clearly defined set of goals and objectives than in the case of those created by traditional politicians. Two examples of parties created by nonpoliticians are the Canadian New Democratic Party that emerged out of the Cooperative Commonwealth Federation and the Party Québécois that emerged from the separatist movement in Quebec. Canadian Liberal Party and Conservative Progressive Party at federal level and the Social Credit Party of British Columbia at provincial level are examples of parties created by politicians.

There is no particular formula that determines the number of parties needed by a community or country. It is safe to assume that the existing electoral market place of a community or country and its electoral system determine the number of its parties that play a role in its political arena; not all the parties that get registered in a community are able to secure seats in the legislature. For example, there are 44 political parties registered in British Columbia, but only two of them are currently represented in the legislature. It has been observed that the influence of the electoral system of a democracy on its number of political parties is significant. The different electoral systems now used in democracies can be broadly categorized into two groups: winner-take-all systems and proportional systems. The winner-take-all systems, like the current electoral system in British Columbia, reward large parties, giving them a larger share of seats in the legislature than their share of votes. This penalizes smaller parties and encourages them to amalgamate. In the process, any winner-take-all system generally ends up with two major parties that dominate the electoral competition, sometimes with a third on the fringes. In contrast, the proportional systems allow parties to get their share of seats in the legislature in proportion to the votes they receive, provide opportunities for new parties to emerge, facilitate multiparty competition and result in a larger number of parties in the legislature.

Political parties do the same type of work in all democracies. They articulate and promote ideas and interests, recruit party candidates for office, put forward party platforms, campaign for votes at the time of elections, and organize and run governments and oppositions.

There have been some opinion polls conducted to find out how Canadians look at parties and what they do. According to the polls, a majority of Canadians are ambivalent about political parties and how they operate. Sixty-nine percent of Canadians think that those who get elected to parliament soon lose touch with the people (Carty, 2004a). Seventy-four percent think, "we could solve most of our big national problems if we brought them back to the grassroots level" (Citizens' Assembly on Electoral Reform [Citizens' Assembly], 2004b). Eighty-two percent believe that we should have better laws if members of parliament were able to vote for what they thought was best rather than having to vote on party lines. Sixty-nine percent agree that without political parties there cannot be true democracy (Carty, 2004a).

(xiii)   Party discipline:

Each political party stands for its own values, ideas and interests. These values, ideas and interests center around three basic questions on human needs: WHAT? HOW? and FOR WHOM? Voters join political parties that have values, ideas and interests closest to their own. As a result, the members of any given political party try to work together to achieve their common goals and aspirations. At times of elections, the individual parties prepare and put forward election manifestoes or platforms explaining their policies and programs of action in pursuit of their interests. There is agreement among the leaders, candidates and members of every party for upholding and following its declared policies and program of action. The leaders, candidates and members of every party also campaign together on its agreed policies and program of action to win the election. This assumes that after an election, the winning candidates of any given party would work and vote together as a team in the legislature either in government or in opposition. One would also expect them to defend each other and their leadership, both within and outside the legislature. This type of electoral politics in a multiparty democracy has the following basic features:

- Voters enjoy a collective government choosing capacity;
- The government formed at an election will be able to claim a mandate for an identifiable agenda;
- The government will have an enduring political base to depend on; and
- Voters will be able to hold the government accountable.

If a party, in government or opposition, is to be successful in this type of politics, its elected members need to stick to its platform in the legislature. Political parties tend to discipline their elected members who act contrary to party line. A vast majority of voters appear to think that party discipline is not a good thing for their interests. For example, an opinion poll suggested that eighty-two percent of voters believe that they would be better off if MLAs or MPs voted the way their constituents thought rather than on party lines (Carty, 2004a).

(xix)   Reform Impulses:

Some electoral issues have always remained at the center of discussions on electoral reform in British Columbia and Canada. These issues include equality of votes, artificial majorities, wrong winners, oversized governments, and under-representation of women and minorities. For voter equality in an electoral system with single member ridings, there should be an equal number of people living in every riding. Historically, there have been huge differences in population among different ridings in both British Columbia and Canada. Despite numerous steps taken to improve the situation, large inequalities still existed in the 1980s.

For example, in the 1983 election in British Columbia the number of registered voters in the ridings of Surrey and Atlin were 56,576 and 4,195, respectively; the population ratio of the two ridings was 13:1. Rita Johnston (Social Credit Party) won the Surrey seat with 38,081 votes, while Al Passarell (NDP) won the Atlin seat with only 1,587 votes. The person who lost to Rita Johnson received 34,082 votes. This was more than 28 times of that of the winner in Atlin.

After the adoption of the Canadian Charter of Rights and Freedoms in 1983, some citizens went to court to force the BC government to deal with this issue. After hearing the related cases, the BC Courts and the Supreme Court of Canada declared that the BC legislative map was unconstitutional. This led to two important developments: the adoption of a new set of ridings of somewhat equal population and a system to regularly update their boundaries to keep up with future population increases and movements. These new developments resulted in lowering the population imbalance among the ridings in a significant manner. In the 2001 election, the ratio of the population of the biggest riding (Saanich N & the Islands) to that of the lowest (Peace River South) was 2.3:1. The voters registered in the two ridings were 37,480 and 16,028, respectively. Some argue that this difference is still too big, and must be corrected.

Artificial majorities are very common in Canadian legislatures. In British Columbia, only once (2001 election) in the last half-a-century did a political party won a majority of the votes. Every government during this period had a majority of seats in the legislature. This stems from the present electoral system where one wins a seat by securing the highest number of votes, and not necessarily more than 50% of the total votes cast in a riding. If many candidates belonging to a party manage to win their seats with less than 50% support at the poll, it could end up with a majority of seats in the legislature with less than 50% of overall support. Some believe that such artificial majorities are not necessarily bad as they provide stable one-party governments with full accountability. Critics say that artificial majorities provide false legitimacy that allows governments to impose their preferred policies with no adequate support for them in the electorate.

Wrong winners come about when a party wins a lot of seats by small margins and loses others by large amounts. These situations also can give more seats to a party with overall lesser vote margins. For example, in the 1996 BC election, NDP secured six of the ten seats in the Vancouver area with 91,446 votes, while the Liberal party won only four seats with 92,782 votes. With similar results in other parts of the province, NDP managed to win a majority of the seats in the legislature in that election, although the Liberal Party received 36,000 more votes province-wide. This was the only time BC had wrong winners. There were other instances of wrong winners in both provincial and federal elections in Canada: Manitoba (1945), Quebec (1966, 1998), Nova Scotia (1970), New Brunswick (1974), Ontario (1985), Saskatchewan (1986, 1999), Newfoundland (1989), and Canada (1957, 1979).

The discussion under the heading 'Government Dominated Legislature' above has already covered the issue of oversized governments.

The underrepresentation of women and minorities in the legislature has been a subject of discussion in all democracies for a considerable time. In western democracies, some have made more progress in this regard compared to others. Scandinavian countries with women making up to 36–42% of their national legislatures are at the top of the list, while Italy, Greece and Japan with less than 10% of women in their legislatures are at the bottom. Canada takes a place in between with women making about 20% of its national (federal) legislature. A more detailed examination of the women percentages in national legislatures of major post-industrial democratic societies shows that a country's electoral system influences its extent of women representation. For example, the average women percentage in countries of proportional representation (list) systems is 29.5% while that of those with plurality/majority systems is 16.9%. Countries with mixed systems stand in between with 19.4% of women in their national legislatures. These different electoral systems and how and why they produce different results will be discussed later in the book.

4.3   Nature of electoral systems in democracies

Professor Carty's presentation to the Citizens' Assembly on February 7, 2004, on Democratic Electoral Systems covered this subject. Electoral systems organize, shape and govern the election process of democracies. In the election process, politicians organize themselves in a certain way and compete among themselves in their campaigns for public support. Voters look at the choices offered to them and vote for the politicians and their parties that appear to be most acceptable to them. At the end of the election, votes cast by voters get translated into seats in the legislature. The process by which this happens in a democracy depends on the type of electoral system it has.

There are three basic characteristics of electoral systems:

1.   District magnitude;
2.   Ballot structure; and
3.   Electoral formula.

District magnitude refers to the number of representatives to be chosen from a particular riding, electoral district or constituency. Ballot structure refers to the type of choices voters get on their ballot on the day of the election. The electoral formula refers to the mathematical formula that translates votes cast by voters into seats in the legislature. These characteristics are different aspects of a whole, rather than three separate entities. The combination of the three characteristics is a matter of choice of any given community. These characteristics are discussed in more detail below as they play an important part in any electoral system analysis.

4.3.1 District magnitude

District magnitude (DM) of a riding can be low or high, depending on its number of constituents. Generally democracies try to ensure that all their elected representatives represent the same number of constituents, within workable limits. Accordingly, a riding of twice the population of a single member riding of DM of one would become a riding of DM of two; it would elect two representatives, instead of one. There is no need for the DM to be the same in all the ridings in a democracy.

It would be less complex if all the ridings of a democracy have the same population, and, therefore, the same DM. This is, however, not always possible as the distribution of the ridings in a democracy is also influenced by the geographic, cultural, demographic, and economic diversity within its local communities. In the current electoral system in Canada, the DM is one across all its federal ridings. All provincial ridings in British Columbia also have a DM of one. In the past British Columbia had some multimember ridings of DMs of greater than one at the provincial level.

The increase of the geographic area of a riding tends to increase its population, and this may call for a corresponding increase in its DM. In its extreme sense, a democracy could consider its entire country as one big riding and have a DM equal to the total number of seats in its legislature. This, in fact, is the case with both Israel and the Netherlands where the DMs are 120 and 150, respectively.

At the same time, there is a growing interest in modern democracies to see that the strengths of political parties in the legislature truly reflect the depths of support they have in the electorate, in a proportional manner. This can materialize only with multimember ridings of DMs greater than one. The greater the size of the ridings and their DMs, the higher the degree of party-based proportionality the legislature could achieve. It works best in Israel and the Netherlands, where the entire nation is treated as one riding with DM equal to the total number of seats in the legislature. The impact of DM on party-based proportionality in the legislature is further discussed later in the book.

4.3.2 Ballot structure

The ballot structures used in modern democracies offer a range of choices to the voter, from a single choice for a candidate or party to numerous preferences over a number of parties and candidates. In some democracies the voter has the choice of voting for one party, but also some candidates of another. In some, voters are even able to attach different levels of importance among a number of candidates belonging to the same party or across different parties.

The ballot structure also has the ability to influence the nomination process of political parties and the balance of control between parties and voters with respect to who get elected as representatives. For example, if the ballot requires the voter to vote only for a party in a multimember riding, the party leaders would make their own lists of candidates for the riding and choose the order of preference among them in the final selection of their winning candidates. In this system, the leaders of parties are the ones that decide who actually get elected from their parties. Alternatively, if the voter were also expected to show his or her order of preference among a number of candidates belonging to a party, the voter would decide its winning candidates.

The ballot structures used in Luxembourg and Switzerland are considered as most flexible with regard to the above features. For example, the Luxembourg ballot paper in particular offers the voter as many votes as there are seats to be filled in a multimember riding. The voter has the following three choices in casting the votes:

1. Cast a 'list vote' for a party, giving one vote to each of the party's candidates (bloc vote);
2. Cumulate two personal votes on one candidate, attaching different levels of importance among candidates (cumulative vote); and
3. Vote for candidates on more than one party list.

4.3.3 Electoral formula

Electoral formulae establish the mathematics and procedures for transferring votes into seats in the legislature. Three main features characterize this process:

1. The number of votes required by a candidate to be elected as a member of the legislature (referred to as the *Quota);*
2. The minimum number of votes a party should secure before it can gain any representation in the legislature (referred to as the *threshold);* and
3. The basic principles that govern the process of transferring votes to seats: *plurality, majority,* or *proportional.*

Democracies build their own electoral formulae by choosing a combination of these three basic features. Different electoral formulae can result in different election results with respect to who actually win seats in the legislature.

4.4   Five basic families of electoral systems

There are many electoral systems in modern democracies. As shown in Figure 4.1, they can be classified into the following five basic families:

1. Plurality systems;
2. Majority systems;
3. Proportional representation list (PR-List) systems;
4. Proportional representation by single transferable vote (PR-STV) systems; and

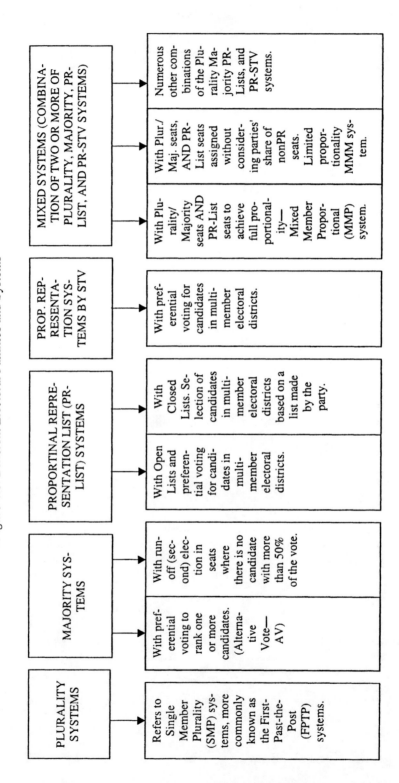

Figure 4.1: Different Electoral Families and Systems

PLURALITY SYSTEMS	MAJORITY SYSTEMS		PROPORTINAL REPRE-SENTATION LIST (PR-LIST) SYSTEMS		PROP. REP-RESENTA-TION SYS-TEMS BY STV	MIXED SYSTEMS (COMBINA-TION OF TWO OR MORE OF PLURALITY, MAJORITY, PR-LIST, AND PR-STV SYSTEMS)		
Refers to Single Member Plurality (SMP) systems, more commonly known as the First-the-Post (FPTP) systems.	With preferential voting to rank one or more candidates. (Alternative Vote—AV)	With run-off (second) election in seats where there is no candidate with more than 50% of the vote.	With Open Lists and preferential voting for candidates in multi-member electoral districts.	With Closed Lists. Selection of candidates in multi-member electoral districts based on a list made by the party.	With preferential voting for candidates in multi-member electoral districts.	With Plurality/Majority seats AND PR-List seats to achieve full protionality—Mixed Member Proportional (MMP) system.	With Plur./Maj. seats, AND PR-List seats assigned without considering parties' share of nonPR seats. Limited proportionality MMM system.	Numerous other combinations of the Plurality Majority PR-Lists, and PR-STV systems.

5. Mixed systems.

Each of these basic electoral families is discussed in detail below.

4.4.1 Plurality Systems

In plurality systems candidates seek election in individual, geographically identifiable electoral districts or ridings, and the most popular candidates in them become the winners. The candidates may or may not represent political parties, and winners do not necessarily get more than 50% of voter support. Plurality systems applied for single member ridings are also referred to as Single Member Plurality (SMP) or more commonly as FPTP systems.

The FPTP system is currently used in Canada, both federally and provincially. The other countries that use FPTP system include Bangladesh, Chile, India, Malawi, Nepal, Pakistan, Philippines, South Korea, the United Kingdom, the United States, Thailand and Zambia. Under FPTP systems, the DM can be just one or greater than one. The DM is one in all the above mentioned countries, except in Chile, South Korea, and Thailand. There is no need for DM to be the same in every riding. South Korea with varying DM is an example in this regard.

The ballot structure in democracies that use the FPTP system can appear in numerous forms. The ballot typically contains a list of names of candidates and specified places beside them for voting with a simple mark, usually a cross (X) or a tick. Where DM is greater than one, the voter may get the same number of votes as the number of representatives to be elected. If not, the number of votes the voter gets could be lesser than the number of representatives ('limited vote'). At the same time, the voter may have a choice to cast all his or her votes in favour of just one candidate ('cumulative vote') or candidates of one party ('bloc vote'), as already discussed under 'Ballot Structure' above.

The electoral formulae of the FPTP system are simple in nature and easy to understand: in all FPTP systems, candidates with the greatest number of votes in their favour become the winners. So, in the FPTP system, votes are first counted for candidates in each electoral district, and those (one or more according to DM) with the highest number of votes are declared as duly elected representatives for the district.

There are some significant advantages and disadvantages of the FPTP system. The main advantages are in the areas of local representation, accountability, style of government and representation, simplicity, and transparent ballot counting. The representatives elected for specific and identifiable areas under the FPTP system can speak authoritatively for their area and place its issues of interest or concerns on the public agenda. Voters also have an identifiable representative who can be contacted locally at times of their need. This promotes local representation with a direct link between voters and their representative in every electoral district. Local representation in turn promotes accountability of representatives towards their voters.

Style of government and representation under the FPTP system is significantly different from those under other electoral systems in a number of ways.
First, the FPTP system promotes the formation of majority governments that
could claim an electoral mandate and have a security of tenure for the lifetime of
the legislature. This gives such governments opportunities to confidently plan
and implement their intended programs as they wish, even when there is strong
resistance from the opposition. This winner-take-all feature in the FPTP system
promotes two-party competition, reducing the strength of minor parties and
marginal interests. Major democracies of the FPTP system, including the United
States and the United Kingdom, clearly testify to these scenarios. At times of
elections, voters of such countries primarily look for choices in government.
Another important feature in the FPTP system is the equal standing of all elected
representatives in the legislature, unlike in mixed systems (discussed later). The
elected representatives of FPTP countries share some common obligations towards their electorates, and the nature of the relationship between representatives and their voters in them is the same.

Perhaps the most strikingly advantages of the FPTP system are its simplicity and transparency in counting the vote. In the FPTP system, voters are simply
asked to indicate their preferred candidate from a list of names shown on the
ballot. The counting of votes is also equally straight forward. In the FPTP system, the vote counters only need to sort votes among candidates and count the
number of votes each one of them has received. The results of this simple counting process immediately identify the winner. Thus, the entire counting process
and the identification of the winner are transparent. This adds legitimacy to the
process and the government it produces.

The weaknesses of the FPTP system include the lack of votes-to-seats proportionality, inadequate minority representation, unequal votes, domination of
the legislature by the government, sharp swings in public policy, less voter
choice, and voter apathy. Under the FPTP system the number of seats a party
gets is not proportional to its share of votes at the election. The FPTP system favours large parties at the cost of smaller ones, as demonstrated in the 2001 general election in BC. This creates artificial majorities in government, shuns minority views in the legislature, and makes votes unequal and even redundant (or
wasted) in the process of electing representatives. Because of this situation, voters, especially those who support minor parties, treat elections under the FPTP
system with apathy. The domination of the legislature by the government is a
very common feature in the FPTP system. This results from the two-party adversarial politics in the legislature the FPTP system usually promotes. In such
politics, the legislature cannot play an effective role in holding the government
accountable between elections; the FPTP system normally does not produce
strong Oppositions in the legislature. With a strong dose of party discipline, requiring all representatives to vote on party lines, government could take full
control of the legislature. In such situations, local and minority interests get
mostly ignored. This type of governance and politics remain the same irrespective of the party that forms government under the FPTP system. The changes in
government under the FPTP system bring sharp swings in public policy, as the

new governments come and undo or even reverse the programs implemented by their predecessors. Thus, the FPTP system gives the voter stable governments, but not stable public policies. The voter choice in the FPTP system is limited to singling out a candidate from a list of names that appear on the ballot. This is usually a simple either–or choice between two major parties. Other electoral systems, offer the voter much more choices.

4.4.2 Majority Systems

Majority systems have been designed on the fundamental principle that the winning candidate at an election must obtain more than 50 percent of the vote. This is guaranteed in the FPTP system when there are only two candidates; when there are more than two candidates, the FPTP system may or may not produce winners with more than 50 percent of the vote. The majority systems always produce winners with more than 50 percent voter support, irrespective of the number of candidates. For this, the majority systems eliminate the least popular candidates and redistribute their votes to the remaining candidates. Democracies with majority systems do this in two ways.

Some countries of majority systems conduct a second round of voting with the two candidates who have polled the highest and the second highest number of votes in the first round. The election held between the two results in a winner with more than 50 percent of the vote. France has used this system when no candidate gets a majority of votes (50% + 1) in the first round of voting.

Some democracies of majority systems achieve the same results by asking the voters to rank candidates on the ballot in order of their preferences. This is generally referred to as the system of Preference Voting or Alternative Vote. It helps to produce winners with more than 50 percent voter support in just one round of voting. In this system, once the voters vote, the counting will first concentrate on their first preferences. This may or may not produce a winner with 50 percent voter support. If it does not, then the least popular candidate is eliminated, and his or her votes will be redistributed to the remaining candidates based on the second choice indicated in them. This process continues until a winner finally emerges with more than 50 percent of the voter support. Table 4.1 below shows how this process unfolded in a 1998 Australian federal election. As can be seen from this example, in this process the one who gets the highest number of first choice votes may or may not end up as the final winner. Irrespective of this, the winner will always have support from more than 50 % of the voters who took part in the election. The same process of counting can be used to elect more than one candidate, when the DM is greater than one. The website *http://www.seo.sa.gov.au/flash.htm* of the State Electoral Office of South Australia shows an animated example of the majority systems.

Democracies that adopted majority systems have done so with different intentions. For example, France adopted the second ballot system for its National Assembly hoping to reduce its representation of small parties, forcing their supporters to align themselves with one of the two large party groupings. This, in

Table 4.1: An Alternative Vote election result: division of Hinkler (Queensland) in the 1998 Australian federal election

	Count One	Next Count	Count Two	Next Count	Count Three	Next Count	Count Four	Next Count	Count Five
Paul Neville (National)	26,471	+45	26,516	+223	26,739	+807	27,546	+8877	36,423 Elected
Cheryl Dorron (Labour)	29,021	+39	29,060	+353	29,413	+987	30,400	+5533	35,933
Ray Pearce (Green)	1,139	+48	1,187	Excluded					
Marcus Ringuet (Hanson's One Nation)	13,739	+61	13,800	+169	13,969	+441	14,410	Excluded	
Lance Hall (Australian Democrats)	1,677	+116	1,793	+442	2,235	Excluded			
Cindy Rolls (Citizens' Electoral Council)	309	Excluded							

Source: Farrell (2001, p.58)
Original source: Australian Electoral Commission

fact, resulted from the use of the second ballot, although some small parties continued to influence French politics. In contrast, Australia adopted the Preferential Voting system to reduce the strength of a major party in the legislature. This helped a non-Labour coalition to do that at the expense of the Australian Labour Party. In time, however, the Australian Preferential Voting system has generally benefited its large parties. BC experience with the Preferential Voting system in 1952 and 1953 is different to that of France or Australia. BC adopted the Preferential Voting system to preserve a Liberal/Conservative government against the CCF/NDP. This did happen to some extent. However, the real beneficiary was a new party, Social Credit, which managed to keep the CCF/NDP out of office.

Majority systems have a number of advantages. They produce single-party or well-established coalition governments, provide an identifiable local representative for each area (when DM is one), enable the supporters of minor political parties to contribute to the choice of large party candidates, and keep representatives and the governments they make accountable through direct electoral contests.

Majority systems have three main disadvantages. First, the second ballot system requires two sets of elections, and the Preferential Voting system needs a more complicated ballot. Second, even with a second ballot or the alternative voter preferences, many voters do not contribute to electing any representative. Third, the majority systems, like the FPTP systems, encourage two-party competition, distort the votes-to-seats relationship, and shun the views of minorities and special interest groups from the discussions in the legislature. This, in turn, allows government to dominate legislature, sometimes with "friendly dictatorship."

4.4.3 Proportional Representation – List (PR–List) Systems

Proportional representation (PR) systems have been designed to ensure that the range of opinion in the legislature reflects the range of opinion in the electorate. In these systems parties or candidates secure seats in the legislature in proportion to their share of the vote. There are two major types of PR systems: PR-List systems and PR-Single Transferable Vote (PR-STV) systems.

PR-List Systems are designed based on three basic principles. First, they are party based systems in contrast to FPTP or Majority systems that are candidate based; in the PR-List systems, the contestants are political parties. Second, the main focus of PR-List systems is to distribute seats among parties rather than to elect individuals. Third, PR-List systems provide parties with their share of seats in proportional to their share of the vote.

PR-List systems can work only with multimember electoral districts, where DM is greater than one. As DM increases the seats-to-votes proportionality also increases. DM can be low as two or high as the total number of seats in the legislature as in the Netherlands and Israel. When the whole country is not considered as one single electoral unit, the different electoral districts within its jurisdiction need not have the same DM. At the same time, there can be several (mostly two or three) levels of tiers of electoral districts for the purpose of seat allocation among different parties. This allows votes that fail to contribute to seat allocation at the first tier level to be considered at the next level. Even if the whole country is considered as one electoral unit as in the Netherlands and Israel, the winning candidates can be drawn from regional lists, based on the voter support in different regions. A majority of the PR-List countries have only one tier of electoral districts. Such countries include Argentina, Brazil, Bulgaria, Finland, Portugal, Mozambique, Spain, Switzerland, Turkey, and Uruguay. The countries of two tiers include Belgium, Denmark, South Africa, Norway, Poland and Sweden. Greece has three tiers of electoral districts.

In PR-List systems, parties put forward their lists of candidates at elections. The ballot structure decides which of the candidates so listed by the parties get the seats they win. PR-List countries use two distinct types of candidate lists: Closed Lists and Open Lists. In the Closed Lists systems, voters' choice is limited to the selection of a party of their choice. Winning candidates of a party are drawn from its list of names in the order they appear on it; if a party qualifies for only one seat, the candidate whose name appears at the top of its list gets it. A majority of PR-List countries use closed list systems. These countries include Israel, Norway, Sweden, and the United Kingdom (European Parliament).

In the Open List systems, voters can show their preferences among the candidates whose names appear on party lists. The countries that use Open List systems include Austria, Belgium, Finland, and Switzerland. Choices available under the Open List systems can allow the voter to choose either candidate or party (e.g. Belgium), among candidates of a preferred party (e.g. Finland), or even more than one candidate or party (e.g. Switzerland). By choosing either candidate or party, the voters can influence the place of candidates on their party lists. By choosing among candidates of the same party, voters, instead of parties, decide which candidates qualify for seats. Just as in Closed List systems, even if the whole country is considered as one electoral unit, the winning candidates can be drawn from regional lists. The choice of voting for candidates on more than one party list is known as *panachage*. On average, about eight percent of Swiss voters and 18 percent of Luxembourg voters have made use of this choice; Switzerland and Luxembourg give most choices to the voter. For example, the Luxembourg voter has as many votes as there are seats to be filled. The voter has three choices. One choice is to cast a list vote for the party of his choice, giving one vote for each of its candidates. Another choice is to give up to two cumulative votes to a preferred candidate. At the same time, the voter does not have to select candidates from one single party. Instead, the voter can cast his or her votes to candidates on more than one party list.

The electoral formulae in PR-List systems are more complex than in the FPTP or Majority systems. PR-List systems use mathematical formulae to allocate seats among parties in proportion to their votes. These formulae divide PR-List systems into two main categories: Largest Remainder Systems and Highest Average Systems.

The Largest Remainder systems establish a Quota to determine the number of votes needed for a seat, assign seats first according to the number of full quotas won by parties and then in the order of the 'remainders' after allowing for full quotas. This method is demonstrated with the help of a hypothetical example in Table 4.2 below. The total valid votes and the number of seats assumed are 1000 and five respectively. The quota has been calculated as 200 (Hare Quota, discussed later) by dividing the total number of valid votes by the number of seats.

Table 4.2: A hypothetical example of the Largest Remainder system

Total valid vote = 1000
Number of seats = 5
Hare quota (1000/5) = 200

Political Party	First Round Votes	Hare Quota	Seats	Second Round remainder	Seats	Total Seats
Blue	360	200	1	160	1	2
Red	310	200	1	110	0	1
Orange	150	-	0	150	1	1
Green	120	-	0	120	1	1
Psychedelic	60	-	0	60	0	0

Source: Farrell (2001, p. 72)

In this example, the parties Blue and Red got a seat each by securing enough votes to qualify for a Quota. Then the remainders of the party votes (after allowing for full quotas) qualified the parties Blue, Orange, and Green for a seat each. The total number of seats each party got was the sum total of seats it secured on quota and the remainder. It is interesting to note here that the Green Party had only 120 votes, 80 votes short of a quota, but managed to secure a seat under the remainders. Seats are assigned under the remainder column only to get enough seats to complete the total number of seats required. At the same time, the seats assigned under the remainder column help to produce proportional results. Using a lower quota can lessen the role played by the remainder column in assigning seats. This would make it more difficult for smaller parties to win seats. Over the years, different formulae have been developed to calculate the quota. The three main quotas used are shown below with their mathematical formulae, based on assumed values of 1000 and five as the total valid votes and the number of seats, respectively:

1. Hare Quota: votes ÷ seats
       $1,000 \div 5 = 200$

Learning Phase

2. Droop Quota: [votes ÷ (seats + 1)] + 1
$$[1,000 ÷ (5+ 1)] + 1 = 167$$
3. Imperiali Quota: votes ÷ (seas + 2)
$$1,000 ÷ (5+2) \quad = 143$$

Hare and Droop quotas are more widely used. Denmark, Columbia, Costa Rica, Madagascar are among the countries that use the Hare Quota, and Greece, South Africa, and Czech Republic use the Droop Quota.

The Highest Average systems divide the votes received by each party by a series of divisors, say 1, 2, 3, 4, etc., to produce a series of average votes, and assign seats among parties based on the averages, starting from the highest. Table 4.3 below demonstrates how the voting in the hypothetical example explained above (1,000 votes and 5 seats) under Largest Remainder systems now works under a highest average system of divisors 1, 2, and 3.

Table 4.3: A hypothetical example of the operation of the d'Hondt highest average system

Total valid vote = 1000
Number of seats = 5

Political Party	Votes	Votes Divided by 1		Votes Divided by 2		Votes divided by 3	Total seats
Blue	360	360	1st seat	180	3rd seat	120	2
Red	310	310	2nd seat	155	4th seat	103	2
Orange	150	150	5th seat	75			1
Green	120	120					0
Psychedelic	60	60					0

Source: Farrell (2001, p. 74)

The d'Hondt divisors are the most widely used divisors. The countries that use the d'Hondt divisors include Argentina, Austria (at higher tier), Belgium, Brazil, Finland, Israel, Luxembourg, Mozambique, the Netherlands, Portugal, Spain, Switzerland, Turkey and Uruguay. Denmark, Norway, and Sweden use the modified Sainte-Lague divisors. The pure Sainte-Lague divisors are rarely used. New Zealand uses them as part of its new electoral system. Arend Lijphart has noted that the use of Sainte Lague divisors very closely approximates proportionality and treats large and small parties in a perfectly even-handed way (Farrell, 2001, p77). The Modified Sainte-Lague divisors tend to somewhat assist small parties. On the scale of proportionality, the Modified Sainte-Lague system lies somewhere in between d'Hondt and pure Sainte-Lague systems.

Academic reviews of all the electoral formulae used in both largest remainder and highest average systems show that the largest remainder system with Hare Quota produces the most proportional results. For example, David Farrell says,

According to Arend Lijphart's research, separate from the effects of DM, the electoral formula which produces the most proportional result is the largest remainder system with the Hare quota; modified Sainte-Lague highest average forms an intermediate category; and the least proportional systems are d'Hondt highest average and largest remainder with the Imperiali quota (Lijphart 1986a, 1994a) (Farrell, 2001, p78).

If more than one tier is used in electing representatives, there is no need to use the same electoral formula at all tier levels. At the same time, many PR-List systems have a *threshold* of a minimum percentage of the vote a party needs to win to qualify for its share of the seats, irrespective of the electoral formula.

The threshold may even require a party to secure a seat at the first tier level (Spain) or at the national level (Austria) or both, in addition to the minimum percentage of the vote. Table 4.4 below shows the threshold levels of some PR-List countries. The countries that do not use a threshold include Dominican Republic, El Salvador, Finland, Honduras, Ireland, Nicaragua, Portugal, South Africa, Switzerland, and Uruguay.

Different combinations of DMs, ballot structures and electoral formulae are designed for achieving desired electoral results. Table 4.5 shows such combinations of DMs, ballot structures and electoral formulae in three democracies, and the outcome of their recent elections.

There are some significant advantages and disadvantages of PR-List systems. The main advantages include fairer (than in FPTP and Majority systems) or more proportional representation of parties in the legislature based on voter support, decrease if not complete avoidance of 'wasted votes,' strengthened role of legislatures in choosing and checking on the government, and higher voter turn out at elections. The fairer representation of the parties in the legislature based on voter choice encourages more parties to compete. It also makes it possible for minority views to be heard in policy discussions in the legislature. This helps legislatures elected under the PR-List systems to pass more stable policies. Having no wasted votes helps to give those who traditionally ignore elections a renewed sense of importance to their votes. The strengthened role of legislatures under PR-List systems helps to avoid dominant single-party majority governments and 'friendly dictatorships' that act in disguise of democracy.

As their disadvantages, the PR-List systems often fail to form single party majority governments and do not give the voter identifiable local representatives or a clear choice of government at elections. Some also see that PR-List systems lead to proliferation of minor parties. Single party governments can claim a mandate and quickly carry out a plan of action without much hassle, while coalition governments under PR-List systems have to take time to make compromises among their coalition partners before implementing any program. The

Table 4.4: Threshold levels of some PR-List countries.

Threshold For	Threshold	Countries
For a local seat	3% of the electorate in the district	Argentina
	Reached the quota in the district	Brazil
	4% of the national vote	Bulgaria
	50% of the district quota	Costa Rica
	5% of the national vote (10%, 15%, & 20% for coalitions of two, three, & four parties).	Czech Republic
	3% of the national vote	Greece
	5% of the national vote	Mozambique
	5% of the national vote (8% for coalitions)	Poland
	3% of the national vote (8% for coalitions)	Romania
	3% of the national vote	Spain
	4% of the national vote or 12% of the local district	Sweden
	10% of the national vote and the district quota	Turkey
For a seat at higher level	One local seat + 4% of the national vote	Austria
	33% of the quota in at least one of the districts of the Province	Belgium
	1 local seat, 2% of national vote or a determined no. of votes in 2 of the 3 geographic areas of the country	Denmark
	3% of the national vote	Greece
	1.5% of the national vote	Israel
	0.67% of the national vote	The Netherlands
	4% of the national vote	Norway
	7% of the national vote	Poland

	3% of the national vote	Romania
	5% of the national vote	Slovakia
	4% of the national vote	Sweden
	10% of the national vote and district quota	Turkey

Source: Citizens' Assembly (2004d)

Table 4.5: Combinations of District Magnitudes, Ballot Structures and Electoral Formulae

Country	District Magnitude	Ballot Structure	Electoral Formula	Threshold	Election Results
Israel	120 (whole country)	Vote for a Party, Closed Lists	Highest Average with d'Hondt divisors	1.5% of the national vote	2003 election—13 parties won seats; the largest got 29% of the seats
Sweden	Variable	Vote for a party & candidates, Open Lists	Highest Average with Modified Sainte-Lague divisors AND two tiers, 2nd corrective (14% of seats)	4% of national or 12% in local district.	2002 election—7 parties won seats; largest got 41%.
Austria	Variable	Vote for a party & candidates, Open Lists	Largest Remainder with Hare quota at lowest level & Highest Average with d'Hondt divisors at higher tiers, three tiers in all.	4% of the national vote or one local seat.	2002 election—Four parties won seats; largest got 43%. Took three months to form a coalition government.

Source: Citizens' Assembly (2004c)

lack of identifiable local representatives makes it difficult for voters to keep individual politicians accountable.

4.4.4   Proportional representation systems by STV

PR-STV systems are proportional representation systems designed to produce legislatures that mirror voter support for candidates, not parties. Like PR-List systems, PR-STV systems operate with multimember districts with DMs greater than one. Political parties also operate as in PR-List systems and submit their (party) lists of candidates at elections. Voters, however, can vote for their preferred candidates, even across party lines. Unlike PR-List systems that reflect the support for political parties, PR-STV achieves proportionality by adding the preferences of voters for individual candidates.

Malta (since 1921) and Ireland (since 1922) are the only countries in the world that use PR-STV systems for electing members for the legislature at national level. PR-STV systems are used in Australia for electing members for its Senate (1949), Tasmanian state assembly (1909), Australian Capital Territory (1995) and Western Australia upper house.

As the voters' choices are based on candidates instead of parties, PR-STV systems have an anti-party flavour. At the same time, at elections candidates have to compete with those of the same party, as in PR-List systems with Open Lists. In addition, the voter's ability to choose candidates across party lines tends to weaken party discipline of candidates, before or after elections.

As in PR-List systems, DM must be greater than one, and it does not have to be the same for every electoral district. The proportionality of election results increases with increased DMs. The DMs used in the countries of PR-STV systems range from 2 to 7: Ireland 3, 4, & 5; Malta 5; Australian Senate 2 & 6; Western Australian upper house 5 & 7. These DMs are generally low compared to those under PR-List systems. The higher the DM under a PR-STV system, the bigger the number of candidates the voter has to consider at elections.

The ballot structure of PR-STV systems is similar to that of the Alternative Vote (AV) system. The voters need to rank the candidates, not necessarily among those of the same party. Voters may be asked to show their preferences (1, 2, 3, etc.) for a minimum number of candidates, lesser or equal to the number of seats. The grouping and ordering of candidates on the ballot paper can differ from one democracy to another. The names of candidates can be grouped under their respective parties in an alphabetical order. As an alternative, names of all candidates can be listed in an alphabetical order without grouping them under party names; the party names can appear in front of candidate names. There are many more options available for grouping and ordering of candidates.

The electoral formula used in PR-STV systems is somewhat more complex than those of other electoral systems. The basic principle used in the PR-STV electoral formula is that a candidate needs to get a quota of votes to get elected, as in the Largest Remainder formula under PR-List systems. The quota usually used in the PR-STV systems is the Droop quota. It is calculated by dividing the total valid votes in the electoral district by its total number of seats plus one, and adding one to the answer, as shown below:

Quota = [{(Total number of valid votes) ÷ (Number of seats + 1)} + 1]

According to this equation, the quotas as percentages of total valid votes for DMs 2, 3, 4, 5, 6, and 7 are 33.3%, 25.0%, 20.0%, 16.7%, 14.3%, and 12.5%, respectively. There is a mathematical process to determine the winning candidates who manage to get the required quota of the preferential votes cast by voters. The process begins with the counting of the first preferences for each candidate. If a candidate has adequate first preferences to qualify for a quota, he or she is declared duly elected. If a candidate has more than a quota, the surplus is transferred to other candidates based on the second preferences indicated on the ballot. Any candidate who gains a quota as a result of this transfer is then declared elected. This process continues until all the required representatives are elected or there are no more surpluses with any candidate but still more candidates need to be elected. In the latter case, the least successful candidate is excluded, and his or her votes are redistributed to other candidates not yet elected according to the second preferences on the ballot. This process of distribution of surpluses followed by the exclusion of the least successful candidates continues until the required number of representatives are elected. The website *http://www.seo.sa.gov.au/flash.htm* of the State Electoral Office of South Australia has an animated demonstration of this process. The website *http://election.polarbears.com/online/online.htm* gives the results and the distribution of voter preferences of the 2002 Irish election.

As their main advantages, PR-STV systems give more power and a wider range of choices to the voter and produce proportional election results with a close match between the seat and vote shares of parties. The voter has the opportunity to vote for individual candidates as well as parties. In addition, the voter can choose among candidates of the same party, as in PR-List systems with open lists, or different parties. The ability to choose among candidates of different parties helps to reduce the animosity and hostility among voters and candidates on party lines. This, in turn, reduces the adversarial nature of politics in the legislature. The benefit of proportionality with matching seat/vote shares of parties in PR-STV systems with candidate based voting is particularly interesting.

As for disadvantages, PR-STV systems have complex preferential ballots, do not produce a single identifiable local representative, encourage regional politics, and weaken party control. The complexity of the ballot of the PR-STV systems depend on the extent of voter choices offered to the voter; the more the voter choices the more the complexity. The lack of an identifiable local representative is common to all proportional representation systems. All PR systems, not only PR-STV systems, do not often produce majority governments. The focus on candidates in place of parties at times of elections tends to result in regional issues based politics rather than party politics on a broader base. This can be somewhat counterproductive in democracies designed to work on party basis.

Further it weakens party control of candidates 'and elected members, leaving party organizations lesser efficient and effective.

As the PR-STV systems are practiced by a comparatively small number of countries, there is not much experience to go by in analyzing their advantages and disadvantages. For example, experiences in Ireland and Malta, which are not ethnically or religiously diverse, cannot help to assess the performance of PR-STV systems in terms of minority representation. Another reason of concern is that the experiences of PR-STV systems so far have not been consistent. For example, while the norm under PR-STV systems is to have more than two parties and coalition governments, Malta has continued to develop a two-party system and most of the governments in Tasmania have been single party governments. At the same time, in their Senate elections Australian voters have turned their PR-STV system to a PR-List system with closed lists by using the option of voting 'above the line' on the ballot showing a single party preference. As a result, candidates are now elected always in a party preferred order, as in the case of PR-List systems with closed lists.

4.4.5 Mixed systems.

Mixed systems are combinations of two or more of the above described four basic electoral families (Plurality, Majority, PR-List, and PR-STV) and their different electoral systems. Some democracies have established mixed systems as a means to obtain the advantages of the different basic electoral families and their systems while minimizing their disadvantages. There is no one distinct way of mixing the different basic electoral families and their systems in forming a mixed system. For example, Australia and Japan use different electoral families for different choices (national assembly, Senate). The United Kingdom uses different families to elect different levels of government. Germany uses a mix of systems in all its regions, and elects half of its 600-member parliament using the FPTP system and the other half using PR-List Largest Remainder system with Hare quota. France uses different systems in different regions, with a combination of FPTP-Majority rules in small districts and PR-Lists in larger ones. In Canada, both Alberta and Manitoba have used two different systems, one for the rural areas and the other for urban areas. They both used the Majority system with single member districts for rural areas and the PR-STV system with multi-member districts for urban areas. Austria uses different electoral formulae at different stages of seat allocation: PR-List Largest Remainder with Hare quota at the lower level and PR-List Highest Average with d'Hondt divisors at the higher level. The possibilities for combinations of the different systems of the four basic electoral families are infinite. The different mixed systems can produce representatives with different constituencies, mandates, responsibilities and roles.

The general purpose of mixed systems is to try and achieve some balance between the following two political objectives:

1.   Identifiable local representation, and

2.   Some measure of proportionality between seats and votes among different political parties or groups that take part in the electoral process.

A close review of the characteristics of the different electoral families shows that these objectives are mutually exclusive. For example, FPTP or Majority system gives the voter an identifiable local representative. These systems, however, do not produce proportional results. At the same time, the PR-List systems produce proportional results, but do not give identifiable local representatives.

Mixed systems have been generally established with either different electoral families and systems across an entire democracy or different families and systems in different places (regions) in a democracy, the former being more common. In the more common case, some members are elected under the FPTP or Majority system with identifiable local districts, while some form of a PR system elects the others. The different characteristics that apply to local districts (including DM, plurality or majority, preferential vote or not) and the PR system (including DM, open list or closed list, formula, seat allocation by region or the entire system, threshold) depend on the features of the specific electoral families and systems that constitute the mixed system.

Mixed systems of this kind with different electoral families and systems across the entire democracy can be further classified into two basic groups, depending on the extent of proportionality they achieve. In one group, the seats under the PR system are used to top up the numbers of seats the different parties have won at the local districts, making the seat totals of the parties proportional to their vote totals, in a compensatory manner. For example, if a party won 10% of the seats at local district level but had received 25% of the popular vote, it would get enough PR seats to give it 25% of the seats in the legislature. This kind of system that brings overall proportionality in a mixed system is generally referred to as Mixed Member Proportional System or simply MMP system. It has been adopted by Germany and New Zealand. If a party wins more local district seats than what it is entitled under PR, Germany allows the party to keep them and brings overall proportionality to the legislature by temporarily increasing its size.

In the other group of mixed systems with different electoral systems across a democracy, votes-to-seats proportionality applies only to the seats run under PR. This kind of mixed system is referred to as Mixed Member Majoritarian (MMM) system. It is more widely used than the MMP system. The countries that use the MMM system include Japan and Italy. This system helps small parties to get some supplementary seats. It, however, helps the bigger parties more at the same time. As a result, the MMM system is considered to be highly disproportional.

In either group of mixed systems of this kind the local districts become larger than those under FPTP or Majority system. This results in heavier constituency workload for elected members. At the same time, the number of PR seats should be high enough to reach a reasonable level of proportionality. Experts believe that there should be at least one-fourth seats under PR to achieve overall proportional outcomes. Germany and New Zealand have 50% and 40% of list seats, respectively. The degree of proportionality the mixed systems produce also depends on the size of the legislature. For example the New Zealand Royal Commission that recommended the MMP system also recommended that the size of the legislature should be increased from 95 to 120.

Another interesting feature in mixed systems of this kind is the ability for a candidate to seek election both in a local district and under a PR list. This helps parties to give their prominent members a double opportunity to seek election. This also means that candidates defeated in local district elections can be elected from PR lists. In Japan, such candidates are jokingly referred to as "Zombie politicians."

There are different rules used by democracies of mixed systems of this kind for dealing with vacancies created by local district members in the legislature between elections. They are replaced either by the next available person on the party list or through a by-election. Germany uses the former method, while New Zealand uses the latter. In the case of a vacancy created by a list member, the person next in the list always fills the vacancy. A vacancy can be created by the death, incapacitation, or voluntary departure of an elected member. It is also generally assumed that if a member changes his or her party affiliation, it is deemed to have created a vacancy. New Zealand strictly applies this principle.

The most important advantage of having mixed systems of this kind is their ability to deliver favourable results under two or more basic electoral systems at the same time. For example, the MMP system is capable of delivering both local representation and votes-to-seats proportionality at the same time. Being proportional, mixed systems also encourage small parties. This helps to ensure that the range of opinion in the legislature reflects the range of opinion in the electorate. At the same time, mixed systems create two types of members, constituency members and list members. Constituency members owe their position to the voters in their local districts, while list members owe their position to voters in a bigger geographical area and their party leaders who make party lists at the time of election. This helps the elected representatives to focus on local, regional and national issues in a somewhat balanced manner; it avoids preoccupation of all elected representatives with local issues. The two types of members can also lead to two types of parties. Larger parties that have a bigger chance to win local district seats tend to do more constituency work, while smaller parties tend to promote particular issues to gather support across local district boundaries hoping to get some PR seats. This may be viewed as a disadvantage of mixed systems of this kind.

Let us now examine mixed systems with different electoral families and systems in different regions within a democracy. They are designed to respond to diverse representational challenges in different communities. The primary distinction of the needs of voters in this regard comes from the differences between sparsely populated rural areas and dense urban areas. Voters in the rural areas depend on their representatives to a greater extent (than in urban areas) due to four main reasons. First, rural areas do not have adequate public services and infrastructure, requiring the representatives to deal with a wide range of issues and concerns. Second, the rural voters do not have easy access to public officials, and expect their representatives to assist in dealing with them. Third, the representatives of rural districts find very difficult to get around in their large size districts and be accessible to their voters as in urban districts. Fourth, political parties and other interest groups also find very difficult to involve voters in larger rural districts and to get an adequate level of their participation in the political process. Mixed systems with different families in different regions have been designed to meet such challenges, with the majority or plurality system with single member seats for thinly populated areas and the PR-List or PR-STV system with multimember districts for dense urban areas. The proportionality of the overall system depends on the balance between the two kinds of seats.

4.4.6 Historic perspective

The early electoral systems used by democracies were based on the principle of plurality. Majority systems were adopted in the 19th century as an improvement to the plurality systems. By the early decades of the 20th century, the growth in franchise brought in a new dimension to the politics in the democratic world. This was due to a new possibility that workers could organize themselves politically and take over government. The rulers of the time feared that in time workers would form majority governments, as has been the general case up to then, and implement their programs without having to listen to the opinions of others. In responding to this new situation, the rulers of the time started to adopt PR systems, so that no one interest group could form government by majority.

Then, the last two decades of the 20th century once again became a period of electoral system revival. These revivals started in the post-communist democracies in Europe and later spread to already established democracies. By the late 1990s, eighteen post-communist countries adopted four kinds of new electoral systems: PR-List (9), mixed (5), majority (3), and PR-STV (1). Four of the nine PR-List countries (Czech Republic, Latvia, Poland and Slovenia) opted for open lists, while the rest (Bosnia, Moldova, Romania, and Slovakia) adopted closed lists. After experimenting with their new systems, six of the 18 new democracies had another round of electoral reform by 2002.

All the three countries that adopted majority systems (Albania, Macedonia, and Ukraine) changed to mixed systems. Two of the countries that adopted mixed systems changed to PR-List systems. The only country that adopted a PR-STV system (Estonia) changed to a PR-List system. There also have been some changes to the original thresholds that ranged from 3% to 5%; the maximum increase was 2%.

The electoral reforms in established democracies occurred during the 1980s and 1990s at both national and regional levels. The established democracies of major electoral reforms at national level include New Zealand, Italy, Japan, Venezuela and Israel. New Zealand changed its electoral system in 1993 from the FPTP system to a mixed system, MMP, similar to the one practiced in Germany. Italy changed its electoral system in the same year from a PR-List system to MMM. Japan changed its electoral system to MMM from a semiproportional (SNTV) system. The United Kingdom appointed a royal commission, Jenkins Commission, in the mid–nineties to look into electoral reform for its House of Commons elections. The commission followed a lengthy process in 1997-98, and recommended a mixed system as practiced in Germany, but with the Alternative Vote option for constituency elections (as in Australia) and Open Lists for PR elections (as in Belgium). It is not yet known whether these electoral reform recommendations would be implemented. Meanwhile the British are continuing to use their FPTP system for electing members to their (national) House of Commons.

The UK and Canada are two established democracies that have initiated significant measures of electoral reform in the recent past. In the United Kingdom, three regional assemblies, Scottish, Welsh, and London, have adopted mixed MMP systems, with constituency elections based on FPTP system and PR elections with Closed Lists. The Northern Ireland Assembly has adopted a STV system. The British also uses a variation of the Alternative Vote (AV) system to elect their Mayor of London. In this modified AV system, the voter is required to rank only two candidates. British have given a special name, Supplementary Vote (SV) system, to this modified AV system. At the same time, British elect their members to the European Parliament by a PR-List system with closed lists. Chapter one describes the electoral changes implemented in Canada.

4.5   Assessing and choosing electoral systems

Each of the four basic electoral families: plurality, majority, PR-List, and PR-STV, can encompass a wide variety of different electoral systems. Every such electoral system has its own advantages and disadvantages. Because of this, some democracies have adopted mixed systems in an attempt to obtain the advantages of the different electoral families and systems while minimizing their disadvantages. As stated before, the possibilities for making such mixed systems are infinite. But none of the electoral systems, mixed type or not, can meet 100 percent of all the electoral preferences of a democracy; there is no perfect electoral system.

Each of the electoral systems has its own characteristics, affecting the political landscape of a democracy in a unique way. Votes-to-seats proportionality, the number of surviving political parties, the extent of women and minority representation are some of the direct effects of electoral families and systems. For example, PR-List systems produce more proportional results with increased women and minority representation, compared to plurality and majority systems. The number of parties under PR-List systems is also generally more than that under Plurality systems. At the same time, voters and parties engage in political activities differently under different electoral systems. For example, under PR-STV systems, a candidate should resort to strategies to get preferential votes from voters belonging to all political parties, while under the plurality systems one would have to attract voters with the strength of his or her own party platform.

Some electoral systems produce stable, majority governments, while some others tend to produce coalition governments that may or may not be equally stable. Stable, majority governments are able to make hard decisions and act fast when necessary. Majority governments also can be held accountable for what they do, unlike in the case of coalition governments. At the same time, some majority governments can become arrogant and unwilling to compromise on anything. At times they even lead to 'friendly dictatorships,' as discussed before. Coalition governments may or may not be able to make hard decisions or act fast when necessary. Such governments, however, may develop stable policies, that may survive future government changes.

Only under some electoral families and systems the voter can have an identifiable local representative. Some mixed systems can give the benefits of both local representation and proportionality, which are normally mutually exclusive. However, such systems produce two types of members and parties. Some view this as a disadvantage, while others see it as a distinct advantage. Some electoral families and systems lessen the control of elected representatives by their respective parties or their leaders. This is also viewed as an advantage as well as a disadvantage, depending on how one looks at. Table 4.6 on the next page shows which electoral families/systems are likely and not likely to provide the three basic electoral features identified by the Assembly members: proportionality, local representation, and voter choice.

The above shows that different electoral systems can offer different results, and at least some of the results can be perceived as advantages or disadvantages, depending on how one looks at them. Therefore, any attempt to choose an electoral system for a democracy must begin with a clear identification of the kind of politics its citizens wish to have. Once the kind of politics a democracy wants is known, an electoral system can be chosen to help create the desired political environment. As stated earlier, the kind of politics a democracy desires depend on many factors, including its own history, political culture, and social environment. A democracy must first explore all related questions its citizens might have to determine the kind of politics that best serves them. These questions can include the following:

- Do we want adversarial or consensual politics?
- Do we prefer majority governments, minority governments or coalition governments?
- How can we make our representatives and government more accountable to us?
- Should the legislature have more power to oversee government?
- Do we need strong voter link to our representatives? If so, is it a must to have a locally elected identifiable representative?
- How important is to have seats/votes proportionality in the legislature?
- Should we have more choices on the ballot?

Table 4.6: Basic Features of Main Electoral Families/ Systems

Feature	Plurality	Majority		PR-List		PR-STV	Mixed-MMP	
		With AV Voting	With Runoff Second Election	With Open Lists	With Closed Lists		PR Open L & AV Const. Seats	PR Closed Lists & Plu. Const. Seats
Proportionality				Yes	Yes	Yes	Yes	Yes
Local Representation	Yes	Yes	Yes	Yes	?	Yes	Yes	Yes
Voter Choice —Party		Yes		Yes*		Yes	Yes*	
—Candidate	Yes	Yes	Yes	Yes		Yes	Yes	Yes

* With provision to vote across party lines

- Should there be more women and minority representation in the legislature?
- How can we encourage more people to make use of their democratic right to vote?
- Are there any votes that do not contribute to the election of representatives? If so, how do we avoid such wasted votes?
- Are our votes equal?
- Is our electoral system too complicated or simple enough for everyone to understand? and
- Has the existing system contributed to any political scandals? If so how and why?

The answers to these and other related questions the citizens of a democracy may ask determine the main characteristics of the political set up they long to have. These characteristics formulate the basis of a new electoral system. The design of a new system can then begin by choosing appropriate electoral system features, including DM, Electoral Formula and Ballot Structure, that can help to build a new political climate with the desired characteristics. This is not a straightforward process, as there may not be one set of system features that fully satisfy all the identified characteristics.

The final choice of the system features can be made only with some trade-off. Table 4.7 below demonstrates this process, based on some assumed characteristics of a new system desired by a democracy.

4.6   Impact of electoral system reform

Going by the experience of countries that have gone through electoral reform, it is difficult to predict all the effects of any particular electoral reform. The effects of a particular electoral system change in one country may not apply exactly the same way to any other. The effects of electoral reform on a democracy primarily depend on how its politicians and voters respond to the changes resulting from it. It is also possible that some of the trade-offs a democracy chooses in the design of a new electoral system can be unique, and, as such, there is no previous experience to go by in predicting its effects.

The early years of electoral reform are particularly important. It is essential that all politicians and voters be fully informed of the changes being made and what can be expected of them in the short term and long term. Politicians' behaviour during the early years of electoral change can significantly influence its process and effects.

Experience so far shows that it is premature to gauge the particular effects of any electoral system change after one or two elections. It takes time for the new rules to settle down and get established. Politicians and voters also take time to adjust to their political environment created by a new electoral system. Generally, the actual effects of an electoral change can be seen after at least five or six elections. For example, some see that having two types of representatives,

Table 4.7: Relationship between political culture and electoral system features

	Political Culture Characteristic	Electoral System Features		
		District Mag. (DM)	Electoral Formula	Ballot Structure
1	Strong stable government	Small DMs and Small Districts	Non or Semi PR + Legal Threshold	Closed lists
2	Legislature con-trolled Government	Large DMs and large Districts	PR or Semi PR	Open lists, AV for any NonPR Component
3	Close voter link or Local representa-tion	Small DMs and small Districts	Mixed or STV	Open Lists or STV
4	Seats-to-votes proportionality	Large DMs and large Districts	PR-List, MMP, STV	PR-Lists, STV
5	Maximum voter choice	Large DMs and large Districts	PR, STV	PR-Open Lists, STV
6	More women and minority Representation	Large DMs and large Districts	PR	PR-closed lists
7	Encourage voters to vote & end wasted Votes	Large DMs and large Districts	PR-List, MMP, STV	PR-Lists, STV
8	Equality of the vote	DM based on population	Any	Any
9	Simplicity	Small DMs and small Districts	NonPR (SMP)	Closed lists

local district representatives and list representatives, as a problematic issue under a MMP or MMM system. This appears to be a genuine concern when we
look at New Zealand, which implemented its MMP system in 1993. This is,
however, not true in Germany, which adopted the same system much earlier.

One should be extremely cautious in trying to assess the effects of any particular electoral system based on long experience elsewhere. For example both
Ireland and Malta adopted PR-STV systems in early 1920s, but show different
performance levels in some areas. In Ireland, 13.3 percent of elected officials are
women, compared to 9.2 percent in Malta. Irish system produces some independent representatives, when Malta has failed to produce any in the last 55

years. Modern Malta has virtually a two-party system, unlike in modern Ireland. Furthermore, the experiences of Ireland and Malta, which are ethnically and religiously homogeneous, may not apply the same way to democracies of multiethnic or multireligious societies.

4.7   Demographics of British Columbia

British Columbia is a multiethnic, multireligious and multilinguistic society. The 2001 census has identified 61 ethnic groups. A majority (56%) of a total population of 3,868,870 claim single origins in these ethnic groups. Others claim that they belong to the same ethnic groups, but have mixed origins. The people who claim Canadian, Chinese, English, East Indian, German, Scottish, North American Indian, Dutch, Filipino, Italian, Ukrainian, and French are the biggest single origin groups, in that particular order (BC Stats, 2005). Visible minorities account for 22% of the total population. According to a Statistics Canada report released on March 22, 2005, nearly one of every three people living in BC would belong to a visible minority group in 2017 (Statistics Canada, 2005).

Thirty five percent of the people living in BC do not claim any religion. The rest of British Columbians claim 33 religions. The most populous religion is Roman Catholicism; 17.2% of the total population claims this religion. United Church (9.4%), Anglicanism (7.7%), Christianity n.i.e (5.2%), Sikhism (3.5%), Baptism (2.8%), Lutheranism (2.6%), Buddhism (2.2%), Protestantism n.i.e. (2.0%), and Islam (1.5%) appear after that in that order of strength in numbers of people who claim them (BC Stats, 2005).

As for language, 73% of British Columbians have claimed English as their mother tongue, while only 1.4% have claimed French. This means more than 25% of British Columbians have claimed nonofficial languages as their mother tongue. According to 2001 census, there are 47 such nonofficial languages. The leading nonofficial languages so claimed include Chinese, Punjabi, German, and Tagalog, in that order (BC Stats, 2005).

4.8   Preliminary Statement

At the end of the learning phase, the Citizens' Assembly issued an eight-page preliminary statement to the Province. It started with a brief description of the Assembly process and the work completed by the Assembly during its Learning Phase. This was followed by an account of the Assembly's assessment of the existing electoral system in British Columbia and possible approaches to alternative electoral systems based on the electoral values of British Columbians. Finally, the preliminary statement stated that the Assembly members were eagerly looking forward to hearing a full expression of public views on these matters at the upcoming public hearings. A complete list of the proposed public hearings appeared on the last page of the eight-page statement.

In its account of the existing single-member plurality FPTP system, the preliminary statement pointed out a number of its strengths and weaknesses. The nature of local representation, accountability, style of government, simplicity, familiarity and transparent vote-counting were all shown as the strengths of the FPTP system. The lack of votes-tò-seats proportionality, government-dominated legislatures, and adversarial nature of politics with sharp swings in public policy with changes in government were listed as its main weaknesses.

As for alternatives, the preliminary statement said that the Assembly members studied a wide range of alternative electoral systems and their impact in other democracies. In addition, the statement said that the Assembly members paid special attention to the basic values that underlie the different alternative systems, and how they relate to those of British Columbians. The Assembly members thought, the statement further said, that local representation, votes-to-seats proportionality and voter choice were the most important basic values of British Columbians. In inviting the public to express their views, the statement stated that the Assembly members would like to hear if the public shared these basic values, and what kind of choices they would like to see at the polls. Further, the statement affirmed that the Assembly members were also anxious to hear what kind of electoral systems their fellow citizens believed could best express their common values.

The preliminary statement also gave contact details for information on how to register to present one's views at a public hearing and make a written submission to the Assembly for the consideration of its members. The preliminary statement was made available in four languages: English, French, Chinese and Punjabi. This allowed as many British Columbians as possible to take part in the dialogue on electoral reform.

CHAPTER 5
PUBLIC HEARING PHASE

5.1   Spreading the word

The preliminary statement of the Citizens' Assembly became the main tool of communication to inform the general public about the upcoming public hearings on electoral reform. The statement was first posted on the Assembly websites and emailed to all those who were registered to receive Assembly newsletters electronically. All this was done by the second week of April 2004. Those who received the preliminary statement by email included trade unions and many business groups. This was followed by the dispatch of hard copies of the statement by mail to Assembly members and a number of other sources of interest throughout British Columbia. The members of the Citizens' Assembly received the number of copies they had individually ordered for distribution to the public in their local communities. The Assembly members also made arrangements to speak to local community groups, such as schools, service groups, government employees, women's groups, business associations, professional associations, and church groups, hoping to generate interest in the upcoming public hearings in their communities. The nonmembers who received hard copies of the preliminary statement include the following:

- Social studies departments in schools throughout BC;
- Political parties in BC, 44 in all;
- Members of the BC Legislature;
- Members of Parliament and Senators from BC;
- First Nations groups and Chiefs in BC;
- Libraries in BC;
- Provincial government agents in BC;
- People who had made special requests for copies; and
- People who received the Assembly regular newsletters by mail.

By this time, the Assembly public website had a significant amount of learning materials for the general public to learn about the Assembly and different political systems and their implications. These materials include 14 fact sheets, audio and video versions of the Assembly learning phase, and links to numerous sites that discussed electoral reform issues. The specific topics discussed in the 14 fact sheets were as follows:

- Fact Sheet 1:   Politics in BC: What do we need?;
- Fact Sheet 2:   Assessing electoral systems;
- Fact Sheet 3:   Legislatures, elections, representation, parties;
- Fact Sheet 4:   Electoral experimentation in BC;
- Fact Sheet 5:   Why electoral Reform?;
- Fact Sheet 6:   Understanding electoral systems;
- Fact Sheet 7:   Electoral systems;
- Fact Sheet 8:   Majority systems;
- Fact Sheet 9:   Plurality systems;
- Fact Sheet 10:   Proportional representation – list systems;
- Fact Sheet 11:   Proportional representation – single transferable vote systems;
- Fact Sheet 12:   Mixed electoral systems;
- Fact Sheet 13:   Implications of electoral systems; and
- Fact Sheet 14:   Global activity in electoral reform.

Meanwhile, the Knowledge Network TV Channel gave a helping hand in getting the message about the public hearings to the general public. On April 1, 2004, it began broadcasting a three-to-four-minute long vignette featuring the Citizens Assembly. The vignette encouraged the public to participate in the Citizens' Assembly process, starting with the public hearings scheduled for May and June. Then on April 13, 2004, the Hansard TV, also known as the Legislative Channel, began to broadcast the plenary sessions of the Assembly held during its learning phase. This round of broadcast of the first six weekends of the Assembly proceedings ended on April 30, 2004. The same TV channel repeated the broadcast later in May/June 2004; the repeats started on May 25th and ended on June 3rd.

At the same time the Assembly members became very active in their communities with their speaking engagements. They also began to engage the media in numerous ways in publicizing the upcoming public hearings. The Assembly staff made sure that the Assembly members received all the communication tools they required for their speaking engagements as well as public hearings. The communication tools used by the Assembly members in their speaking engagements included a Power Point presentation, overhead slides, two videotapes, and some handouts. The Assembly members used overhead slides for their presentations only where the Power Point presentation was not possible due to logistic reasons. One of the two videotapes had the same short vignette as the one the Knowledge Network was broadcasting. The other was a 14-minute video that provided an overview of the Citizens' Assembly as well as a summary of electoral options. The handouts distributed to the attendees at the members' speaking events include the 14 Fact Sheets mentioned above and two additional information sheets. One of the additional information sheets was named

"Backgrounder," which, among other things, explained how the public could get involved in the Citizens' Assembly process. The other additional information sheet explained the specific mandate of the Citizens' Assembly.

At their speaking engagements, the Assembly members encouraged those who were present to make written presentations to the Assembly and share their ideas with others at the upcoming public hearings. At the same time, the Assembly members informed those who were present when and where the hearings would take place in their local communities. The Assembly members had also undertaken to post Assembly posters of the hearings at strategic locations in their areas during the same period; every Assembly member was given a minimum of 20 posters, some much more upon specific request. Often, some of those who attended the speaking events of the Assembly members assisted them in posting the public hearing posters on a voluntary basis. Each poster showed the date and time, venue, and other related information regarding the upcoming public hearings in a local community.

Meanwhile, the Assembly members engaged the media to draw public attention to the upcoming Assembly hearings in a number of ways. Some wrote columns for their local newspapers. Paul Harris, Assembly staff member, helped them to complete the columns they wrote for their local papers, and worked with them to get the columns published in a timely manner. At the same time, some members wrote Letters to the Editor. All the published columns and Letters to the Editor written by Assembly members made an appeal to the public to participate in the Citizens' Assembly process by sending written submissions and sharing their views on electoral reform at the public hearings. As all this was happening, a number of well known and not so well known newspaper columnists, both in BC and outside, joined in with their own writings on the Citizens Assembly and its process, including the public hearings. The newspaper columnists' writings were generally appreciative of the Assembly's process and emphasized the need for the public to participate in it. The column of Greg Neiman in Nanaimo Daily News (Neiman, 2004), a reproduction of what had earlier appeared in the Red Deer Advocate of January 13, 2004, is particularly interesting in this regard. Among other things, it said:

> Every country has its mythic icons, images of those moments frozen in history that people use to define their identity as citizens.
> These images are a kind of shorthand to explain the higher ideals of a people. For instance, Britain the signing of the Magna Carta, where the notion of divine right of kings was ended; the United States has its Declaration of Independence, which codified the notion of equality of all people; France has the storming of the Bastille. Canada has Meech Lake.
> Actually, we have a lot more than that. Our national icons include Confederation, the famous image of the Last Spike at Craigellachie, Vimy Ridge and the patriation of our Constitution, to name a few.
> Perhaps, in a year or so, we will have one more.
> Recently, British Columbia struck a unique committee to decide how that province will form its government. What is amazing about this exercise is not how badly electoral reform is needed in this country, but rather it is the courage

and confidence of the elected legislators to stand by and let the decisions rest with the people.

The only people left in Canada who prefer our first-past-the-post system of electing governments are the elected governments themselves. How else could an established government maintain their overwhelming grip on power, often supported by a minority of actual votes?

So to see the process put into place in B.C. is almost enough to restore one's faith in Canadian democracy.

Some writers, however, had some adverse comments on the assembly process. For example, in their writings, Vaughm Palmer (Vancouver Sun) and Les Leyne (Victoria Times–Colonist) both stated that the Assembly was leaning toward a form of PR even before the public hearings. Few politicians joined the fray expressing their concerns as well in this regard. In response to these concerns, some Assembly members wrote back (columns and Letters to the Editor) explaining that the Assembly had not made up its mind on a particular type of electoral system as yet. The letter of Assembly member Shoni Field published in both the Vancouver Sun and the Victoria Times–Colonist (Field, 2004) is particularly interesting. It alludes to some contents of the Assembly's preliminary statement that may have caused the confusion as to whether or not the Assembly had already made up its mind on a particular electoral system. This letter said:

> I am concerned lest British Columbians get the impression that the Citizens Assembly has already made up its mind. We have not.
>
> There is a difference between Proportional Representation systems and proportionality, the characteristic. The Assembly has not identified a preference for any one system. Our preliminary findings were that some degree of proportionality might be desirable for BC. We also stated that some degree of local representation was important (which happens to be a strong feature of our current plurality system) ...
>
> The intention of our Preliminary Statement was to start a discussion with British Columbians. If we hear that proportionality is far more important than other considerations, we would recommend a Proportional Representation system. Or if local representation outweighs all other factors, we might recommend that the current system be retained. Or, we might hear that British Columbians want a balance between these two values, leading us to recommend another system altogether. The only certainty at this point is that Citizens Assembly members have not made up their minds.

Meanwhile, there were media interviews with some Assembly members. Local newspapers, radios and TV channels, all devoted some time for such interviews. These media interviews started sometime in March, while the Assembly was still in its learning phase. There were also panel discussions on some TV channels normally with one or two Assembly members on the panel, and some others in the audience. For example, on May 25, 2004, 8:00 p.m. to 9:00 p.m., the Watch the New VI channel (Victoria based) broadcasted a live panel discussion with Assembly members Diana Byford and Darren van Reyen on the panel and more than half a dozen other Assembly members from the Vancouver Island in the audience.

Spreading the Assembly word in BC schools continued without drawbacks. In response to the initial information package sent to schools, many Grade 11 Social Studies teachers showed interest to get down classroom copies of the Preliminary Statement of the Assembly; Government Studies is part of the Grade 11 curriculum in BC. At the same time, the Assembly members were also contacting their local Grade 11 Social Studies teachers, offering to talk to their students. This lead to a series of talks to Grade 11 students throughout BC by Assembly members. The Assembly members who gave these talks let the teachers know about the Assembly resources for the classroom located on the Learning Resources Section of the Assembly public website. A lesson plan for holding a Model Citizens' Assembly was also posted on the website.

The Rockridge Secondary School of West Vancouver seized the opportunity and held a Model Citizens Assembly on Wednesday, April 21, 2004. More than 50 students took part in the event. It lasted for three and a half hours. During this period, they discussed which electoral system would best meet BC's needs. Interestingly, they also discussed how to get more young people involved in the democratic process. At the end, the students came up with a proposal to be presented by five of them to the Assembly members at a local public hearing, scheduled for Wednesday, June 2, 2004. The proposal of the students was for a mixed electoral system, with 50% of the seats in the legislature to be filled with constituency level representatives under a majority system and the remaining 50% of the seats to be filled under a PR system. The Model Citizens Assembly also had small group breakout sessions just as in the real Assembly. The Social Studies teacher of the school organized the event, and five Citizens' Assembly members served as the facilitators for the group breakout sessions. The five Assembly members who took part in this process were Neall Ireland, Chérie Mostrovich, Firmin Hung, Julie Boehmer and John Mak. As the news about this special event spread around the province the students of other BC schools began to show more interest to know about the Citizens' Assembly and its process.

The media reported what some members of the Citizens' Assembly did to publicize its public hearings and the highlights of what was heard at the hearings held. In addition, the media gave publicity to many columns and articles written by journalists on related issues. For example, the Vancouver Sun of Saturday, May 1, 2004, carried a page long feature article written by Neil Hall on some alternative electoral systems submitted to the Citizens' Assembly. This article also talked about the Model Citizens' Assembly of the Rockridge Secondary School (Hall, 2004). On Thursday, May 6, 2004, the same newspaper carried a column written by Neils Veldhuis and Jason Clemens on the activities of the Citizens' Assembly. This column expressed the view that the Preliminary Statement of the Assembly left the reader with a strong impression that it was already leaning towards greater proportionality. This column also argued that proportionality is likely to produce less effective, larger coalition governments, which would result in lower rates of economic growth and higher taxes. More newspapers had columns, feature articles and news items about the Citizens' Assembly and related matters. At the same time, the Citizens' Assembly ran paid advertisements in local community newspapers about the public hearings (Veldhuis and Clemens, 2004).

The Preliminary Statement of the Citizens' Assembly, learning resources of the Assembly website, speaking engagements and media interviews of the Assembly members, newspaper columns and feature articles on matters related to the Assembly, Letters to the Editor by some Assembly members, school events modeling the Assembly, and special broadcast programs run by Hansard TV and Knowledge Network, all helped to generate immense interest in the Assembly process and hearings among the general public. The large number of people who made written submissions or lined up for presentations at the Assembly hearings testified to this.

By mid–April 2004, there were only 200 written presentations to the Citizens' Assembly and 100 persons registered for verbal presentations at its public hearings. By about the same time, there have been 16,000 unique visitors from 120 countries to the Assembly public website, which was launched at the end of November 2003. This gave an average of 234 unique visitors per day. The Citizens' Assembly Members' Newsletter of October 5, 2004, said, "The Assembly's public website passed a noteworthy milestone this past weekend (October 2), with our one-millionth pageview" ("Website Milestone," 2004). The number of written submissions rose to 400 by mid-May, 700 by mid-June, and to 1,600 by mid-September. The number of persons registered for verbal presentations rose to almost 400 by mid–June.

5.2   Hearing format

The Citizens' Assembly members had discussed and agreed how to conduct public hearings, before they ended their learning phase. According to this agreement there would be formal and informal hearings. The number of people attending a hearing and the number of its registered presenters would determine whether it should be conducted formally or informally. Where either number was significant, a formal hearing would be held. Where either number was not significant informal hearings would be conducted. The hearing floor layouts for the two types of hearings were different, especially as far as the way attendees were seated. In the formal hearings attendees would sit on rows of chairs as in a theatre, while in the informal hearings attendees would be seated in a semicircle or U-shaped sitting arrangement. In either case, presenters would speak from a podium. After their presentations, presenters would answer questions from the Assembly members and other attendees. The Assembly members present at the hearing would stay back and determine if any of the presentations made at the hearing should be recommended for presenting to the Assembly plenary session in early September.

The conduct of a pubic hearing involves a number of people playing some key roles. For this, the Assembly members agreed to have a registrar, media liaison officer, note taker, local host and a facilitator. In addition, there would be supporting staff to assist the registrar. The Assembly staff, with one exception, would play these roles: the local host would be one of the Assembly members present. The registrar would provide the administrative support needed. This would include putting the hearing room to order with proper seating arrangements, hanging posters, displaying handouts, maintaining a record of attendance, collecting and recording presentation materials, and ensuring that facilities are appropriate and refreshments are available. The registrar would also ensure that the Assembly members on the hearing panel would have their name cards properly displayed.

The media liaison officer would act as the Assembly point of contact for the media. As his or her specific functions, the media liaison officer would answer questions from media personnel, introduce them to Assembly members, take pictures, and prepare a news release for distribution. The note taker would record the hearing and prepare two summaries, one for each presentation and the other for the hearing as a whole. There would be an audio recording equipment to assist in recording the proceedings. The note taker's summary of each presentation would include some details of the presenter, a brief description of the presentation, key recommendations made, questions asked by the audience, the presenter's answers to those questions, and any key observations made by any member of the audience, with "quotable quotes," as deemed necessary. The summary of the hearing as a whole would include who attended, key recommendations heard, and key themes presented and discussed during the hearing.

The local host would officially open the hearing at the appropriate time. His or her first task would be to welcome the members of the public to the hearing, and introduce the Assembly members on the panel. After that the local host would explain to the house the purpose of the hearing, review the agenda for the hearing, and invite the public to complete the survey form handed over to them at the time of their entry to the hearing room; the completed survey forms could be handed in at the hearing or mailed to the assembly office at a later time. The local host would then introduce the 15-minute video specially prepared for the hearings, and play it for the audience. At the end of the video show, the local host would handle follow up questions. In doing this, the local host would get other Assembly members present involved in answering the questions. Once there are no more questions from the audience on the video and related matters, the local host would introduce the facilitator for the hearing. The facilitator would be responsible for managing the hearing. At the end of the hearing, the local host would thank everyone present for participating in the hearing and officially conclude it with closing remarks.

The facilitator would first thank the local host for introducing him or her to the audience, and introduce other members of the Assembly staff present and their specific roles for the day as registrar, media-liaison officer, note taker, and so on. After that the facilitator would explain to the audience how the day's presentations would be conducted. He would also inform the audience that the proceedings of the hearing would be recorded and the summaries of the presentations would be shortly posted on the Assembly website. The facilitator would further advise the audience that the media may be present and photographs may be taken as the hearing proceeds. Regarding the questions after each presentation, the facilitator would ask the members of the audience to limit them to those seeking clarification or added information on what the presenter has already presented. The facilitator would make it very clear that there would be a time to express opinions and differing views after the presentations. As for the timeframe, the facilitator would let everyone know that the time slot allocated for each presentation is 20 minutes: the first 10 minutes for the presentation itself and up to 10 minutes thereafter for any questions seeking further clarification or additional information on what has been said. Every speaker would be given a 1-minute warning before his or her time was up. The facilitator would first call for the presentations listed on the day's agenda, and after that call for any other presentations from the attendees, if any.

The main task of the Assembly members present at a hearing would be to listen to presenters and ask questions to fully understand their specific electoral reform proposals and their potential implications. In addition, the Assembly members would seek input from the public on the basic electoral values, such as local representation and proportionality, which are important to be considered in making an electoral choice for British Columbia. At the beginning, the Assembly members present would greet and welcome attendees as they arrive and make them feel welcome and comfortable. During the hearing, the Assembly members would not engage in a debate about the merits of a proposal made by a presenter or express a preference for any particular electoral system. Assembly members on the panel would also not engage in any arguments with their fellow panel members or the members of the public.

The Citizens' Assembly first identified the need for 49 public hearings, three hours of hearing at each. One more hearing was later added, as more people showed interest in making presentations than originally expected. This brought the total number of hearings to 50. The first of the 50 hearings was scheduled to take place in Vancouver on May 3, 2004, and the last in Kelowna on June 24, 2004. The hearing added later was scheduled to be held in Vancouver on June 12, 2004. The author participated as a panel member in three of the hearings, two in Surrey and one in Sechelt in the Sunshine Coast. He also played the role of the local host of one of the Surrey hearings.

5.3   What was heard

The Citizens' Assembly members heard lots of ideas, both within and outside the Assembly mandate, from a significant number of presenters at the Assembly public hearings. These were the largest set of public hearings ever held in British Columbia. In the 50 Assembly public hearings, 387 people made formal presentations and offered recommendations on electoral reform. Many more members of the public who joined in made informal presentations, offering more recommendations. According to Assembly records 2,742 members of the public attended the hearings. Table 5.1 below shows the extent of public participation at the hearings conducted by the Citizens' Assembly (2004) and the BC Federal Electoral Boundary Commission (2002) for comparison purpose.

Table 5.1: Comparison of the extent of public participation

Details	BC Citizens' Assembly on Electoral Reform Public Hearings, 2004	BC Federal Electoral Boundary Commission Public Hearings, 2002
Number of public hearings	50	12
Number of presenters	383	136
Number of public attendees	2,742	~ 400

Source: Carty, K. (2004b)

A number of presenters who took part in the Citizens' Assembly public hearings came from far away places. For example, one traveled from New York City to make a presentation at a public hearing held in Vancouver, while there were some who traveled from other parts of Canada. The number of presentations made at the public hearings held in the Lower Mainland was 153, while those made at the hearings held in The Islands, Interior/South East, and Northern BC were 85, 82, and 63, respectively.

Fourteen presenters made their presentations at more than one hearing. Eleven of them made their presentations at two hearings, while the remaining three made their presentations at three hearings. Most of the presentations made at the 50 Citizens' Assembly public hearings were on the Assembly's mandate. A vast majority of them called for change in the BC electoral system, while a small minority spoke in favour of the existing electoral system, FPTP (Single Member Plurality System).

The presenters who advocated change criticized the existing electoral system for a number of different reasons; there was, however, no perfect agreement among them as to what was really wrong with the existing system. The lack of fairness in election results, adversarial nature of politics in the legislature, dominance of a two-party system, friendly dictatorships, wrong winners, and artificial majority governments were among the reasons for which they criticized the existing electoral system. Most of these presentations strongly advocated proportional representation. Those who did this were of the opinion that some kind of proportional system would be the answer to most of the weaknesses of the existing system. These presenters did not elaborate on the extent of proportionality they preferred. As for different electoral systems, the presenters referred to all the three major proportional electoral systems: PR-List, Mixed proportional, and PR-STV. Among these proposals, those supported the Mixed Member Proportional (MMP) system outnumbered all others by a very clear margin.

Table 5.2 summarizes the different issues addressed at the public hearings and the geographic distribution of related presentations. The issues addressed by some presenters outside the Assembly mandate include democratic elections and

Table 5.2: Issues addressed at Citizens' Assembly public hearings

	Issue/Category	Interior/ South East	Lower Mainland	Northern BC	The Islands	Total
1	Change-Other	2	16	9	8	35
2	Democratic elections	4	11	1	1	17
3	Democratic government	8	15	8	11	42
4	Electoral system change:	67	118	42	64	291
5	- Citizens' Assembly type	1	6	2	2	11
6	- List proportional	1	6	3	5	15
7	- Majority system (AV, Run off)	6	9	5	7	27
8	- Mixed – other	3	1	1	3	8
9	- Mixed Proportional (MMP)	46	72	22	41	181
10	- NOTA	2	6	2	2	12
	- STV	5	8	3	7	23
12	Electoral system current	2	13	2	5	22
13	Local representation	18	38	22	15	93
14	Proportional representation	65	101	37	62	265
15	Underrepresented groups (women, ethnic, First Nations, ethnic)	23	26	16	17	82
16	Voter choice	60	91	38	56	245

Source: Citizens' Assembly (2004m, p.75)

democratic government. Some of the presenters who raised such issues appeared to have erroneously thought that the subject matters they discussed fell under the Assembly mandate. Others may have made use of the Citizens' Assembly public hearing opportunity to vent their grievances on the present governing system as a whole, disregarding the specific mandate of the Citizens' Assembly. The presenters in the former category dwelt on issues such as party discipline in the legislature, election financing of political parties, under representation of women and minorities, the need for lowering the voting age, voter turnout, compulsory voting as in Australia, giving tax credits as an inducement to vote, and the role of political parties. These presenters made a number of recommendations relating to elections, although they were not directly related to the Assembly mandate. Such recommendations include the following:

- Direct voting for the premier of British Columbia;
- Selection of representatives by a random process;
- Creation of some aboriginal electoral districts;
- Abolition of all political parties, and having elections with only independent candidates; and
- Banning of antidemocratic political parties.

The presenters in the latter category spent their time in talking about issues such as the processes used by parties to nominate their candidates, weighted votes for elected representatives, midterm elections, a bicameral legislature for British Columbia, limited terms for elected representatives, adversarial behaviour in the legislature, broken political promises, taxation, Republican status for Canada without a constitutional monarchy, and many more.

The issues addressed within the Assembly mandate were seen in two major areas: 1. electoral values and 2. electoral systems. The electoral values discussed were proportional representation, voter choice, local representation and better representation of women and minorities. There were presenters from all the regions of British Columbia among those who advocated these electoral values. Proportional representation and voter choice were the electoral values heard most at the hearings; almost 70 percent of the presenters advocated proportional representation, while more than 60 percent wanted to see enhanced voter choice.

As for electoral systems, only about six percent of the speakers (22) advocated the existing FPTP system. Eighty percent (291) of the rest (361) wanted to see some change. In their presentations, those who advocated the existing FPTP system focused on its strengths and the disadvantages of changing it to a proportional system. These presentations had lots of counter arguments to those who spoke in favour of proportional representation systems.

In their arguments, the advocates of the existing system pointed out that it has provided for the most part stable governments that could claim and efficiently implement electoral mandates over the past 133 years. These governments, they said, have remained accountable at all times, and have provided the voter with an identifiable local representative. They further pointed out that the existing plurality system is simple, familiar to the people, and has a transparent vote-counting process that determines the winners almost immediately. The proportional systems, they argued, have lots of flaws. The governments formed by proportional systems are often unstable, ineffective, inefficient, and costly. A person could get elected under some PR-List systems (Closed Lists) by having his or her name included in a list prepared by a party, even without the benefit of direct endorsement by the electorate. Proportional systems also give too much power to small parties, inconsistent with their political bases, and often produce coalition governments. A small party may even have the power to make or break a coalition government led by a major party at any time. At the last Citizens' Assembly public hearing held in Kelowna on Thursday, June 24, 2004, Jim Nielsen, a former BC cabinet minister for 11 years, passionately spoke on these and other disadvantages of proportional systems, and concluded, "A former premier of the province said Proportional Representation is for losers. That is perhaps the only time I have agreed with Glen Clark" (D. MacLachlan, personal communication, June 25, 2004).

Those presenters who wanted to see electoral change advocated seven different electoral models. These models include Mixed Member Proportional, Majority, STV, and List Proportional. More than 62 percent of those advocated change showed their preference for the Mixed Member Proportional (MMP) system. The second popular choice among them was the Majority system at 9.3 percent, and the third was STV at near eight percent. The level of support for these electoral options among the presenters looked similar in all the regions of BC. For example, the support levels among the presenters for MMP in Interior/ South East, the Lower Mainland, Northern BC, and the Islands were at 69%, 61%, 52%, and 64%, while those for STV were at 8%, 7%, 7%, and 11%, respectively.

The presenters who advocated proportional systems put forward many arguments in support of their position. According to these arguments, the coalition governments produced by proportional systems would change the politics of British Columbia for the better. Such governments, they said, would foster cooperation and harmony among diverse political groups and parties in the legislature, and produce policies on consensus. Such policies would be more likely to remain stable with any change in government. Those presenters further argued that proportional representation systems would put an end to wasted votes, improve voter turnout at elections, and give more opportunities to women and minorities to enter legislature. Above all, they pointed out that proportional representation systems would ensure the range of opinion in the legislature reflects the range of opinion in the electorate.

A number of presenters who advocated change to proportional systems also raised the issue of local representation. Some of these presenters stressed the point that any further increase in the size of existing rural electoral districts, which were already much larger in size than those in urban areas, would weaken local representation for the rural voter. These presenters made a special plea to the Assembly members to take this point into consideration in designing any form of proportional system. This matter was more regularly raised in the public hearings held in the rural areas of British Columbia. At the same time, some presenters questioned the validity of local representation in any system with excessive party control over voter representatives.

Some of those who advocated change to proportional systems also called for a threshold requirement for a party to first qualify for seats. These presenters were aware that such thresholds would affect proportionality to some degree. They, however, advocated thresholds as a means to exclude fringe parties. The thresholds proposed by these presenters ranged from two to 10 percent of the popular vote. In general, most of the speakers who advocated change did not go into more specifics of the particular electoral systems they preferred. They showed confidence in the Citizens' Assembly to work out all outstanding details.

The presenters who advocated the Majority system took time to explain that under this system one could get elected as a representative only with more than 50% of voter support. Among other benefits of the Majority system, these presenters pointed out, enhanced voter choice is an important one. A few of these presenters even suggested that the preferential voting by ranking candidates under the majority system could produce proportional results at elections, which, in fact, is not true. There was such confusion among some presenters who advocated proportional systems as well. For example, some of these presenters talked against political parties, while advocating party based and party driven proportional systems.

According to the advocates of the NOTA system, a NOTA option on the ballot is necessary for the voters who do not wish to support party-chosen candidates or independents. These voters, the NOTA advocates argued, abstain from voting or spoil their ballots under other electoral systems. The NOTA advocates also pointed out that once the NOTA option is supported by a majority of voters at an election a caretaker government could be formed with representatives randomly selected from those who had voted in favour of the NOTA option. Such a government, they said, would become a 'nonadversarial Constituent Assembly.'

Meanwhile, a number of presenters who made presentations both within and outside the Assembly mandate stressed the need for the final report of the Citizens' Assembly to be in a clear, simple language. These presenters also stressed the need for a well-planed process to educate the public on the rationale of the Assembly's final decision, especially if it becomes a subject of a province-wide referendum. One common premise across all presentations was their outpouring confidence in the Citizens' Assembly that it would do the job it had been assigned in an exemplary manner.

5.4 Written presentations

The Citizens' Assembly started to receive written submissions in November 2003, even before it began its plenary sittings. Figure 5.1 below graphically demonstrates the rate of increase in written submissions after the Assembly started its plenary sessions in January 2004. By the end of January 2004 the Assembly received 41 submissions, and this number increased to 59 by the end

Figure 5.1: Inflow of Written Submissions

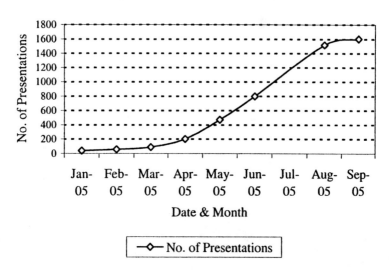

of February 2004 and to 89 by the end of the learning phase of the Assembly in March 2004. During the public hearing phase of the Assembly, which began with measures to generate interest in the Assembly process among the members of the public, the inflow of written submissions shot up rapidly. With the new submissions received in April (115), May (270+), and June (170+ to June 20th), the total number of submissions passed the mark of 800. This number later increased to 1,519 by August 13, 2004, and to 1603 by the set final deadline for written submissions, Friday, September 27, 2004.

A vast majority of the written submissions to the Citizens' Assembly were from the residents of British Columbia. Only six percent of the 1603 written submissions received were from outside British Columbia: four percent from other provinces of Canada and 2% from outside Canada. Table 5.3 on the next page shows the origins of the 1603 written submissions.

The written submissions made looked different in size and content. A review of the first 700 submissions processed by the Assembly staff showed that 95% of the submissions were limited to five pages or shorter. Much more than one-half (67%) of the total number of written submissions had only one page, with the shortest having only three words! Eighteen percent of the total number of submissions had two pages. Some (10%) had attached documents, while several of the presentations were duplicates. In one particular case, five different individuals made the same submission. There were also people who sent in more than one submission; highest being 11.

Table 5.3: Origins of written submissions

Origin	Submissions		Submitters	
	Number	%	Number	%
British Columbia	1530	95.45	1383	96.11
Ontario	30	1.87	17	1.18
Manitoba	4	0.25	3	0.21
Quebec	4	0.25	3	0.21
Yukon	2	0.12	2	0.14
Newfoundland	1	0.06	1	0.07
Nova Scotia	1	0.06	1	0.07
Nunavit	1	0.06	1	0.07
Total from Canada	*1573*	*98.13*	*1411*	*98.05*
United Kingdom	16	1.00	14	0.97
U.S.A.	8	0.50	8	0.56
New Zealand	2	0.12	2	0.14
Australia	1	0.06	1	0.07
China	1	0.06	1	0.07
Finland	1	0.06	1	0.07
Germany	1	0.06	1	0.07
Total from outside Canada	*30*	*1.87*	*28*	*1.95*
GRAND TOTAL	1603	100.00	1439	100.00

Source: Citizens' Assembly (2004m, p.82)

Most of the 1603 written submissions received by the Citizens' Assembly varied widely in content. A vast majority of them (1442) advocated electoral system change, while only a small minority (44) wanted to retain the existing FPTP electoral system. Others dealt with issues related to the Citizens' Assembly process (71), minority representation (22), and regional representation (32). There were also submissions that dealt with issues outside the mandate of the Citizens' assembly, as already discussed.

Most of those who advocated electoral change also indicated some preference to an alternative electoral system. More than half of the submissions that favoured change proposed a mixed member proportional (MMP) system. Another 20 percent of the submissions favoured proportional representation in a general way. Some of the submissions were not clear whether they were in favour of MMP or PR-List systems. On the whole, the research staff that did the analysis of the submissions felt that "It is likely that somewhere between 70% and 80% of submissions which identified a particular electoral system favoured MMP of some kind" (Citizens' Assembly, 2004m, p. 85). Another about 13% of the submissions favoured proportional representation by single transferable vote (STV). The Majority system with Alternative Vote (AV) was mentioned in four percent of the written submissions as an alternative electoral system.

Table 5.4: Written submissions by electoral system

Electoral Systems	Submissions		
	Number	%	%
Alternative vote (AV)	50	3.7	3.119
Mixed member proportional (MMP) (This includes a wide range of MMP systems)	849	63.1	53.0
Proportional Representation (PR)	277	20.6	17.280
Single transferable vote (STV)	170	12.6	10.6
TOTAL	1346	100.0	84.0
TOTAL SUBMISSIONS	1603		100.0

Source: Citizens' Assembly (2004m, p.84)

Table 5.4 above shows a breakdown of the written submissions by most frequently mentioned electoral system. All the submissions that indicated a preference for an alternative electoral system did not describe the preferred option in detail as mentioned earlier. The Citizens' Assembly research officers compiled a list of submissions of four or more pages, and identified 80 of them with some preference for an alternative electoral system. These 80 submissions had considerable commentary on a particular electoral system. Table 5.5 below shows a breakdown of these 80 submissions of four or more pages by electoral systems they discussed.

Table 5.5: Electoral systems dealt with in some detail in longer submissions

ELECTORAL SYSTEMS	LONGER SUBMISSIONS	
	Number	%
Alternative vote (AV)	10	12.5
Approval voting	2	2.5
Borda Count	3	3.8
First past the post (FPTP)	4	5.0
Mixed member proportional (MMP)	42	52.5
Proportional representation (PR)	2	2.5
Single transferable vote (STV)	14	17.5
Other systems	3	3.8
TOTAL	80	100.0

Source: Citizens' Assembly (2004m, p.85)

According to the details given in table 5.5, a clear majority of the people who made the written presentations in question have indicated their preference for the MMP system. The PR-STV system is a distant second in their order of preference. The 'Borda' system listed in the table has not been separately discussed in this book. In this particular system, voters rank the candidates and assign points to them, say 3 points to the candidate ranked first, 2 to the one ranked second and 1 to the one ranked third. At the time of counting, the points for each candidate on all ballots are added up to determine the winner with the most number of cumulative points.

Meanwhile, the author analyzed the 84 submissions the Assembly received between August 13, 2004 and the final submission deadline, September 27, 2004. Table 5.6 below shows the electoral system preferences shown in them.

Table 5.6: Electoral system preferences in 84
submissions received after August 13, 2004

	Preferred electoral system	No. of presenters
1	MMP	28
2	PR-List	19
3	Mixed—other than MMP	6
4	Alternative Vote	4
5	PR-STV	2
6	Others	1
7	Outside CA mandate	24
	TOTAL	84

Here again, a clear majority of the people who made the written presentations in question have indicated their preference for the MMP system. Unlike in the earlier case, PR-List systems appear as a distant second in the electoral preferences shown in the presentations; PR-STV system appears as the fifth preference.

5.5   Prince George meeting

The Prince George meeting scheduled for June 26–27, 2004, took place as planned. It was the first time all the Assembly members got together after they disbanded at the end of their learning phase on March 21st, 2004. The get-together started with a colourful reception arranged by the local Assembly members at the Coast Inn of the North in the center of Prince George city on Friday evening, June 25th. The reception was more like a family reunion with lots of hugs, greetings, and chitchats among the Assembly members and staff. Live music, appetizers and a cash bar entertained the attendees. On the invitation of the organizers of the event, some local dignitaries came in and graced the occasion. Mayor Colin Kinsley, Mayor of the City of Prince George, and Charles Jago, President of the University of Northern BC, were among them.

The Saturday and Sunday meetings that followed were held at the Prince George Civic Centre. The members devoted the entire Saturday meeting to review what British Columbians were saying to them through written submissions and presentations at the Assembly public hearings. The total number of presentations made at the public hearings was 387 as stated earlier, while the number of processed written submissions made by then stood at 700; about 200 written submissions received by them had not been processed yet.

The review of the public hearing presentations began with a short address by Professor Carty, Chief Research Officer. In this address Prof. Carty gave an account of the principle messages conveyed to the Assembly during its public hearings, based on written reports on them. After his address, the Assembly members broke up into discussion groups to review the principle messages discussed by Prof. Carty, based on their own experiences. This process was then repeated for the Assembly members to identify key messages to the Assembly through written submissions. This was done with the help of an introductory presentation by Prof Sharman, Associate Research Officer. After the two rounds of group reviews, the Assembly members looked at the key public messages together in a plenary session.

In the same plenary session, the Assembly also set a deadline of August 13, 2004, for receiving further written submissions. It was agreed that all written presentations until then would be processed and made available to the Assembly members before they begin their deliberation phase in early September. Submissions made afterwards also would be processed, but the Assembly members did not guarantee that they would be reviewed by September. In addition, the Assembly members also thought that it would be advantageous for them to build a list of "must read" written submissions, based on their own readings.

After many hours of group and plenary discussions on the key public messages to the Assembly on electoral reform, the Assembly members relaxed and enjoyed a special presentation by Dr. Leo Perra, Chief Operating Officer. This presentation named "Beyond Hope" gave an interesting BC profile, capturing the socioeconomic and geographic landscape of all the regions of British Columbia, and brought the Saturday program of the Assembly to an official closure. On the same day, at lunch break the Assembly members posed for a group picture in front of the Price George Civic center.

The Assembly reconvened the next day at 8:30 a.m. at the Civic Centre for a plenary session. The main item on the day's agenda was to discuss a process for decision making during the Assembly Deliberation Phase in the fall. Before going into that subject, the Assembly members first discussed whether or not the Deliberation Phase plenary sessions should be open to the public; The Gibson Report that was instrumental to the Assembly mandate had recommended that the Learning Phase should be open to the media and the public but it should be left to the Assembly members to decide whether the Deliberation Phase should have a similar open process. Following some discussions on the subject, the Assembly members decided to have their Deliberation Phase plenary sessions as well open to both the media and the public.

After that, Dr. Blaney, the chair of the Assembly, introduced the main subject of discussion for the day with a proposed decision tree and a process for the Deliberation Phase. His proposal was based on earlier discussions of the Assembly members on the subject at the end of the Assembly Learning Phase. The Assembly members then broke up into their discussion groups to review what the chair had now proposed and to discuss any new ideas on the subject. After their group discussions, the Assembly members reconvened for their last plenary session in Prince George. In this plenary session, the Assembly first heard from the different groups what they had discussed on the issues in question, and then tried to bring consensus among themselves as to how best they would conduct the Deliberation Phase in the Fall. The general agreements made during this discussion include the following:

- The decision tree should be reproduced in the form of a chart showing specific decisions to be made during each weekend during the Deliberation Phase, a critical path for decision making;
- The priorities and values of the Citizens' Assembly members should be the basis of discussion and ultimate decision;
- The Assembly members should be sensitive to minority concerns as well as regional differences, and try to understand how to integrate them in making electoral choices;
- All major decisions should be made in plenary sessions;
- Reporting back to the Assembly plenary sessions from discussion groups should be improved by having prior agreement among the members of each group for its reporting content, incorporating both majority and minority views and avoiding repetition in group presentations, and, where possible, by having one synthesized report from the different group reports;
- The Assembly research staff would prepare and submit some helpful tools, including a guide to electoral systems and a guide to submissions, to the Assembly members for their use in the Deliberation Phase; and
- The Assembly members should prepare for the Deliberation Phase, especially in regard to their understanding of the different electoral systems and their own choices on electoral values and priorities.

With these agreements the Assembly members and staff ended their Prince George sessions. The agreements required them to complete the tasks they had undertaken during the summer that had just begun. The same agreements also set the tone for the Assembly Deliberation Phase in many ways.

CHAPTER 6
DELIBERATION PHASE

6.1   Some preparations

The Citizens' Assembly reconvened on Saturday, September 11, 2004, at its usual meeting place, the Wosk Centre for Dialogue, Vancouver, to begin its Deliberation Phase. By this time a process for the deliberation phase and a critical path for decision-making had been drafted with input (by mail) from the Assembly members, as a follow up to the Prince George discussions. In addition, Assembly members had also received an electoral system chart with some explanatory notes that could help to better understand the different electoral systems advocated in the written submissions they received. Meanwhile, the Assembly's selection committee on plenary presentations had met over the weekend of July 10th, and selected nine presentations from those heard at the public hearings. The committee members had selected these presentations based on quality, mandate, balance and representativeness, presenter's history, and merit, as previously arranged. The Assembly members had agreed earlier that they would listen to the presentations selected by the committee in a plenary session during the first weekend of their Deliberation Phase. This was, in fact, the first item in the agenda of the first Saturday of the Deliberation Phase.

6.1.1   Plenary presentations

The names of the nine presenters selected for plenary presentations and the topics of their discussions were as follows:

1. Ian McKinnon, Electoral Reform—Taking into account political parties and governance issues;
2. Bruce Hallsor, Comparison of STV and MMP systems;
3. Tom Hoenisch, MMP system;
4. Katherine Gordon, MMP system;
5. Julian West, STV system;

6. Nick Loenen, Preferential Plus: A new effective made-in-BC voting system to elect MLAs;
7. Mayor Chris Morey, rural perspective;
8. Arpal Dosanjh, Majoritarian Preferential Voting: The wisest option; and
9. Jim Neilsen, First Past the Post system.

These presenters made their presentations to the first plenary session of the Assembly's Deliberation Phase in the order in which their names appear in the above list. Each presentation was followed by a question and answer session. The Assembly members had come up with a consolidated list of questions on their presentations beforehand, and the presenters had been informed of them in advance. This made the question and answer period most productive. There were, however, some impromptu questions in addition to the advance questions. The Assembly had asked all the presenters to stay for the entire day, giving an opportunity to its members to chat with them informally during coffee breaks and over lunch.

In their presentations, two presenters strongly resisted any change to the existing electoral system, while six others advocated change to a new electoral system of their choice. At the same time, one presenter was ambivalent about change, but argued against bigger ridings, especially in remote and rural regions of the province. Ian McKinnon of Victoria and Jim Nielsen of Peachland, a former BC health minister, were the presenters who spoke against any change to the existing electoral system. McKinnon stressed the need for the Assembly to consider how any potential change of electoral system would affect government and political parties and consequences of repeated minority governments some electoral systems could often produce. In comparing the existing FPTP system with the proportional and mixed systems, he said:

> The First Past the Post system tends to mean significant local independence in determining who will be the local candidate. ... There is a tendency for looser central party control over the choice of candidates. ... In contrast, list-based Proportional Representation systems tend to give more power to the central party apparatus. A mixed system ... can also lead to power being exercised by a highly centralized party organization (Citizens' Assembly, 2004f).

Regarding the consequences of minority governments, he said, "Recurring minority governments drive Canadians crazy" (Citizens' Assembly, 2004f). In his defence of the existing electoral system, Nielsen said that there was no perfect system of electing members to the BC legislature, and that British Columbians have been choosing their representatives, for the most part, over 133 years by the FPTP system. In response to a question on the representation of minorities and minority views, he said:

> What is a minority? One person? Two people? ... There are many ways of expressing minority views. It doesn't mean they have to be in the legislature. I have got a minority opinion. I would dump the Queen. I would sell the CBC.

Why should I be in the legislature just because I have a minority opinion? ("Sept. 11—Saturday session," 2004, pp. 2–3).

When he was specifically asked to comment on the plight of the Green Party that failed to secure a single seat in the legislature with 12.4% of the vote under the FPTP system he was defending, he said:

Twelve percent is not a winner. Somebody who has competed in the Olympics and has come in fourth 20 times is not a winner. Just because you have some candidates, and some people voted for you, does not mean you should be in the legislature ("Sept. 11—Saturday session," 2004, p. 3).

Presenters Bruce Hallsor, Tom Hoenisch, Katherine Gordon, Julian West, Nick Loenen and Arpal Dosanjh all advocated electoral change. Hallsor said that either a MMP system or a STV system would best suit BC. Both Hoenisch and Gordon preferred MMP. West preferred a modified version of the STV system, with "circuits" within multimember electoral districts, so that an individual MLA represents each area and community. He also proposed that urban constituencies could have as many as five to seven members while the rural ones should be limited to two to three members.

Loenen (Fair Voting BC) recommended a new electoral system designed by him for BC named Preferential Plus system. He explained that this new system would have preferential voting in multimember ridings for urban areas and single-member ridings for rural areas. He wound up his presentation expressing his desire to see BC change its electoral system by 2009 and Canada follow suit. In this regard, he specifically said:

This is my dream, that starting in 2009 in Victoria, we will have the essence of responsible government, and it will move east and permeate Ottawa. The greatest democratic deficit is not in Victoria; it is in Ottawa. .... If we have a major accomplishment, it will be like in England where (Prime Minister) Tony Blair had 137 members of his own party vote against his involvement in Iraq. Can you see that happening in Canada? If that were to happen in Canada, that would be wonderful ("Sept. 11—Saturday session," 2004, p. 2).

Meanwhile, Arpal Dosanjh expressed his preference for the Majority (AV) electoral system. He explained that any change to the existing electoral system would pose some element of risk, as any new system would have its own advantages as well as disadvantages. In his arguments in favour of the majority (AV) system, he said:

There is little risk at all in moving to this system (and) it does improve on our current system. ..... Other models may have great advantages, but also great disadvantages. ... Since a winning candidate requires 50% support of those voting, the constituency may feel the elected candidate more legitimately represents the riding than a candidate elected with less than 50%, a common occurrence in the current system ("Sept. 11—Saturday session," 2004, p. 2).

Mayor Chris Morey, Mayor of Fort Nelson, expressed the view that local representation was particularly important in remote and rural regions, and that it should continue under any new system. For this, she said it was important to avoid any new electoral system that would require larger electoral districts. In further explaining the type of problems that come with larger electoral districts (ridings) she referred to the Northern Health Authority and said:

> Increased ridings just don't work. Look at our health authority, the Northern Health Authority. You're looking at a region that looks after the health interests of one-third of the people of B.C. It is too large, too unwieldy. It does not address sub-regional issues, as it should. .... No discredit to the people who are directors of the health authority; it just doesn't work ("Sept. 11—Saturday session," 2004, p. 2).

These nine presentations on the first day of the Deliberation Phase of the Citizens' Assembly helped the Assembly members to cross a bridge between two important Phases of the Assembly process: from a well-known Public Hearing phase to an unknown and unpredictable deliberation phase.

6.1.2 Training for consensus building

The tasks now ahead of the 160 voting Assembly members were not easy, especially compared to those in the Learning and Public Hearing phases of the Assembly. The Learning phase helped the 160 members of varying backgrounds to first come to a level ground in terms of the knowledge of different electoral families and systems in democracies. Then, during the Public Hearing Phase that followed, they listened to what other British Columbians had to say about electoral reform in BC. During the same period, the Assembly members also read more than 1600 written submissions to the Assembly. After all that, they were now required to deliberate among themselves and choose the best electoral system for BC. Despite their common knowledge and experience gained during the Learning and Public Hearing Phases, it was obvious that the Assembly members would have different opinions on the issues that would be discussed during the Deliberation Phase.

Democracy requires all opinions to be well heard and respected. At the same time, democracy requires a meaningful process for people of all opinions to sit together and have productive discussions for making decisions. The key to all this is the ability of all who take part in democratic processes to deal with inevitable conflicts that can come up in their discussions. For this important reason, the chair of the Assembly arranged a highly informative session on *Consensus decision-making and conflict resolution* for its members during the second weekend of the Deliberation Phase. It was first arranged for the evening of the Saturday of that weekend, and was later advanced to the Saturday morning. Michael Fogel, a highly regarded specialist in negotiations and conflict resolution, conducted the session in the form of a "workshop." This workshop gave the Assembly members, and perhaps all others closely watching the Assembly proceedings, much needed hope that the Assembly would be able to complete its Deliberation Phase in a productive manner.

6.1.3 Critical path for decision-making

The Assembly Chair presented to the Assembly the draft critical path for decision-making during its second weekend. This was an attempt to reach a final agreement on the critical path by the Assembly members. After a fresh round of plenary discussions on the subject, the Assembly reached a final agreement on the Critical Path, with the following nine steps of ten distinct decisions:

1. Decision 1: Review and confirm electoral values;
2. Decision 2: Choose two electoral options ("A" and "B") that could achieve our goals;
3. Decision 3 & 4: Build best option "A" for BC, and Build best option "B" for BC;
4. Decision 5: Compare options and then choose the best electoral alternative;
5. Decision 6: Reassess and reconfirm the merits of the existing system;
6. Decision 7: Compare best alternative system against existing system and choose one;
7. Decision 8: Decide on the basic recommendation;
8. Decision 9: Draft report and other considerations; and
9. Decision 10: Approve Final Report.

Each of the Critical Path decisions was voted and approved by the Assembly members, decisions 1 to 5 by majority and the rest by consensus. At the same time the Assembly members agreed to treat Decisions 3 and 4 as one single step in the Critical Path process. The adoption of the Critical Path by the Assembly members installed in them a new sense of timely commitment to the deliberation process they were in.

6.1.4 Fresh look at values

The Assembly had earlier agreed that any system best for BC should be underpinned by the basic electoral values of British Columbians. Therefore, reaching a final agreement on the basic electoral values remained as the first task in the Assembly decision-making process, as identified by the above critical path.

For this, the Assembly arranged its members to revisit and reconfirm the electoral values they had identified during the Assembly Learning Phase, especially in view of what they had heard and read in the subsequent Public Hearing Phase.

In this task, the Assembly members first broke up into 10 discussion groups and identified one least important and three most important electoral features in

BC politics. After that each group reported its findings to a plenary session. In this exercise, some groups reported more than three most important features. Table 6.1 below shows most important and least important electoral features identified by the 10 groups.

Table 6.1: Most important and least important electoral values of British Columbians as identified by Citizens' Assembly members

Group	Most important	Least important
1	Local representation, Increased proportionality, Voter choice	SMP[2]
2	Seats won mirror votes won, Local representation, Voter choice, Lessen party discipline, More constructive civilized parties	SMP
3	Voter choice, Seats mirror votes, Local representation, minority option—social and cultural representation in legislature	SMP
4	Voter choice, Local representation, Proportionality, minority option—social and cultural representation in the legislature	SMP
5	Seats mirror votes, Local representation, Multiparty competition	SMP
6	Seats mirror votes, Voter choice, Multiparty competition, Local representation, District size	SMP
7	Local representation, Voter choice, Seats mirror votes	SMP
8	Seats mirror votes, Socially and culturally representative legislature, MLAs represent local constituency, System should encourage multiparty competition, Simplicity in ballot	SMP
9	Local representation, Seats mirror votes, Candidate and party representation, minority option—social and cultural representation	SMP
10	Candidate and party votes, Seats mirror votes, Multiparty competition	SMP

The most striking aspect observed was that all the 10 groups identified the SMP (FPTP) system as the least important feature. This and the importance all the 10 groups attached to proportional representation as one of the three most important electoral features have ruled out the SMP system. Another interesting observation was that some groups used different names to denote the same electoral feature. For example, references to "increased proportionality," "seats mir-

---

[2] SMP is not an electoral value or a single feature in an electoral system. Every Citizens' Assembly group, however, indicated SMP as their least important electoral feature.

ror votes," and "seats won mirror votes won" meant the same thing. In the same vein, the references to "MLAs represent local constituency" and "local representation" denoted the same interests. The references to "candidates and party votes' and "voter choice" also could be considered in the same manner.

Table 6.2: Assembly group support for each of the distinct electoral features

	Electoral feature	*No. of supporting groups*
1	Proportionality	10
2	Local representation	9
3	Voter choice	8
4	Minority—social and cultural representation in the legislature	4
5	Multiparty competition	4
6	District size	1
7	Simplicity in ballot	1
8	More constructive civilized parties	1
9	Lessen party discipline	1

Table 6.2 above gives a breakdown of the distinct electoral features the different groups identified and the number of groups that supported each of them. It clearly shows that the Assembly members' discussion groups had identified proportionality (seats to mirror votes), local representation and enhanced voter choice as the three most important electoral features of British Columbians, in that particular order. Minority representation in the legislature and multimember competition came next in line in the order of importance. In a plenary session held on Saturday, September 25, 2004, the Assembly members reached an agreement by consensus to accept the first three key electoral features as the most important ones to be considered in selecting an electoral system for British Columbia. This completed Step 1 (Decision 1) of the critical path of the Assembly decision-making process.

Interestingly, the Assembly members had considered the same three key system features as the ones most important to them some months back during their Learning Phase. This shows that the public input during the hearings had remained consistent with the Assembly members' opinions in this regard.

There were, however, two main surprises in the members' choices in electoral features. First, excessive party discipline had been a hot topic of discussion in the Assembly from its inception. Many presenters at the Assembly public hearings also spoke against excessive party discipline. Only one of the ten Assembly members' groups had, however, treated lesser party discipline as one of the three most important features. Second, during the learning phase of the Assembly, there was general consensus among its members that they were opposed to any system that would require further increase in the size of electoral districts. However, as in the case of party discipline, only one group identified district size as one of the three most important features.

6.2   Narrowing down electoral options

The mission now ahead of the Assembly members was to look for electoral families and systems that would uphold and retain the electoral features identified as most important to British Columbians. For the accomplishment of this mission, it was important that every Assembly member represented the wishes of not only the voters of the electoral district from which he or she had been selected but those of all British Columbians. The Assembly chair, in fact, took time to make this particular point very clear at a plenary session of the Assembly held on Saturday, September 25, 2004.

Two presentations made by Professor Carty, Chief Research Officer, to the Assembly's plenary sessions on Sunday, September 12, 2004, and Saturday, September 25, 2004, initiated plenary discussions with a view to narrowing down electoral options. In his presentation of Sunday, September 12th, he discussed in detail the extent to which each of the five basic electoral families could accommodate the three key electoral features in a comparative manner. As for proportionality, the PR-List and Majority electoral families were ranked the highest and lowest, respectively. The Mixed and STV families were ranked together next to the PR-List family, and the Plurality family came in between the Mixed/STV and Majority families. For local representation, the electoral families STV, Majority, Plurality, Mixed, and PR-List were ranked in that order, with STV as the highest or the best. The electoral families were not ranked in that manner for voter choice. Instead, typical ballot forms under the five different electoral families were discussed as shown below:

- Plurality family:
  Simple mark beside candidate's name;
- Majority family:
  Rank candidates 1, 2, 3;
- STV family:
  Rank candidates 1, 2, 3;
- PR-List family:
  Indicate party preference by selecting list or candidate;
- Mixed family:
  Constituency seats—Simple mark beside a candidate's name or rank candidates 1, 2, 3,
  and
  PR seats—PR list voting (Closed Lists) or simple mark(s) beside preferred candidates (Open Lists);

This presentation of Prof. Carty finally summarized how the five main electoral families are likely to accommodate the key electoral features identified by the Assembly members in a table form. Table 6.3 is a truncated version of this summary.

Table 6.3: Status of key electoral features in different electoral families

Electoral Feature		Electoral Families			
	PR-List	Mixed	STV	Plurality	Majority
1 Proportionality	Yes	Yes	Yes	No	No
2 Local representation	No	Yes	Yes	Yes	Yes
3 Voter Choice: across party	Possible	Possible	Yes	No	No

Professor Carty's presentation of Saturday, September 25, 2004, entitled "Defining Key Elements & Identifying Alternative Systems," outlined a process of elimination to short list the electoral family options. This process eliminated the PR-List family for its least performance in local representation, and the Majority and Plurality families for their least performance in proportionality. The existing plurality system would, however, be looked at again later in the process in making a final decision as to the best electoral system for British Columbia. All this meant, only Mixed and STV families were now left with as possible alternatives to the existing system for further consideration.

After each of the above presentations, the Assembly members raised many questions, especially regarding the status of the key electoral features under different electoral families. Some brought new arguments to the debate. For example, a number of Assembly members argued that the nature and extent of local representation under STV systems was similar to that of PR-List systems with Open Lists. Some emphasized the point that in both STV and PR-List systems with open lists the voter could be given the option of voting across party lines. After a lengthy discussion on these and other related matters, the Assembly members finally settled for the Mixed and STV families as possible alternatives to the existing system in the afternoon plenary session of Saturday, September 25th. This completed the Step 2 (Decision 2) of the Critical Path of the Assembly decision-making process.

6.3   Building best STV & Mixed options

The next step (step 3) of the Critical Path required the Assembly to build the best STV and Mixed electoral options for BC. The Assembly members first deliberated on the STV electoral family during the remaining plenary sessions of the same weekend, and agreed on some basic features for the best STV option for BC. After agreeing on the basic features of the best STV option, the Assembly members spent most of their next weekend sessions (October 16/17) in designing the best Mixed option for BC. Tables 6.4 and 6.5 below show the specific features built into the best STV and Mixed options for BC.

By and large, the details built into the best STV option were sufficient to compare it with any other electoral option. This, however, could not be said

Table 6.4: Details of the best STV option for British Columbia

	Electoral System Feature	Decision	Remarks
1	District magnitude	Minimum of 2 for rural areas and 4 – 7 for densely populated areas.	
2	Quota	Droop, to be decided, if STV is finally selected.	Droops Quota makes it easier for small parties to win the first seat.
3	Ballot form	Grouping by party, randomized names and randomized parties.	No enthusiasm for having pictures on ballot.
4	Ballot completion rules	Voters to express as many preferences as they desire.	No support for ranking entire ballot.
5	Filling vacancies	By by-elections with Alternative Vote.	Little support for SMP for by-elections.
6	Transfer votes	Full transfer count for replicability.	Not a major concern at this stage.

Table 6.5: Details of the best Mixed electoral option for British Columbia

	Electoral System Feature	Decision	Remarks
1	Mixed kind	MMP	Members agreed by consensus. Little support for other mixed systems, including MMM & MMP-Lite.
2	Constituency List balance	Constituency seats—60%, and List seats—40%	Members' preferences: 60/40—78, 50/50—41 & 66/33—22
4	Type of lists	Open Lists	Members' preferences: Open lists—135 & Closed lists—8
5	Determination of proportionality.	Provincially determined.	Members' preferences: Provincially—111 & Regionally—29
7	Candidates in either or both parts: Lists & Constituencies	Parties can decide to run candidates in either or both parts of MMP.	
8	Constituency seats rules.	AV will be used for constituency elections.	AV—99 FPTP—43
9	Two choices	Candidate and Party	
10	Filling vacancies	Constituency seats by Alternative Vote.	Decision by consensus. List seats – to be decided, if MMP is finally selected. Agreed list seats belong to the party.
11	Threshold	3%	Members' preferences: For regular elections: 3%—67, 5%—46, & Natural—32% For run off elections: 3%—93. 5%—48%
12	Others	To be decided, if MMP is finally selected.	

about the best Mixed option, as it was not built to a degree where it could be compared with other electoral options to the same extent. The Assembly failed to find adequate time to build the Mixed option model to the same level as that of the STV because of the time frame slotted for the remaining tasks of its decision-making process.

The basic Mixed (MMP) electoral features left to be decided later include the following:

- Formula for allocating PR seats
- List access by parties
- Possible overhang seats
- Vacancy rule for list seats
- Ballot forms
- Appropriate regions

With the design of the basic features for the best STV option and some important features for the best Mixed option for BC, the Assembly members could only partially complete the step three (Decisions 3 and 4) of the Critical Path of the Assembly decision-making process.

Meanwhile, the process of building the best STV and Mixed options for BC as alternatives to its existing SMP (FPTP) system also set the tone for the Assembly members' debates that followed on their preferences among those three electoral systems. The debate between those who preferred the best STV option to the best Mixed option and those who thought the other way about, in particular, became the most intense debate in the Citizens' Assembly on Electoral Reform.

6.4   Choosing the best alternative option

According to the original plans, the Assembly should have made a decision (Step 4, Decision 5) on the best alternative electoral system to consider in relation to the existing SMP system by the end of the third weekend (October 16/17) of the Deliberation Phase. This decision was now postponed to the Saturday of the next Assembly weekend, scheduled for October 23/24. That was when the formal debate on MMP vs. STV was expected to begin on the floor of the Assembly. This debate, however, started informally six days before, with the buildup of the two best alternative options (MMP and STV) during the previous weekend. The Assembly members, in fact, walked out of the Asia Pacific Hall at the end of their Sunday plenary session of the previous weekend (October 17th) arguing about the merits and demerits of the two best options they had built.

As the author was getting ready to leave his seat in the Asia Pacific Hall that Sunday, four other Assembly members approached him to discuss something "very important." They said that there was an urgent need for someone to start a "thread" on MMP in the Assembly electronic discussion forum, as all the contributors to it so far had "ganged up" against MMP. Their writings, one of the four members said, were one-sided, and had already convinced many Assembly members to vote for STV on "false" arguments. The author did not have any opinion on what they were complaining about, as he had not often visited the particular thread in the Assembly members' website. He, however, decided to open a new thread to facilitate an open website debate on MMP-STV as soon as possible.

Later on the same day the author opened his new "thread' under the heading STV vs. MMP in the discussion forum of the Assembly members' website. In this thread, the author gave his arguments in support of the MMP option, and invited others to come up with their opinions on the two options in question. Within hours the usual contributors to the discussion forum supporting STV joined the debate. They questioned the validity of the arguments the author made in support of MMP, some in a mature, objective manner and some with less objectivity. At times, the author found very difficult to respond in a timely manner to the counter arguments they all made. On some occasions, the few who were supporting MMP in the web debate had written encouraging notes for the author. For example, one member wrote, "RB, I am glad you made your post, and I hope you continue to make more! Don't be intimidated by this crowd … we need to hear strong arguments on both sides" (Citizens' Assembly, 2004h). As the days passed by, the web debate on MMP-STV became more tense and nail-biting. At a time of war of words between the two sides, one Assembly member wrote:

> I hope you and RB and Rick keep posting. I think you represent views of many in the assembly who are quieter. As I read the posts I can see that a person with a different view might not want to take on the STV advocates. … But hey, it could be worse, we could be in the legislature screaming obscenities at each other, this is far more civilized (Citizens' Assembly, 2004h).

In all, fifteen Assembly members took part in this website debate on MMP-STV, and ran through 54 separate submissions of 57-page length in six days. It continued in the thread even after the author responded to the last round of comments opposing the MMP option, with a closing remark that said, "Thank you all for your comments. See you at the Assembly tomorrow morning. With regards to all!!!."

The arguments made by those who advocated MMP covered eight different areas: proportionality, local representation, voter choice, party discipline, two types of MLAs, women and minority representation, DM, and system complexity. The arguments in support of STV covered the first five of these areas. The specific arguments made in favour of MMP and STV in these areas in the website debate are summarized below:

1. Proportionality

For MMP
- Proportionality ensures that the range of opinions in the legislature reflects the range of opinions in the electorate—through political parties.

MMP is specifically designed to do that. STV promotes voters to concentrate on local personalities (not parties), and, therefore, cannot
achieve the same results.
- Party system will continue under STV as well. For it to bring proportionality, however, the voter should have the freedom to vote for a
party without being influenced by local personalities. STV does not allow this.
- Researchers have found that by its very nature, STV is less proportional
or quasi proportional (Farrell, 2001, p.155).
- STV is counterproductive to the Westminster style multiparty democracies that can bring proportionality through parties.

For STV
- According to a proportionality matrix from New Zealand (NZ) & Ireland based on elections since 1948 (*NZ introduced MMP only in 1993*),
disproportionality of Ireland and NZ are 5.8% and 6.3%, respectively.
This shows that STV Ireland is more proportional than MMP NZ. [*The
proponent of this argument, however, agrees that such a comparison
with only 11 years of MMP in NZ is not dependable*]
- In MMP, the size of the legislature needs to increase with "overhang
seats" in the event a party gets more constituency seats than what it gets
under PR to bring proportionality. STV brings proportionality without
any change to the number of seats in the legislature in all situations.

2. Local Representation

For MMP
- MMP elects constituency representatives as in SMP. MMP is still better than SMP, as the voter also has List MLAs to depend on.
- STV does not elect constituency MLAs as in MMP or SMP.
- Under STV, the voter will have only List MLAs to go to at times of
need.
- MMP List candidates would be spread around the MMP district.
- MMP can give better LR to the rural areas in the North by carving 6
constituency seats out of the present ten (on assumed 60:40 split). This
would give the voter a local MLA for an area equal to 1.67 times the
size of the present constituency and 4 PR MLAs.
- The candidate(s) a voter votes for may or may not win under STV or
MMP. Despite this MMP gives the voter an identifiable local MLA and
PR MLAs that belong to the party of his/her preference. But under
STV, if a voter's candidate(s) looses, there is neither an identifiable local MLA nor any other MLA of common interests.

For STV
- Being a candidate based system, STV produces MLAs better known to
voters. This gives better local representation than under party based

MMP.

- Although STV can give only regional (STV Districts) MLAs, they are going to be spread out around the STV District. This assists in local representation.
- STV can improve LR in rural areas by lowering DM to 2. This is a good solution to the North, with two MLAs for an area equal to on average twice the size of the present constituency.
- In STV, the candidate the voter votes for automatically becomes his or her local representative.

3. Voter Choice

For MMP

- MMP can give the same amount of voter choice as in STV, with AV constituencies and Open List PR seats; MMP can allow voting across parties too, if deemed desirable.
- MMP gives the voter an identifiable local MLA, as in SMP. This is a voter choice STV cannot give.
- Record of independent candidates under STV is very poor. STV Malta failed to produce any independent candidate for the last 50 years.
- In voting on party lines under MMP, voters relate to choices on all aspects of life covered by party platforms. The candidate based voting under STV narrows down these choices to single or limited local issues.

For STV

- Voter choice depends on the size of the STV District. In big STV districts, voters can vote for small party candidates hoping to get elected. It is also not too difficult for independent candidates to win.

4. Party Discipline

For MMP

- BC has a Westminster type party-based democratic system. Different parties are opinionated differently, and voters make choices based on what opinions they need to be represented in the legislature. That is how the legislature is expected to reflect the range of opinions in the electorate. This system can work effectively only with some party discipline to ensure MLAs do not go outside their party policies. Both MLAs and parties can betray voters. In the case of MLAs, there is a recall system in place. In the case of parties, voters can boot them out at a general election.

For STV

- By being a candidate-based system, STV reduces party discipline of MLAs. This helps MLAs to better represent their voters.

5.   Two Types of MLAs

For MMP
- Having two types of MLAs under MMP is very advantageous. Their efforts to work together help all regions (and constituencies) develop faster by taking mutual advantage of local resources in a coordinated manner. It also helps reduce NIMBY (Not in my backyard) challenges when it comes to development issues that are of benefit to regions.

For STV
- MMP produces two types of MLAs with different interests, at constituency and regional levels. STV does not produce two types of MLAs.

6.   Women and Minority Representation

For MMP
- Women and minority representation in PR and MMP countries is much higher than in STV countries. For example, Women representation in STV Ireland and Malta are only 12% and 9.2%, while that of MMP Germany is 30.7% (Farrell, 2001, p.157).

7.   District Magnitude

For MMP
- MMP can have higher DMs than in STV. This also means MMP can give more proportional results. The need to lower DM to 2 in rural areas under STV will have adverse effects on proportionality.

8.   System Complexity

For MMP
- MMP has a transparent and simple counting process that can determine winners immediately. It is not so under STV; STV counting is both complex and obscure. In Australia, voters have turned their STV system to one of List type because of the difficulties they faced with the STV system.

Source: Citizens' Assembly (2004h).

The last entry in the MMP-STV website debate appeared on Friday, October 22, 2004, at 12:14 p.m. The same afternoon Assembly members had to travel to Vancouver for that weekend's Assembly sessions, where they would conduct an open debate on the same subject. A number of Assembly members who had read the contents of the website debate congratulated the author for opening the STV vs. MMP thread in the Assembly members' Discussion Forum. They said that mainly STV virtues were told and repeated in the discussion forum before, and the new thread brought in a new dimension to the MMP-STV debate with equally sounding virtues of the MMP system. They were, however, concerned that a majority of the Assembly members may not have had the bene-fit of reading the website debate, as many members did not have a habit of visit-ing the Assembly websites on a regular basis.

The MMP-STV debate on the floor of the Assembly started on Saturday, October 23, 2004. The debate began after some discussions about a procedure and some ground rules to be followed by all taking part in it. As for the proce-dure, the chair would first ask someone from one of the two sides to speak for a few minutes explaining the option preferred, and call for a couple of people who would argue differently. After this is done with both sides, the floor will be opened to all members for further arguments. At some point the chair would ask the members whether they are ready to vote on their positions. If the members were not ready to vote when the chair calls for that the debate would continue. When the members are finally ready, they would vote by secret ballot. Once voted, the Assembly staff would count the votes in front of four scrutineers in a room away from the Assembly meeting. The chair would select the scrutineers. The chair appointed Campbell Sharman, one of the Assembly research officers, as the returning officer for the day.

The Assembly members themselves had selected both MMP and STV as two best alternatives for further consideration. Most of the members who took part in the debate, however, took strong positions for one of the two systems in preference to the other. As the debate continued more and more members spoke with passion and vigour in support of their arguments. The assembly had not witnessed before the amount of enthusiasm and excitement among its members seen during this debate. The occasional sounds of applauses and even whistling in jubilation added some joy and impetus to the heating up arguments on both sides. In all, 57 Assembly members spoke during the debate, and they made 100 separate submissions that ran into 28 Assembly transcript pages. Some members were still not prepared to end the debate when the chair had to finally call for a deciding vote.

In this lively MMP-STV debate, the Assembly members touched on issues in all the areas discussed in the website debate over the previous week, though not necessarily in the same manner. In addition, the Assembly debate touched on some new areas. These new areas include rural needs, voter apathy, public input, and some general topics. The general topics covered political culture, safe seats, wrong winners, incentives for parties to clean up their acts, and Zombie politi-cians. The main points made by the Assembly members in arguing for and against MMP and STV in this debate in all these areas are summarized below:

1. Proportionality

- Under STV, both proportionality and local representation act together, whereas MMP separates them.
- MMP gives the voter the best of both the worlds: proportionality and local representation.

- MMP wants additional MLAS to bring overall proportionality at times. These top-up List MLAs usually come from the opposition.
- STV is an elegant system where proportionality comes naturally.
- DM for constituency seats under MMP is just one. How does the DM of one in MMP constituency seats give more proportionality than in STV districts of DM 2?
- STV provides proportionality, which is not in any way significantly different to that of MMP.
- MMP optimizes both local representation and proportionality.
- MMP provides proportionality by design and not by coincidence.
- MMP produces the most proportional results most reliably.

2. Local Representation

- Locally elected MMP MLAs do not represent the voters who did not vote for them in their districts.
- Identifiable local/ constituency MLAs under MMP in rural areas will take their constituency concerns to Victoria.
- Local representation is better under MMP for both the rural and urban voter. MMP gives the voter an identifiable local representative and a number of PR representatives to go to. STV can give only STV-District representatives.
- STV is fairer, as it produces MLAs more representative of the people, not parties.
- STV gives more effective local representation. If a voter contacts all his/her STV representatives, they will scramble over each other to get back to the voter.
- Under MMP, there will be a party and chosen candidate(s) carrying the voter's interests.
- Candidates will be more responsible to the voter under STV, as it promotes competition among them all, irrespective of parties they represent.
- Representatives elected under candidate-based STV would be more accountable to the electorate.
- Under MMP a voter can reach his/her constituency MLA as now. That is what the voter wants at times of need. The suggestion that under STV the voter can approach all STV district MLAs is not workable. The voter is not going to spend time trying to speak to all of them.
- MMP optimizes both local representation and proportionality.
- STV MLAs would know voters' needs better than MMP List MLAs.
- MMP is a dynamic system that can better respond to the diversity of British Columbia.
- STV encourages MLAs to serve the voter and to understand the relationship they have with the voter.

3. Voter Choice

- Have not seen any evidence that points to MMP with Open Lists is necessarily better than STV.
- STV allows the voter to choose candidates across parties. It would, however, be difficult for MLAs of different parties to unite on the issues of the voter's interests.
- MMP offers more meaningful choice. The voter can vote for a known local candidate and a party representative.
- MMP has more voter choice with one vote for candidates and one vote for party. STV gives only one vote (for candidates).

4. Party Politics and Discipline

- It is better to have a system that improves the existing party system in preference to one that suppresses it. Voters should be voting for values/policies, and for a group (not an individual) that has a commitment to uphold & implement them.
- The need for electoral reform has come about because of the problems created by parties, not candidates. STV is the best solution for that.
- MMP forces voters to vote party lines. This is not a solution to a large section of people who do not believe in party line voting. MMP excludes these voters. STV does not.
- STV reverses the process for party policy making for the better. First, candidate-based elections elect representatives, and they go and frame their party policies, addressing the voter's interests.
- In a party-based system, parties can create dictatorships and dynasties through party discipline.

5. Two Types of MLAs

- MMP produces two tiers of MLAs, while STV does not.

6. Women and Minority Representation

- According to David Farrell (Farrell, 2001, p.151), STV permits the possibility that voters of main parties get one (or two) constituency representatives they can approach. This means candidates of smaller fledging parties would find more difficult to get elected.
- Independents will have more chances under STV.
- STV encourages independent candidates to run and be elected. This also reduces party discipline.
- MMP allows small parties and more of them.
- It is difficult to believe that MMP would increase minority and women representation in legislature.

- Over the last 50 years, in Ireland only one party has obtained more than two percent of the vote nationally and failed to gain a seat.
- MMP fosters inclusivity and attracts minorities, First Nations people, and women who want to get involved in politics in a better way.

7. District Magnitude

- STV is more flexible. It gives DMs varying from 2 to 7.

8. System Complexity

- Under MMP, voters have a clearer idea as to how their votes are translated to seats.
- Simplicity is not a concern.
- The MMP model designed by the Assembly is more complex than its STV model; STV looks less complex.

9. Rural Needs

- MMP gives better voter choice to rural voters, as under STV only major parties have any chance of winning a seat in rural areas.
- MMP, unlike STV, translates votes to seats throughout the province in the same manner, and acts the same way and benefits the voter the same way throughout BC. STV cannot do this. Under STV, especially the rural voter is disadvantaged and treated differently.
- DM of two in STV for rural areas simply not acceptable, as it compromises the interests of the rural voter.
- STV may not give proportionality to the North, but it would better provide all the three basic needs of proportionality, voter choice and local representation as a whole
- MMP serves all equally but STV creates two tiers of voters.
- STV does not look at the province in a wholesome manner.

10. Voter Apathy

- MMP is the better solution to voter apathy and low turnout at elections. It allows small parties and more of them.
- STV can do better in addressing the issue of voter apathy.

10. Public Input

- The strong support for MMP and very weak support for STV at public hearings and written submissions cannot be ignored. BC Voters would easily understand and support MMP because of the widespread support for it.

- It is true that there was overwhelming support for MMP at public hearings and in written submissions made to the Assembly. But the Assembly members must decide for themselves.
- It is important to have a system that looks after the interests of the province as a whole, and not as a community of individual isolated regions.

12. General Arguments

- MMP with AV for constituency seats and Open Lists for PR seats is a unique MMP model. It does not have the weaknesses of other MMP systems in the world, and it has been specially designed to meet BC needs. It is the best MMP model in the world, and it would serve BC best.
- Under STV there will not be safe seats for anyone.
- Both, voting for an individual and voting for a party are necessary. MMP gives this option. A party vote is essential to address provincial issues.
- MMP model designed with AV constituency seats and Open List PR seats will not have safe seats for anyone.
- The light-hearted culture in Ireland, where STV works well, is particularly interesting.
- STV provides for an enriched legislature because it allows for an influx of fresh new parties and balances this with the stability and wisdom of established large parties.
- MMP provides incentives for parties to clean up their acts.
- STV can do better in improving the political culture of BC.
- Allowing candidates to have their names in both constituency and List elections under MMP is not acceptable. It could elect candidates defeated at constituency level as MLAs.
- MMP avoids further fragmentation of local communities, accelerate development in all regions, and bring greater prosperity to all British Columbians.

After bringing the MMP-STV debate to a closure, the chair asked the Assembly members to mark their ballots selecting either MMP or STV as the best alternative electoral system for BC. The results of the voting showed that the vast majority of the members preferred STV to MMP: 123 for STV and 31 for MMP. Accordingly, the chair declared that the Citizens Assembly on Electoral Reform had duly selected the STV electoral system as the best alternative electoral system for BC. This has now completed the step 4 (Decision 5) of the critical path of the Assembly decision-making process.

A close review of the numerous arguments brought forward by Assembly members in this debate shows that some of them were ill-informed or had only limited knowledge about MMP and STV systems. For example, one member said that under STV, the candidate one votes for automatically becomes his or her local representative. This gives the wrong impression that every voter would get at least one MLA he or she has voted for. Another member arguing for STV asked how could the MMP constituency seats of DM one be more proportional than the STV districts of DM two, when MMP manages proportionality at regional or provincial level. Some members made statements without any form of supporting evidence. For example, one member stated that independent candidates would have more chances of winning under STV, when available statistics clearly show otherwise. Another Assembly member said that simplicity was not a concern, when many Assembly members as well as almost all the presenters at the Assembly hearings had advocated simplicity as an essential element in any new system for BC.

At the same time, during this debate few Assembly members also posed themselves as experts on electoral systems. For example, one Assembly member who supported STV said that although there was overwhelming support for MMP at the public hearings of the Assembly and in the written submissions it received, he had come to the Assembly with the ability to think for himself. Instead of trying to show that he could think better than all those who argued for MMP and elevating himself to a position of an expert of some sort, he should have responded to the specific arguments of MMP supporters explaining why he still preferred STV.

6.5   One more look at the existing electoral system

The next task of the Citizens' Assembly was to make a decision between the existing electoral system, SMP, and the best alternative system chosen, STV. For this the Assembly first had one more look at the existing system. This time, it was done in comparison with the best alternative system chosen. The Assembly spent most of Sunday, October 24, 2004, in doing this. It began with a special presentation prepared for this purpose by Professor Carty, Chief Research Officer. A question and answer session followed the presentation. After that the Assembly members broke up into their discussion groups and further deliberated on the subject.

Professor Carty's presentation included an assessment of the strengths and weaknesses of the SMP (FPTP) system in comparison to those of an alternative PR system, and tried to identify the potential effect of the recommended PR alternative (STV) on the system of government in British Columbia; the mandate of the Citizens' Assembly specifically required it to take into account the potential effect of its recommended model. In doing this, Professor Carty said that there was a need to find out what could be gained and lost by a change. At the same time, he continued, the Assembly members should ask two important questions. First, could a change address the weaknesses of the existing system without giving up its strengths? Second, are the potential gains to be made worth the costs? Professor Carty ended his presentation by explaining that the Assembly members had to consider difficult trade-offs in selecting one system in preference to the other, and that they should feel confident in making their final decision in favour of SMP (FPTP) or STV.

The main arguments discussed during the presentation and the follow-up discussions as to why people perceive the existing SMP (FPTP) system as a weak or preferred system are given below:

Weak System
- Promotes an overly adversarial type of politics;
- Produces disproportional election results, with seats-votes imbalance;
- Larger parties get more seats than they deserve at the expense of small parties;
- Produces wrong winners;
- Produces artificial majorities in the legislature;
- Produces weak oppositions that cannot effectively check on governments;
- Underrepresents women and minorities;
- With strong party discipline, produces dictatorships and possibly dynasties.

Preferred System
- Promotes broad-based inclusive parties with incentives to reach out to voters;
- Produces stable, majority governments that can claim specific mandates, plan for life of term, implement unpopular decisions, hold elections at predictable times, and be more innovative in making policy;
- Voters can effectively hold their MLAs and government accountable;
- With strong governments, can better defend BC's interest in Federal-Provincial politics; and
- Provides effective local representation.

Professor Carty's presentation also showed electoral advantages of the PR alternative and related governing issues that could be viewed as its disadvantages. The specific advantages and disadvantages of the PR alternative discussed by the Assembly members after his presentation are summarized below:

Advantages of the PR alternative
- Provides more representative legislature, with party-seats in proportion to party-votes and a greater diversity among MLAs,
- All partisan interests are represented in the legislature;
- Does not force small parties to merge with larger ones;
- More control of the government by the legislature than in the SMP system; and
- Provides more kinds of choice for individual voters.

Disadvantages of the PR alternative
- High possibility to form coalition governments, based on post-election bargaining among politicians;
- Governments may not last for full term, as coalition governments can break up any time;
- Voters will not know whom to credit or blame for government's successes or failures; and
- A coalition Premier may not be able to effectively defend BC interests in Federal-Provincial politics.

In his presentation, Professor Carty also looked at the types of government BC would have with a change to a PR alternative system. In doing this, he first gave some examples of what happened with a similar change in New Zealand, and showed the range of coalition possibilities of the left, right and center in BC with a change of its electoral system to a PR alternative. He also pointed out that the voter may or may not know what kind of a coalition government they would get after an election, as the parties may not discuss their potential coalition plans beforehand.

In response to some specific questions raised from the floor after his presentation, Professor Carty clarified the following points:

- There is no guarantee that the PR alternative (STV) is going to solve the problem of underrepresentation of women and minorities. It is determined more by decisions taken by political parties or explicit laws providing for those special needs.

- It could take time to form a coalition government after an election, unless there was an obvious winning coalition. New Zealanders took weeks or perhaps a month to form their coalition government. After the first PR election, politicians learn that they have a new form of legislature and that they have to treat one another differently. Some learn faster than others.

- Under PR systems, often a vote in the legislature after an election decides who would be the premier, and the premier would select his cabinet ministers. Thus the legislature explicitly votes for the government. Germany, Ireland and other PR countries normally form their governments in this manner.

With Professor Carty's presentation and the subsequent plenary and group discussions of the Assembly members, they have now completed the step 5 (Decision 6) of the Assembly decision-making process. The next task of the Assembly was to weigh the merits and demerits of the existing SMP system and the best PR alternative, STV, and make a decision as to which of the two would be the best system for BC. The process for this was similar to the one used to decide the best alternative electoral system on the previous day. Thus, the Assembly members were now poised for another debate, this time on SMP and STV. Voting on the two systems by secret ballot would follow the debate.

6.6   Final choice

The SMP-STV debate among the Assembly members started soon after they returned from their morning coffee break on Sunday. Twenty-eight Assembly members spoke and made 30 separate submissions that ran into 14 pages of Assembly transcript. There were no loud cheers, applauses, or whistling as on the previous day. The media, however, had sent more people to record the events of this day, as the Assembly members were expected to make their final choice on an electoral system for BC; no doubt, this day's Assembly decision between SMP and STV was the one all British Columbians were anxiously waiting for. A decision in favour of SMP on that day would end the Assembly process, acclaiming the status co. A decision in favour of STV would result in a province-wide referendum on the day of the next general election. Perhaps, the MMP-STV debate held on the previous day may become more important for historians. The arguments brought up by the Assembly members in their SMP-STV debate are summarized below:

The arguments in favour of SMP over STV:

- STV provides regional representation and not local representation.
- STV diminishes local representation in rural areas, and has a double standard in local representation, one for rural areas and the other for urban areas.
- Community dynamics in STV districts, especially in the rural areas, would make some parts of the districts completely disfranchised.
- Votes are never wasted under SMP. Those who loose have a chance at the next election.
- Unless one takes it from a provincial perspective, SMP does not produce wrong winners and artificial majorities.
- In STV, a small party or an independent group of MLAs could hold balance of power, and would be able to enforce its policies as a result, although it did not win the election or form government. This causes disproportionality in a different way. This is not fair as much as shutting the voices of such small parties or groups altogether.
- SMP produces majority governments that can make hard decisions and form long-term plans. STV cannot do that.
- In SMP, the voter chooses government in a transparent way, while in STV politicians choose government behind closed doors.
- The existing SMP system could be improved, say with forced by-elections as in Russia, increased DMs, limited voting systems as in

Spanish Senate, and/or nontransferable vote as in Taiwan and Korea, to have majority governments and other voices in the legislature.

- STV brings more conflicts into the legislature, making legislative functions difficult. SMP, on the other hand, promotes to solve the conflicts outside the legislature. This helps the legislature to work better.
- Under STV, no one in the legislature may take responsibility for failures in decision-making. No business or any other enterprise could prosper in that situation. This is important, as there would always be mistakes made under any electoral system.
- Under SMP, BC has improved from being a poor province to a surplus province. This fact should not be ignored.

The arguments in favour of STV over SMP:

- STV provides better local representation, with two or more District MLAs the voter can go to.
- STV does better on all the electoral values identified: local representation, proportionality, and voter choice.
- STV has an inherent quality of accountability, because of the way it acts.
- Better to change to STV and see how it works for BC. If necessary, BC can go back to SMP at a later time.
- SMP system is an elitist system that was designed specifically to meets the needs of a time when only white male who owned property could vote and hold office. It cannot serve meaningfully any more.
- STV system is a much fairer system.
- In STV, different viewpoints are heard and considered in decision-making, unlike in SMP.
- The economics and political systems of PR Germany, Ireland and the Scandinavian countries are not collapsing because of the lack of stability or ability to make decisions.
- In STV, only the votes not cast become wasted votes, while it is not the case with SMP.
- British Columbians asked for change in public hearings. It is time to give them what they want.
- Currently political parties have too much power and control over the legislature, and thereby they dominate the public. STV would stop that.
- STV would put an end to the current adversarial type of politics in the legislature.
- The history of SMP has been one of exclusion (nonlandowners, women, different ethnic and religious groups, & small parties). STV would replace this with participatory democracy.
- STV option gives an opportunity to all British Columbians to decide whether they need a change or not.

- In SMP decisions are made behind one closed door, the door of the Premier. STV changes this situation.
- In SMP, the one who wins may not have the support of a majority of voters; some voters may never see their candidate winning. In 1996 election, in one district 68% of voters did not vote for the winning candidate. Under STV every voter has someone representing his/her points of view in Victoria.
- STV is a solution to voter apathy because of its inclusiveness. SMP cannot reverse the ongoing apathy trend.
- Under STV, politicians would be competing among themselves both within and across party lines for the vote. This puts voters above politicians.
- The electoral system in BC has not changed for a long time, but British Columbians have changed. So the need to change the electoral system.

At the end of the debate the Chair asked the Assembly members to vote on the question, "Does the Citizens' Assembly recommend that the current electoral system (FPTP) be retained? Yes or No" (Citizens Assembly, 2004j). The Assembly members voted on the question by marking 'Yes' or 'No' on their secret ballots. There were 153 votes cast. The result of the voting was overwhelmingly in favour of STV: 142 in favour of STV and 11 in favour of SMP. With these results, the Assembly members chose the STV system as the best electoral system for BC. Accordingly, the Chair declared that the Citizens' Assembly would not recommend that the current electoral system (SMP) should be retained.

Immediately after that, the Chair asked the Assembly members to vote on another question, "Does the Citizens' Assembly recommend that the best electoral system—STV be proposed to the people of British Columbia in a referendum?" (Citizens' Assembly, 2004j). In this voting 146 members voted YES, while only four Assembly members voted NO. The chair then declared that the Citizens' Assembly recommended that the STV system be proposed to the people of British Columbia in a referendum.

These two votes in the Assembly have now completed the Step 6 (Decision 7) of the Assembly decision-making process. By the same voting, the Assembly has also made its final decision on electoral reform. The Assembly, however, had few more tasks to complete during the next two Assembly weekends scheduled for November 13–14 and November 27–28. These tasks included finalizing the chosen STV model design, framing a suitable referendum question, communicating the Assembly message, considerations outside Assembly mandate (Other Considerations), and producing the Assembly's final report.

On the STV model, the Assembly members finally agreed on its outstanding details, including DM, quota, ballot design, and seat vacancies. On DM, the Assembly members reached consensus to remove rural–urban categorization, and in its place to have a range of 2 to 7, with preference given to high DMs. There was also consensus on ballot design: candidates' names to be grouped by party, and party groups to appear in a randomized manner. Candidates' photos would not appear anywhere on the ballot. At the same time, there would be no provision for a single party vote (above the line). On ballot completion, the Assembly members agreed that voters would rank candidates showing one or more preferences. If preference sequence is broken, the ballot would become nontransferable. A single "X" against a candidate's name would be interpreted as a first preference. By-elections would require only a simple majority. At the end, the Assembly came up with a name for the STV model they designed for BC: BC-STV. This name was chosen by a vote on three different suggestions: PR-STV (Proportional STV), CC-STV (Citizens' Choice STV), and BC-STV (British Columbia STV). In this vote, 64% of the votes cast (145) were in favour of BC-STV, 22% in favour of CC-STV, and 14% in favour of PR-STV.

6.7   Framing a suitable referendum question

The discussion on the referendum question started with an initial draft submitted by the Chair in the Saturday afternoon plenary session of the November 13-14 weekend. The Assembly members had a number of comments on the wording of the draft question. A revised version of the question based on the members' comments was later discussed on two other occasions, first in the Sunday plenary session of the same weekend and in the Saturday morning plenary session of the next weekend. After their three rounds of discussions and comments on the subject, the Assembly members finally agreed to have the wording of the referendum question as follows:

> Do you agree that British Columbians change to BC-STV as recommended by the Citizens' Assembly on Electoral Reform? Yes/No (Citizens' Assembly, 2004i).

6.8   Communicating the Assembly message

The last discussion on the Assembly floor was to formulate strategies for communicating the Assembly final message to the public. This discussion started with a Power Point presentation to the Saturday afternoon plenary session of the last weekend by the Assembly's Director of Communication, Marilyn Jacobson. In her presentation, Jacobson made suggestions for final report distribution, supporting the Assembly members with the needed communication toolkits, and educating the youth and local communities. She also made some suggestions for a media strategy and a website strategy for communicating the Assembly final message to the public. According to the presentation and what the Assembly members discussed, the final report would be sent to all libraries, municipal halls, First Nations, High Schools, MLA constituency offices, and Government Agent offices in British Columbia. In addition, copies of the final report would go to all those who provided written submissions to the Assembly and everyone in the Assembly's mailing list. At the same time, a copy of the final report would be mailed to every household in British Columbia. The communication toolkit given to every Assembly member would include Power Point presentation material, fact sheets, Q&A and key messages, a short video about BC-STV, and copies of the final report individually ordered. The public website of the Assembly would be kept alive but in static form. It would have all the exiting information, and some special BC-STV resources, including fact sheets, relevant links, and an animation of vote counting. As a media strategy, all media outlets would be made available with a customized toolkit of information. In their discussions on communication strategies, Assembly members also discussed some innovative ways in communicating on one-on-one basis. For example, one member suggested that the complex vote transfer between candidates at the time of vote counting in BC-STV could be explained in a very simple way by using a few stacks of coins.

6.9   Other Considerations

The thousands of British Columbians who talked to Citizens' Assembly members at public hearings and community meetings had raised a multitude of issues both within and outside the Assembly mandate. The formal presentations made at the public hearings and written submissions also covered issues both within and outside the Assembly mandate. In their deliberations for building the best alternative electoral systems for BC, the Assembly members were expected to consider all the issues so raised by the public that fell under the purview of the Assembly mandate. At the same time, the Assembly members felt that there were five issues in particular outside the purview of the Assembly's mandate that should not go unnoticed. These issues had been echoed in many written submissions and at public hearings throughout the province. Because of the significance of these issues, the Assembly members thought that it was appropriate to include them in their Final Report, not as any specific recommendations but as "other issues raised by the public." These five issues are briefly discussed below:

1.   **Enthusiasm for citizen involvement in electoral reform:**

In every community meeting and public hearing held by the Citizens' Assembly, the members of the public were extremely pleased that the government had entrusted electoral reform to citizens. They were particularly happy about the role played by the Citizens' Assembly and the arrangement to take any proposal of change made by the Assembly, if any, to a referendum. They also showed their confidence in the Assembly members for completing their task in an exemplary manner. Most of the members of the public who advocated change at the public hearings trusted their fellow citizens on the Assembly to decide which electoral system would be best for all British Columbians. Even those who proposed new electoral systems wanted the Assembly members to work out their specific details. Many suggested that the Citizens' Assembly process represented the 'gold standard' for citizen participation in BC, and future governments should maintain it in electoral reviews.

2.   Facilities for access to local MLAs:

The participants of the Assembly community meetings and public hearings throughout BC have indicated that effective local representation is central to how its parliamentary system works. The Assembly members also had identified local representation as one of the three most important electoral core values of British Columbians. All those who expressed this concern have indicated that there are serious challenges in this regard for voters and elected representatives in remote and thinly populated areas of the province. Many urged that the Assembly should bring this matter to the attention of the BC government for a solution. This might call for more resources for elected representatives of large electoral districts to operate more than one constituency office, special allowances for them to make timely and regular visits to all the communities in their districts, and new technology (1–800 numbers and computer-aided communication) that could bring them closer to their constituents.

3.   The role and operation of political parties

Most of the members of the public agree with the Citizens' Assembly that political parties will continue to play an important role in BC's democracy. In their role, political parties provide electoral choices to voters, educate and mobilize them, and contribute to the process of governing. The public also agrees that political parties should remain as voluntary organizations. Many citizens have, however, expressed their disappointment for the lack of minimum standards of openness and democracy within political parties, especially with regard to their internal decision-making processes. In particular, the concerned citizens have raised the issues of excessive party discipline and the questionable nomination processes political parties use for selecting their candidates for elections. The concerned citizens would like to see political parties behave in a more open and transparent manner free from central control.

4.   Public participation in BC's democracy:

Practically at all their public hearings, the Assembly members heard great concern for the declining trend in public participation in BC's democracy that has been demonstrated by the poor turn out at the polls. The Assembly members also heard and agreed that the withdrawal from electoral politics was more prevalent among young people. Many of those who expressed these concerns were worried that if this trend of public participation is left unchecked, it could lead to a real democratic crisis. At the same time, many also argued that not enough progress has been made to open up the electoral system to fuller participation of women and minorities in the legislature. The Assembly members saw for themselves the benefits of having an equal number of men and women and members from as many BC ethnic communities as possible in the Assembly. The Assembly members agreed that this enhanced the legitimacy of the Assembly among the members of the public and helped to bring a wider range of issues and perspectives to Assembly discussions. They further thought that this would provide a powerful lesson to political parties and other organizations in the society. The Assembly members were, however, concerned that they did not hear much from the members of the aboriginal communities at the Assembly public hearings. There were also not much written presentations from the aboriginal communities. Many nonaboriginal British Columbians recognize the fact that many of the aboriginal communities are fully engaged in the life of their own nations, but feel that finding ways to have aboriginals and nonaboriginals in BC work together in their common electoral processes would be advantageous to the province.

The concluding task of the members of the Citizens' Assembly was to prepare its Final Report. They did this with the help of an initial draft document produced for discussion purposes. The Assembly members discussed the draft in two plenary sessions, and approved a final version of the Final Report during the last weekend of the Assembly Deliberation Phase. With this approval of the Final Report of the Assembly and the consideration of the issues outside the Assembly mandate as discussed above by the Assembly members, they had completed the remaining steps (Decisions 8, 9, and 10) of the Assembly's decision-making process.

6.10   Final Report

The Citizens' Assembly on Electoral Reform produced copies of its Final Report for distribution by mid–December. It is a 16-page document, entitled "*Making Every Vote Count: The Case for Electoral Reform in British Columbia*" (Citizens' Assembly, 2004l). By this Final Report, the Citizens' Assembly reported its findings and recommendations on electoral reform to the Attorney General and the people of British Columbia. The Final Report first gives a brief summary of the work of the Citizens' Assembly leading to its final decision. The summary states that for eleven months the Assembly members have studied different voting systems, listened to thousands of British Columbians in 50 public hearings and reviewed 1,603 written submissions. The summary also says, "What we most wanted to learn was what values, hopes and desires should outline our electoral system and which principles should direct our discussions and recommendations," (Citizens' Assembly, 2004l, p.1). All this work, the summary continues, has lead to recommend a STV system, named BC-STV, especially customized for British Columbia, and the new system as proposed is fair, easy to use, and gives more power to the people. After that the summary lays out the final version of the referendum question that would be placed before all the voters of British Columbia at the forthcoming general election, scheduled for May 17, 2005. The referendum question stated in the summary reads, "Should

British Columbia change to the BC-STV electoral system as recommended by the Citizens' Assembly on Electoral Reform? Yes/No" (Citizens' Assembly, 2004l, p. 1).

After its initial summary, the Final Report describes the basic electoral values of British Columbians as identified by the Assembly members, compares the strengths and weaknesses of BC's existing electoral system (SMP) with those of the proposed new system (BC-STV), analyses the consequences of a change to BC-STV, refers to the "other issues raised by British Columbians," and concludes with a description of the Assembly mandate. As for basic electoral values, the report discusses the three basic values the Assembly members identified in their work. The three basic values discussed in the report are fair election results through proportionality, effective local representation, and greater voter choice.

The same section of the report also talks about two issues that had consistently highlighted during the Assembly discussions. One of the two issues refers to the groundswell of opposition in BC to its existing imbalance of power between voters and parties. The report says that the Assembly members believe that the solution to this lies in a new electoral system that encourages voters and politicians to work together in a balanced partnership. The other issue discussed is about the general assumption that single party majority governments are the natural outcomes of elections. The report says that the Assembly members were convinced that the simple nature of majority governments override the basic values of fair (proportional) election results, effective local representation and voter choice, and this needs to be corrected by a system that does not depend on majorities. The report further says that most other successful democracies do not depend on majorities, but have stable and effective governments. These governments, the report adds, are "inclusive of different interests and consensual in making decisions" (Citizens' Assembly, 2004l, p.2).

In its comparison between the existing SMP system and the proposed BC-STV system, the report summarizes the strengths and weaknesses of the two systems. As for strengths of the SMP system, the report points out that it provides effective local representation, accountability and majority governments that can claim and implement a mandate of the people without much opposition. As for its weaknesses, the SMP system provides less voter choice, turns MLAs elected at constituency level into party advocates rather than local advocates as a result of excessive party discipline, and produces unfair, disproportional election results with wrong winners and artificial majorities. The BC-STV system, the report says, will improve the electoral landscape of BC with fair, proportional election results, effective local representation and greater voter choice, in a balanced manner. The report adds that "In the current electoral system, political parties, not voters, control the way MLAs represent their communities. BC-STV corrects this imbalance by being voter-centred and candidate-focused: to be elected, candidates will need to put communities first" (Citizens' Assembly, 2004l, p.5). The report further says that some countries, including Ireland and Australia, have used electoral systems similar to BC-STV for decades, and in

Ireland in particular the government held referendums to abolish STV twice, and failed to get majority support for that on both the occasions.

As for consequences of change, the report points out that the implementation of the proposed BC-STV system would result in changes throughout BC political landscape. The report gives an analysis of the potential changes, as they would apply to voters, candidates and MLAs, parties, legislature, and government. Voters would be able to make more and different kinds of choices, and will have more power than under the existing SMP system. Party candidates will have to compete against those of their own party in addition to the candidates of other parties in trying to get the first preference of the voter. At the same time, as first preference votes alone may not be enough to win, candidates will have to encourage the supporters of other candidates and parties to mark them as their second or third preference. This, in fact, would result in a lesser adversarial nature of politics at times of elections. All this will also redefine the nature of the responsibility and commitment of MLAs towards their constituents and parties. Under BC-STV, MLAS would be encouraged to resist party discipline when it is not in the interest of the communities they represent, strengthening local representation. This would also encourage the MLAs to do their best to ensure that their party's positions would reflect the views of their constituents.

According to the final report, the changes to parties would be mainly three-fold. First, parties would be encouraged to nominate a diversity of candidates within each BC-STV electoral district to appeal to the groups and interests so far underrepresented or not represented under the existing SMP system. Second, parties will find the need to involve more citizens in their party organizations and to make their nomination processes more open and accessible. Third, parties will find difficult to continue with the same degree of party discipline as now, making local representation by elected representatives more meaningful and effective. As a result, a party's strength in the legislature would correctly reflect its strength of support among voters. This would end the ability of parties to win artificial majorities and encourage them to learn to work together for the common good of the province.

As for the legislature, BC-STV would give it back the power to choose and effectively supervise governments. Under the existing system, the final report says, "The presence of strictly disciplined parties, enlarged by artificial majorities, has reversed this principle, making the legislature a creature of the government" (Citizens' Assembly, 2004l, p.7). In the absence of artificial majorities, the report adds, the governments will need to depend on majority support in the legislature. On the part of the MLAs, they would be more sensitive to local interests, and express more often the concerns and hopes of the people they represent in the legislature. Meanwhile, legislative committees will play a more important role in contributing to the formulation of public policies.

As for changes to governments, the final report states that BC-STV would put an end to majority governments with minority support in the electorate and is likely to produce coalition governments, unless a majority of voters support candidates from one party. In any situation, no one party would be able to go ahead and implement its platform without valuable public debate in the legislature. The report further says that the experience of coalition governments in other successful democracies has been positive, and the Assembly members expect BC to have similar results.

Under the heading "Other issues raised by British Columbians," the final report briefly discusses the first four of the five 'other issues' discussed before: 1. Enthusiasm for citizen involvement in electoral reform, 2. Facilities for access to local MLAs, 3. The role and operation of political parties, and 4. Public participation in BC's democracy. The fifth 'other issue' has been separately discussed on page 1 of the report.

The discussion of the Assembly process in the final report begins with the pre-Assembly, member-selection phase, and covers all the three main Assembly Phases: Learning, Public Hearing, and Deliberation. The Assembly mandate appears in the report as outlined in the Order-in-Council: *Citizens' Assembly on Electoral Reform Terms of Reference* issued on May 16, 2003.

In its conclusion, the Final Report says that the Assembly members are confident that BC would improve in its practice of democracy by adopting BC-STV, although it will not answer every call for change or correct all the ills in BC's provincial political system. The final report ends with the Assembly members' claim that "By adopting the BC-STV electoral system the voters will create a system where they, the voters themselves, are closer to the center of the system. In a democracy that is what "fair" is about" (Citizens' Assembly, 2004l). Dr. Jack Blaney, Chair of the Assembly, has signed the final report on behalf of all the 161 members of the Citizens' Assembly on Electoral Reform. The names of the 161 members appear on the inside pages of the front and back covers of the final report. Appendix 6 gives more details of the final report of the Citizens' Assembly. With the publication of the final report, the Citizens' Assembly had now completed its mandate.

The *Technical Report* (Citizens' Assembly, 2004m), a second volume of the Final Report describes all aspects of the Assembly work and deliberations in detail. It is a 102-page document with 25 tables and charts and 27 appendices. The appendices comprise of 162 additional pages of supporting materials.

6.11 Closing down

The members and staff of the Citizens' Assembly worked together to make the closing down of the Assembly as enjoyable and memorable as possible. Their final closing down plan consisted of a certificate presentation ceremony, some photographs for history books, a Saturday night gala, one last round of expressions of appreciation, a closing benediction, and a final goodbye.

The certificate presentation ceremony took place during the Saturday morning plenary session of the last weekend, November 27–28. It was both sensational and colourful. It was attended by both Premier Gordon Campbell and Attorney General Geoff Plant. This was also the first time the Premier or the Attorney General made a visit to the Assembly. After a warm and rousing welcome to the two special guests by the Chair and the members of the Citizens'

Assembly, Premier Campbell presented every Assembly member with a framed commemorative certificate in appreciation of their 'dedicated service to the people and Province of British Columbia as a Member of the Citizens' Assembly on Electoral Reform.' Every Assembly member was also given a photo opportunity with the premier at the time of the certificate presentation. The Assembly members enjoyed throughout the certificate presentation with frequent cheers, applauses, and other sounds of jubilation, as normally heard in a high school or university graduation ceremony. After certificate presentation, Premier Campbell formerly addressed the Assembly.

In his address Premier Campbell expressed his appreciation of what the Assembly members had been able to accomplish and noted that it was now up to the voters of BC to decide in a referendum on May 17, 2005, whether they would go with the recommendations made by the Assembly. In appreciating the Assembly members' role, the premier said:

> You came with open minds. You came with open hearts. You came ready to listen to people. ... Your diligence, your determination, have been exceptional ... It is a great gift you have given to all of us. You have given new life to public life in BC ("Great Gift to BC," 2004).

In his address, Premier Campbell also said that British Columbians were now engaging in a process led by the Assembly leading to the referendum and that engagement was invaluable to the province.

After Premier Campbell's address, the Chair of the Assembly praised and thanked the premier for creating the Assembly, empowering it to make an important public policy decision, and giving it full independence for making that decision. Regarding the level of independence given to the Assembly, the Chair said, "an independence that was real, constant, and greatly valued by all members," (Citizens' Assembly, 2004k). The Chair also added, "No government in any democracy has ever given such a charge to nonelected citizens. You set new rules—the new gold standard—for the true engagement of citizens in democratic governance. .. And it is being copied in Ontario, and watched around the world" (Citizens' Assembly, 2004k). After the Chair's comments the Assembly members and the two official guests moved to the Atrium of the Asian Pacific Hall and posed for a group photograph. This brought the certificate presentation ceremony to a conclusion.

The next closing down event was the evening gala at the Concourse on the same day. A 15-member voluntary social committee of the Citizens' Assembly organized it. Assembly member Gene Quan played the role of the Master of Ceremonies for the evening. The gala started at 6:00 p.m. with self-host cocktails. By this time, the Concourse was well decorated befitting the occasion. One Assembly member, Doug Waller, provided recorded music for the occasion. In doing this, he also coordinated special requests from other Assembly members and staff. After all the participants gathered, dinner was served at about 6:30 p.m. After dinner, the participants settled for the rest of the evening program that included special presentations to the Assembly staff, a skit, and a Hollywood style "Oscar" award ceremony.

In the special presentations, every staff member was ceremoniously presented with a high quality stainless steel mug-flask engraved with the full name of the Citizens' Assembly as a token of appreciation of their excellent contribution to the course of the Citizens' Assembly. There were enough steel mug-flasks in the Concourse to be distributed to the Assembly members as well. The members, however, had to just pick one each when they finally left the Concourse. The mug-flask was viewed by all as a useable memento, compared to the framed certificate distributed to the Assembly members in the morning, to remind of one's personal contributions to the Assembly process.

The skit took the form of a dialogue filled with fun between the Master of Ceremonies and a "professor" associated with the Assembly process. This sparked a new wave of excitement and mirth across the Concourse floor. This atmosphere in the Concourse reached its climax with the award of a number of amusing Assembly "Oscars" in a manner similar to how Academy Awards are presented in Hollywood. The Assembly awards were given in fifteen categories in a hilarious manner. These categories included the best long winded speaker, best following up on what he/she said, best I am smiling so on one notices I don't understand the Droop Formula, best next premier, best encyclopedic brain, best hangover, best northern sob story, best Napper, best hair, tightest sphincter, most photogenic, best dresser, and the best Fist Past the Post advocate. A voluntary 'nomination committee' had picked a handful of Assembly members as nominees for each category and the respective winners. After each award, the winner was given an opportunity to speak a few words, just as in Hollywood. The author was also one of the award winners. The evening gala finally came to a closure at the end of these awards.

The Citizens' Assembly met in plenary the next morning (Sunday, November 28, 2004) as scheduled. This was the very last meeting of the Citizens' Assembly on Electoral Reform in British Columbia. With the approval of the Assembly's final report on the previous day, the Chair found some wiggle room for some closing remarks by the Assembly members who had shown interest in doing so. Before calling for these closing remarks, the Chair invited all staff members of the Assembly, including the group facilitators, to come and join the Assembly members on the floor of the Assembly. After they came and joined the Assembly members, the Chair opened the floor for closing remarks. Fourteen members, including the author, made use of this opportunity. In their remarks, they all were appreciative of the opportunity they had to be part of the Assembly's historic and unique democratic process and the assistance and cooperation they received from the Assembly staff and the general public in accomplishing their Assembly mission. The author, in particular, was also the first member to speak from the floor of the Assembly on the day of its ceremonial opening eleven months back. In his final remarks, the author compared the encounters experienced by the Assembly members during the Assembly process to those of a pregnant woman, and said:

> After an eleven-month pregnancy with usual morning sickness and cramps during the periods of political education, public hearings and deliberations, we finally delivered a baby, BC-STV. The last minute severe labour pains, climaxed

by our historic MMP-STV debate, would, perhaps, remain in our minds forever. Tonight, we are going out of this hall with a commitment to nurture the baby we produced, and present it to our fellow citizens. We all know for sure that our baby will be able to make a difference in the lives of all British Columbians, and, indeed, create history in the democratic world. Some democracies may even try to clone our baby.

The Chair reciprocated the closing remarks of the Assembly members with words of appreciation of the extra efforts made by the Assembly members over the course of the year. After that the Chair invited all participants to give themselves a deserved round of applause. All present joined in and made the loudest and longest applause ever heard in the Asia Pacific Hall. This remarkable applause finally came to an end with Assembly member Reverend Richard Hall taking his position at the podium for the closing benediction. At the end of the benediction, the Chair requested the author to move a motion to adjourn the Assembly, as had been previously arranged. After the words "I move the adjournment of the Citizens' Assembly on Electoral Reform" from the author's mouth, the Chair declared that the Citizens' Assembly had now adjourned. The time of this official closure of the Citizens Assembly on Electoral Reform in British Columbia was 11:11 a.m., Sunday, November 28, 2004.

.

CHAPTER 7
REFERENDUM ON ELECTORAL CHANGE

7.1   Legislative requirement

The recommendation of the BC's Citizens' Assembly for electoral change could be implemented only with enough public support at a province-wide referendum. The Sections 1 and 3(2) of the *Electoral Reform Referendum Act* of BC passed on May 20, 2004, specified the need for such a referendum and the extent of public support required for the implementation of the proposed change.

The Section 1 of the *Electoral Reform Referendum Act*, in particular, specified the need for a referendum as follows:

> If the Citizens' Assembly on Electoral Reform recommends, in its final report, a model for electing Members of the Legislative Assembly that is different from the current model, a referendum respecting the recommended model must be held in conjunction with the general election required under the *Constitution Act* to be held in May 2005 (*Electoral Reform Referendum Act*, 2004, *Section 1*).

The Section 3 (2) of the same legislation specified the extent of public support needed for the implementation of any change proposed by the Citizens' Assembly as follows:

> Section 4 of the *Referendum Act* does not apply and, instead, the results of a referendum under Section 1 are binding on the government only if
>
> (a)   at least 60% of the validly cast ballots vote the same way on the question that is stated for the referendum, and
> (b)   in at least 48 of the 79 electoral districts, more than 50% of the validly cast ballots vote the same way on the question (*Electoral Reform Referendum Act*, 2004, *Section 3*)

The above shows that the threshold fixed for the level of public support required at the referendum was two-fold: 60 percent of the overall provincial support and majority (50 percent + 1) support in more than 60 percent (48) of the 79 electoral districts of the province. This double sixty percent threshold was higher than what was needed for referendums under the *Referendum Act of British Columbia*; the *referendum Act* requires only 50% + 1 majority support province-wide. The *Electoral Reform Referendum Act* makes an exception to the *Referendum Act* by asking for a higher level of support for changing the voting system as proposed by the Citizens' Assembly.

Critics say that the unprecedented double sixty percent threshold set for the 2005 referendum was excessive and lacked precedent. They point out that until this time British Columbia held referendums on a wide range of issues, from enfranchising women to changing the constitution, with a threshold of simple majority, and there was no special reason to increase the threshold to double 60 percent for the referendum on the Citizens' Assembly recommendation. Some of these critics also point out that the Government was able to make a final decision on the Citizens' Assembly recommendation with a vote in the legislature, without holding a referendum.

Those who support the Government do not agree with such criticism. On the double 60 percent threshold issue, they argue that the proposed electoral change needed an exceedingly clear majority mandate for its implementation. This is important, they say, as any future public dissatisfaction on the change could backfire on the Government, if it were implemented with only a simple majority support at the referendum. At the same time, they argue that the Citizens' Assembly approach was developed to give power to the people to make a final decision on electoral reform, and, therefore, a final decision on the Citizens' Assembly recommendation by the BC Legislature is not appropriate.

The increased threshold of public support for the electoral change recommended by the Citizens' assembly called for widespread awareness of the recommended change among British Columbians. This was possible only through province-wide public discussions and debates on the issues around the recommended change before the referendum. Despite this situation, the BC government chose not to spend public funds to engage British Columbians in such widespread discussions and debates on the subject. It only set up an information office within the Ministry of Attorney General to give information on the proposed new electoral system, BC-STV, upon request. The government did not want to promote or sell the Assembly recommendation. Premier Gordon Campbell and his governing party, BC Liberal Party, allowed its MLAs and other members to freely speak for themselves on the referendum issue.

7.2   Those who took the stand

The lack of a government-funded program to educate the public in the event the Citizens' Assembly proposed electoral change always remained a great concern among the Assembly members. All discussions on this issue in their plenary sessions had ended in despair. The Assembly members were told that such a government-funded program was not possible, and that the mandate of the Assembly would end with its Final Report. This put the Assembly members, who had a sense of ownership to the decisions they made as a group, in a vulnerable situation. It was a challenge they failed to avoid. With this challenge, the Assembly members were more determined to spread their message of change to their fellow citizens in BC, and get the required level of public support at the referendum. By the time the Assembly was officially closed, they had gained special skills in communication, media handling, conflict resolution and consensus building through expert-presentations and discussions. They also formed an alumni group to help them to stay in touch with each other and coordinate their activities in spreading their message of change in the province. All these helped the Assembly members to play a significant role both individually and collectively in getting public support for the Assembly's recommendation for change.

Meanwhile, the Fair Voting BC and Fair Vote Canada became immediate allies of the Citizens' Assembly alumni group in supporting the proposed new electoral system, BC-STV. The former SOCRED MLA Nick Loenen led the "Yes to STV" campaign on behalf of Fair Voting BC. He is a long time campaigner for proportional representation. He also played a key role in convincing the government to appoint the Citizens' Assembly. He and his organization were now determined to support the electoral change recommended by the Citizens' Assembly at the upcoming referendum by disseminating correct and helpful information, fostering public discussions, and debating on the subject. Fair Vote Canada had campaigned for electoral change in Canada for many years. Its Victoria and the Greater Vancouver chapters took the lead in supporting BC-STV on its behalf.

As the Citizens' Assembly alumni group, Fair Voting BC and Fair Vote Canada were making a headway in their "Yes to STV" campaign, a new group launched a "No to STV" campaign sometime in March 2005. This new group appeared under the name 'KNOW STV,' and consisted of a number of high-profile British Columbians, including two former SOCRED cabinet ministers, Bud Smith and Bruce Strachan, former NDP MP Anita Hagen, retired union leader Jack Munro and Bill Tieleman, a communication director of former Premier Glen Clark (NDP). The emergence of this high-profile group opposing BC-STV brought the ongoing discussions and debate on the referendum issue to a new dimension.

At the same time, two registered political parties, Green Party of British Columbia and Western Refederation Party of British Columbia, joined the debate in support of BC-STV. After her failed attempt to institute a proportional electoral system (MMP) through an initiative under the *BC Recall and Initiative Act*, the Green Party leader Adriane Carr had closely watched the progress of the Citizens' Assembly. She was the only party leader who attended most of the Assembly plenary sessions as an observer. Her initial reaction to BC-STV recommendation of the Citizens' Assembly was negative, as her preferred option for BC was MMP. Later she and her party took a stand on the referendum question in support of BC-STV, and joined the "Yes to STV" campaign. The Western

Refederation Party of British Columbia is an offshoot of the Western Refederation Party of Canada. Garry Dalton founded the Western Refederation Party of Canada within weeks of its 2000 federal election, primarily to address what he saw as western alienation in Canadian politics. The Western Refederation Party of British Columbia was the only political party other than the Green Party that took an official stand on the referendum question and joined the "Yes to STV" campaign.

Neither of the two main political parties of BC, BC Liberal Party and BC-NDP, took any official stand on the referendum question. The Liberal Party continued to allow its members to freely take part in the referendum debate and express their individual preferences. The NDP remained neutral throughout the debate. The leader of the NDP, Carol James, said that if the BC-STV received the required level of support at the referendum and her party came to power, she would go ahead and implement it. If British Columbians showed that they wanted change but not particularly interested in BC-STV, she added, a NDP government would explore other proportional electoral options, such as the German MMP system.

In time, more groups and individuals joined the referendum debate. These groups in particular consisted of people belonging to more than one political party. Some of these groups, such as the Canadian Taxpayers Federation and West Coast Writers, had been in existence before for different purposes. While the others, such as "STV for BC" and "The Rubble," had surfaced only for the purpose of joining the referendum debate. Those who joined the debate in their individual capacities had varied backgrounds. There were a few former cabinet ministers and other prominent personalities among them. Most of these groups and individuals were in support of BC-STV. Those who did not support BC-STV were against any change to the existing FPTP system. These groups and individuals that joined the debate later brought in new arguments for and against BC-STV. The Citizens' Assembly alumni group, Fair Voting BC, Fair Vote Canada and KNOW STV, however, continued to play the most prominent role in the referendum debate until the Election Day.

The groups and individuals on both fronts of the referendum debate tried to reach the public with their arguments for and against BC-STV through their websites, emails, one-on-one and group discussions, public debates, media interviews, newspaper columns, letters to the editor, and much more. They organized discussions and public debates on the referendum question in colleges, universities, chambers of commerce, seniors' centres, service clubs, public libraries, civic centers, restaurants, churches, and the like. Leading personalities on both the "Yes to STV" and "No to STV" campaigns took part in the debates. Some of those who joined these discussions and debates used to come up with new and innovative ways of explaining the different features of the proposed BC-STV system as well as the existing FPTP system. For example, some who argued for BC-STV used stacks of coins to demonstrate its difficult counting process in an easily understandable way. The students of one high school, Bulkley Valley Christian High School, in Smithers tried to identify whether the BC-STV system or the existing FPTP system could help them in choosing a better pizza. Seventy-four students tried out both BC-STV and the FPTP systems with nine top-pings for three pizzas to choose from to see what kind of pizzas they would get. At the end, with the FPTP system, one-third of the students got pizzas they did not want. With·the BC-STV·system, only two students could not get at least one of their top three preferred toppings on a pizza.

There were two main factors that significantly influenced the progress of the referendum discussions and debates in British Columbia in the spring of 2005. Only one of them had positive influence; the other had negative influence. The one that influenced positively was the Gomery Inquiry, which became a hot topic of discussion throughout Canada. This inquiry was looking into an alleged $250-million sponsorship scandal of the Canadian Federal Government. It was alleged during the inquiry that the Federal Government had dished out millions of dollars of taxpayers' money to their friends and supporters for too little or no work done. In their discussions on the subject many Canadians questioned the limitations of the existing FPTP system in Canada (also in BC at provincial level) in making governments accountable to the voter. This resulted in an in-creased level of interest among British Columbians in their ongoing electoral re-form process.

The factor that influenced the referendum discussions and debates nega-tively was the lack of government funding for organizing and conducting the debates. In the absence of government funding, the groups and individuals that organized referendum discussions and debates had to raise the funds needed for that purpose on their own. The amount of money needed for an effective cam-paign on any side of the referendum debate would amount to millions of dollars. For example, the budget Nick Loenen sketched out for a "Yes" campaign totaled to 1.795 million dollars. Out of this, 1.75 million dollars was estimated for a multimedia advertising campaign. The Vancouver Sun columnist Vaughn Palmer commented on the 1.75 million dollars multimedia advertising cost esti-mate of Nick Loenen, "He wasn't kidding, given the price of advertising space in television, radio and newspapers" (Palmer, 2005a). The remaining 45,000 dollars had been estimated for a full time organizer ($5,000.00), speaking tours ($3,000.00), 10,000 lawn signs ($30,000.00), BC-STV banners and buttons ($2,000.00) and polling ($5,000.00) (Palmer, 2005a). Raising money to meet these needs became a difficult task, especially at a time of a general election, as the referendum campaigners had to compete with major political parties that were also canvassing for donations. Those who led the referendum discussions and debates on both "Yes to STV" and "No to STV" camps experienced this dif-ficulty, but continued with their efforts with limited resources.

On Tuesday, April 19, 2005, Premier Gordon Campbell asked the Lieuten-ant Governor of British Columbia, The Honourable Iona Campagnolo, to dis-solve the BC Legislature and call an election for May 17, 2005. This was not a surprise in any way, as the government had fixed the next election date before-hand; BC is one of the few jurisdictions in Canada to have fixed election dates. The Lieutenant Governor acted on the Premier's request, dissolving the BC Leg-islature with immediate effect. This was the beginning of an official 28-day 'election period.' By this time the Referendum Information Office of the Ministry of Attorney General had distributed an information sheet to British Columbians explaining why and how the referendum would take place on the Election Day. After dissolving the Legislature, the BC Election Office carried a number of advertisements in the media explaining to the public that the voter would have two ballots at the upcoming election, one for the preferred candidate and the other on the referendum question.

7.3   Reaching the public

Three days before the Legislature was dissolved two research groups, Nordic Research and Strategic Council, published the results of two opinion polls on BC-STV. They had conducted these polls between April 13th and 16th. Both the groups were well known for conducting similar opinion polls in the past. According to the results of Nordic Research, 26 percent of British Columbians surveyed would vote 'yes' for BC-STV, and 17 percent would vote 'no,' leaving 57 percent undecided. The Strategic Council results were slightly different: 27 percent would vote 'Yes', 15 percent would vote 'No' and 45 percent undecided.

The groups and individuals on the "No to STV" side were happy with the results of both the research groups as not even one-third of British Columbians wanted BC-STV. Those on the "Yes to STV" front interpreted the results in a different way. They said that if the undecided 57 percent shown in the Nordic results were to vote the same way, the end result would have 60.5 percent in favour of BC-STV. Whatever the interpretation that went with the poll results, neither the Nordic Research results, nor the Strategic Council results gave a breakdown of the level of support for BC-STV at district level. According to the related legislation, a change was possible only with more than 60 percent support province-wide and majority support in more than 60 percent of the electoral districts. At the same time with 45—57 percent of people still undecided, it was clear that more work had to be done in raising awareness of the proposed new electoral system. This was a challenge faced by both the 'Yes to STV' and 'No to STV' camps.

In meeting the challenge, both the camps increased their campaign activities over the days ahead. These activities included public debates, one-on-one and group discussions, and media interviews. Through these activities, they hoped to spread their messages on the referendum question among as many British Columbians as possible. The Citizens' Assembly alumni group and Fair Voting BC took the lead in organizing most of the public debates and discussions. Nick Loenen of Fair Voting BC was at a public meeting almost every night. In summing up his personal observations of the public debates and discussions on the referendum question, Loenen said, "The first reaction people have when they hear STV is always bewilderment. But as they get more familiar with it, the lights start to go on. ... If I only had time to talk to every voter in B. C." (Mickleburgh, 2005a).

Bill Tieleman of "KNOW STV" played the leading role on behalf of the "No to STV" camp in the public debates and discussions. As a way of regular communication with the public, he made use of his weekly columns in the Georgia Strait to express his strong opinions about BC-STV. Neither Loenen, nor Tieleman, was sure what percentage of British Columbians they could reach with their referendum messages by the time of the general election. For this reason, both of them avoided speculating on the results of the referendum beforehand. Regarding those who may not come to know about BC-STV by the time of the election, Tieleman said in mid–April, "If people don't know anything about it, do they vote no, or do they vote yes, or do they not vote on it at all? At this point, it's a mystery" (Mickleburgh, 2005a).

At the same time, there was increased media coverage on the general election and the referendum after the official announcement of the election on April 19, 2005. Such coverage included media interviews, news items about ongoing public debates and discussions, newspaper editorials, musings of newspaper columnists, and the results of opinion polls on the referendum. A number of Citizens' Assembly alumni members were among those who were interviewed by the media. The media reports about ongoing discussions and debates informed the public of the specific arguments raised both for and against the proposed new electoral system. A number of newspaper editorials suggested that BC-STV should be given a chance. The Vancouver Sun, in particular, looked at the pros and cons of both the existing FPTP system and the proposed BC-STV system and took a decision in support of change. In explaining its position, the Vancouver Sun specifically said:

> No one can predict for certain all the effects that changing the voting system will have on life in B. C. But given the current system's flaws, the policy swings and consequent economic turmoil we have seen in the past 40 years, The Vancouver Sun thinks it's worth putting our faith in the Citizens' Assembly and giving STV a try.
>
> It is good to remember that this is an evolutionary, not a revolutionary change and it's not irrevocable. As the Citizens' Assembly itself recommends, after three elections, we must have another referendum to judge whether we made the right choice ("With so many flaws," 2005).

National, provincial, and community newspapers carried columns written by known and unknown writers on the BC Referendum and on electoral reform. Many of them were in support of electoral reform in BC. These writers wrote their columns under different headings, such as "Why I support the STV" (Smyth, 2005), "Don't let chance to make politics work better slip away" (Willcocks, 2005), "If STV fails, it will be years before we get change" (McInnes, 2005a), and "Take STV for a test drive" (Hodgson, 2005). The well-known columnists who wrote against BC-STV include Bill Tieleman and Norman Spector. In one of his columns, Spector wrote:

> STV would produce minority governments, and the spectacle in Ottawa today is discouraging. Moreover, political fragmentation and polarization would grow, as parties catered to the fringes rather than to centrist voters.
>
> No doubt our parliamentary system—built up over centuries by giants like Churchill and Disraeli—can be improved, as our British cousins have been do-

ing. Instead, we're being sold a system devised by an unrepresentative group of British Columbians that very few people in the British Commonwealth use (Spector, 2005).

In April 2005, The Vancouver Sun, The Victoria Times Colonist and Global BCTV News jointly commissioned Ipsos-Reid to conduct an opinion poll on the referendum. The results of this opinion poll, which was conducted province wide from April 23rd to 26th, showed that nearly two-thirds of British Columbians knew little or nothing about STV and that less people knew about it, the less likely they would vote for it. Despite this, the results also showed that 42 percent of the people had decided to vote Yes, while 38 percent wanted to vote No. Two percent had said that they would not vote, and eighteen percent were still undecided. Based on these results, William Boei, a columnist of the Vancouver Sun, concluded, "Electoral reform for British Columbia will be defeated May 17 unless proponents of the single transferable vote system—STV—can pull off a minor miracle" (Boei, 2005).

The increased media coverage given to the referendum and the continued efforts of the "Yes to STV" and "No to STV" camps helped to raise the level of awareness of the referendum and the arguments for and against BC-STV among British Columbians. The two opinion polls taken about a week before the Election Day testify to this. Table 7.1 below summarizes the results of these two opinion polls and the ones held before for comparison purpose.

As shown in table 7.1, the level of support for each side (Yes/No) and the percentage of undecided voters shown in the May 8–10 Ipsos-Reid poll were significantly different to those of the May 9–11 Strategic Council poll. Both the polls show a significant increase in the number of decided voters over a period of four weeks. According to the Ipsos-Reid poll, the proportion of decided voters in favour of STV was 57%, while that shown by the Strategic Council poll was high as 63%. The percentages of voters not yet decided on the referendum question in the two polls had a significant difference of 18%. The Strategic Council May 9–11 poll also showed that a staggering 82 percent of those surveyed still knew little or nothing about the proposed BC-STV system. This showed only a slight improvement from the 89 percent shown in the April 13–16 poll conducted by the same pollster.

The most striking feature of the results of all the polls so far conducted is the relationship, or the lack of relationship, between the number of the people who came to know about the BC-STV system and that of those who had decided to vote at the referendum. Going by the May 9–11 Strategic Council poll, 57 percent of those surveyed had decided which way to vote on the referendum question, although 82 percent still knew little or nothing about the proposed new electoral system. This showed that not knowing enough about the BC-STV would not stop people voting on the referendum question. It is possible that those who had decided to vote Yes on the referendum question without knowing much about BC-STV were making that choice to show their dislike for the existing FPTP system. It is also possible that at least some of these voters were merely expressing their support for the final decision of the Citizens' Assembly, because of its publicized status as a nonpartisan body of ordinary citizens like them. Whatever the reasons for some to vote Yes on the referendum question without knowing enough about the proposed BC-STV system, it was clear that there was a pleasant surprise waiting for those who campaigned for it.

Table 7.1: Summary of referendum opinion polls

	Date	April 13–16	April 14–16	April 23–26	May 8–10	May 9–11
	Company	Strategic Council	Nordic Research	Ipsos-Reid	Ipsos-Reid	Strategic Council
1	Voting YES	27%	26%	42%	47%	36%
2	Voting NO	15%	17%	38%	35%	21%
3	Undecided	45%	57%	18%	13%	31%
4	Will not vote	5%		2%	3%	4%
5	Don't know/No answer/Refused to answer	8%				9%
6	Know a lot about BC-STV	10%		4%		17%
7	Know little or nothing about BC-STV	89%		64%		82%
8	Sum of 3 + 4 + 5	58%	57%	20%	16%	44%
9	% of YES votes	64%	60%	53%	57%	63%

Source: Mickleburgh (2005b), Nordic Research Group (2005), Sauder School of Business, University of British Columbia (2005), and Wikipedia (2005).

The *Electoral Reform Referendum Regulation* required that a copy of the Final Report of the Citizens' Assembly be made available at all voting opportunities for the benefit of those who may not know enough about BC-STV at the time of voting. The voting opportunities included Advance Voting locations, General Voting locations, district electoral offices and the mobile teams who visit hospitals, long-term care facilities and other locations where voting was administered. The 20-page long Final Report was not a document one could read and understand to be able to make a choice between the BC-STV system it recommends and the existing FPTP system in a matter of few minutes. The author, therefore, wrote to the Referendum Information Office located in the Ministry of Attorney General, Victoria, on April 25, 2005, with a special request to consider sending copies of a simpler document on BC-STV to voting facilities. In particular, the author recommended that the brochure named *Electoral Reform Referendum,* which had been published and distributed by the Information Office only a few weeks back, was more appropriate for the intended purpose; it was much shorter and easier to read and understand. The Information Office forwarded the author's request to the Elections BC, which is an independent office responsible for conducting provincial elections in BC, for their consideration. Their final response letter (E-mail) of April 29, 2005, partly said:

> The ballot question refers to the Citizens' Assembly, so the recommendation as made by them is appropriately available as a resource. However, Elections BC does not believe it appropriate to provide other information in the voting place regarding the subject matter of the referendum, just as information regarding political parties and candidates is similarly absent (L. M. Johnson, personal communication, April 29, 2005).

The activities of both the "Yes to STV" and "No to STV" campaigners of the referendum reached a climax during the last few days of the election period. There were TV and radio programs involving them almost every day. More interestingly a good number of high profile former politicians joined them during the last few days. For example, Preston Manning, the founder of the Reform Party of Canada, strongly endorsed that BC adopt the BC-STV system. In particular, he warned that should the referendum fail, politicians would not consult the people on major public policy issues again for decades to come. At the same time two former BC Premiers, Bill Bennett and Dave Barrett, threw their weight behind the No side. The No side campaigners gave publicity to two open letters to BC citizens written by the two former premiers (Downtown Eastside [Downtown], 2005). In his letter, Barret argued that the vote counting formula of the proposed BC-STV system would replace "clear voter choice with academic theory" (Downtown, 2005). He also said in the same letter that "Most importantly voters will loose accountability because they will have between two and seven MLAs representing them in huge ridings. On every difficult issue buck passing and finger pointing would replace true representation" (Downtown, 2005). Bennett's letter also expressed similar sentiments about the BC-STV system. His letter partly said, "In this proposed system you end up with partial votes determining the outcome because of the complicated counting formula. It allows a few to manipulate the outcome of the majority in favour of biased minorities" (Downtown, 2005). The contents of these two letters are given in full in Appendices 7 and 8. Karn Manhas, a retiring BC Liberal MLA was also among the notable personalities that joined the No side of the referendum during the last few days. Three days before the Election Day, Bill Tieleman, who lead the "No to STV" camp, issued his ultimate warning, "If STV passes we will be locked in to a terribly flawed electoral system for three elections and 12 to 15 years" (B. Tieleman, personal communication, May 14, 2005). The day before the referendum, Dr. Jack Blaney, the former Chair of the Citizens' Assembly, said, "If the referendum fails, many Assembly members will be disappointed. ... But the issue engaged the public in a debate about how to reshape democracy in B. C" (Hall, 2005).

7.4   People's verdict

On Tuesday, May 17, 2005, British Columbians finally had their day to vote on the referendum question. They also had to vote in the general election at the same time. The early results of both the general election and the referendum were out by the next day morning. These results had not taken into account the votes cast in *absentia* amounting to about 75,000 province-wide. According to the early results, out of 1,679, 288 voters (55.6 percent of eligible voters) who took part in the election, 1,621,620 (96.57 percent) had voted on the referendum ballot as well. Out of the votes cast on the referendum ballot, 930, 721 had indicated Yes in favour of BC-STV. This amounts to 57.39 percent province-wide support for BC-STV, only 2.61 percent short of the required 60 percent provincial threshold. At the same time, the same results showed that there was more than 50 percent support for the proposed BC-STV system in 77 of the 79 ridings, when the district-wise majority support threshold was only 48 ridings.

Thus, the Yes vote beat the threshold of the number of ridings where majority support was necessary, but missed the one on province-wide support by 2.61 percent of the votes cast on the referendum. There was a possibility that the results of the 75,000 absentia-votes would change these results, but not to the extent of making a difference as far as the required thresholds were concerned. The final results announced on June 2, 2005, did increase the province wide support for BC-STV, but only slightly, to 57.69 percent. The number of ridings where there was more than 50 percent support for BC-STV remained at 77.

Although the support for BC-STV failed to reach one referendum threshold level, it surpassed the level of support the BC Liberal Party received at the same election. In this election, the BC Liberal Party received only 46.03 percent of the popular vote, but still managed to form a majority government. The total number of seats the BC Liberal Party secured at this election was 46. The BC New Democratic Party received 41.27 percent of the popular vote and secured all the remaining 33 seats. The BC Green Party received 9.11 percent of the popular vote, but failed to secure any seats. A close review of the level of support previous winning parties received at general elections in BC shows that only once in the last fifty years a party had come to power with a level of support as high as that for BC-STV (57.69 percent) at the referendum.

The results of the referendum produced a flurry of arguments between its Yes side and No side. Yes side argued that there was justification to accept the results as adequate mandate for the government to go ahead and implement the BC-STV system. In support of this argument, Nick Loenen of Fair Voting BC put forward the following points:

- The 60 % province-wide threshold was not recommended by the Gibson Report, which recommended the logistics of setting up the Citizens' Assembly;
- No other province or country known to Fair Voting BC requires such a high threshold for approving a referendum on electoral reform;

- PEI's referendum on electoral reform required a simple majority (this was, however, later changed to the BC threshold);
- New Zealand's referendum on electoral reform passed with 54% support;
- Both Ireland and Italy twice held referenda on electoral reform requiring simple majorities;
- The BC Referendum Act stipulates a simple majority for any other referendum;
- No former BC referendum has ever required more than a simple majority;
- Referenda on Quebec separation and the Charlottetown Accord involved significant constitutional issues of much greater importance than electoral reform, yet required no more than a simple majority; and
- Nearly all governments in British Columbia are themselves elected with considerably less than 50% support (Fair Voting BC, 2005).

Bruce Hallsor, a cochairman of the Yes to STV camp reiterated the same points and said:

> We are thrilled a clear majority of British Columbians have supported STV. ..
> We have never accepted that a 60 percent threshold is acceptable.... In Quebec, they had two referendums on separation with the threshold at 50 percent. If we can elect a majority government at 46 percent, surely 57 percent should be enough to change our electoral system. .. We are now faced with running elections under a system that British Columbians have decisively rejected (Nagel, 2005).

Citizens' Assembly Alumni group also reacted in the same way. Shoni Field spoke on behalf of the Alumni group soon after the announcement of the early results and said:

> We proudly stand behind the recommendation of the Citizens' Assembly on Electoral Reform. ... The Single Transferable Vote best meets the needs of British Columbians and—with the support of a significant majority—it should be introduced for the 2009 election (Citizens' Assembly Alumni, personal communication, May 18, 2005).

The No side took the position that the above arguments of the Yes side were both too late and wrong. The No side argued that the rules for accepting the referendum results were set long in advance by the BC Government, requiring more than 60% province-wide support and majority support in more than 48 ridings. Any arguments on these requirements at this stage were not appropriate. At the same time, the No side stated that the government rightly decided that any fundamental change to BC electoral system should be made with only a strong consensus of its citizens. Bill Tieleman of No side quoted two previous BC referenda questions, one on the recall of MLAs and the other on citizen initiatives, as examples. In both these cases the voters approved the moves with more than 80 percent support in 1991, before the government finally implemented them. He also said that as far as he was concerned, BC-STV was now a dead issue. A number of other concerned citizens expressed similar views through Letters to the Editor and newspaper columns. For example, in summing up his reaction to the referendum results, Columnist Ted Colley wrote, "STV is for losers, so I'm glad the vote failed" (Colley, 2005).

There was no significant difference in the manner in which the BC Liberal Party Leader Premier Gordon Campbell and the NDP Leader Carol James interpreted the results of the May 17, 2005, referendum. They both recognized that the results showed strong support among BC voters for electoral reform. Gordon Hamilton of The Vancouver Sun reported that in a news conference held at James' Victoria-Beacon Hill constituency office on Wednesday, May 18, 2005, she said:

> The high voter response to STV – single transferable vote – shows voters want a new system. If it is not to be STV, then some other form should be put to a provincial vote at this fall's municipal elections. .. I do not feel that STV was the direction to go; that there were other models to look at (Hamilton, 2005).

The position taken by James to look at other options for electoral reform if BC-STV is rejected at the referendum was consistent with what she had been saying all along before the election. For example, during an interview with Vaughn Palmer on *Voice of BC* on Shaw Cable on BC-STV and the referendum during the last week of April 2005, she said:

> Let's see if people vote in favour. ... If people vote Yes, we will implement that for the following election. .. If people do not vote in favour, but there is a very strong support for some kind of electoral reform, then I think it's important to ... give the voters another option to look at. ... I think, we have the opportunity, then to say 'the voters have very strongly said they want something different.' They're not sure this is quite the right model, so then let's look at another model (Palmer, 2005b).

Premier Campbell also spoke on the referendum results immediately after their release on Wednesday, May 18, 2005, and suggested that the issue of electoral reform should be discussed in the newly elected legislature (BC Liberal 46 seats and NDP 33 seats) to determine the next steps in that regard. In his media interview on Wednesday, May 18th, on the referendum results he specifically said:

> I do think citizens have been pretty clear. There is pretty strong mandate there for electoral reform to take place. ... I think the result is significant, and it is something for all of us to learn from. It may be an opportunity for us to sit down as a legislature and say what can we do as a body that clearly reflects what is a concern for British Columbians (Lee, 2005).

Later, Premier Campbell also suggested that the Citizens' Assembly could be reconvened to provide guidance on how to proceed on electoral reform. In explaining this further he said, "The legislature may even decide that they would like to get back together with the Citizens' Assembly and be guided by some of their thoughts on how we might move forward with them" (Palmer, 2005c).

The NDP Leader James was not in favour of reconvening the Citizens' Assembly. She expressed the view that "It was time to dispense with the Assembly and get on with alternative forms of electoral reform" (Palmer, 2005c). She has also said, "One of her first moves in the legislature will be to press Premier Gordon Campbell to hold a second ballot on electoral reform as early as this fall" (Hamilton, 2005). With these positions taken by Premier Campbell and the NDP Leader Carol James on the BC-STV referendum results, it was clear that the new legislature is poised for a new round of serious discussions and debates on electoral reform in BC.

Meanwhile, an opinion poll released in mid-June 2005 offered some clues as to whether voters who answered Yes to the referendum question did know enough about BC-STV or not. In this poll, Nordic Research found that "Many of those who voted Yes simply wanted change. They weren't necessarily wedded to BC-STV. Many who voted No said they did so because they didn't understand the proposed system" (Palmer, 2005d). Thus, this poll supports the interpretation of the referendum results by both Premier Campbell and NDP Leader Carol James that there was strong support among BC voters for electoral reform and not necessarily for BC-STV. At the same time both the leaders cannot ignore the fact that the referendum got much more support than any of the political parties at the election.

The above shows that the May 17th referendum failed to bring about a new electoral system in BC, but did manage to generate unprecedented interest in and commitment to electoral reform among its voters and legislators alike. It also became clear that the renewed interest in electoral reform in BC was not going to melt away, at least in the foreseeable future.

The new legislature met for the first time on Monday, September 12, 2005. The throne speech by Lieutenant–Governor Iona Campagnolo at the opening of the new legislature announced, among other things, the new Liberal government's plan for electoral reform. According to this plan, the government would hold another referendum in 2008 to give voters a second chance to decide whether the existing FPTP system should be changed to BC-STV. The plan also intended to increase the number of electoral districts by six to 85 under the current electoral system, redefine their boundaries, and establish BC-STV constituency boundaries before the new referendum. The increase in the number of seats in the legislature to 85 was a measure to guarantee adequate representation for rural communities under any electoral system. The government believed that the establishment of BC-STV constituency boundaries would provide the public with a critical piece of information that was missing at the time of the May 17th referendum. According to the plan, the government would also provide equal funding to support active information campaigns for both the supporters and detractors of each electoral model under consideration. The new referendum question would be crafted by the government and debated in the legislature beforehand. Whatever electoral model (FPTP or BC-STV) prevails at the referendum would be in effect for the next provincial election scheduled for May 12, 2009.

Thus, the need for a second referendum on BC-STV has come about because of numerous inadequacies of the way how the first referendum was conducted. The BC government is now hoping to take the challenge of electoral reform to its 'ultimate conclusion' as said in the throne speech with the second referendum scheduled for November 2008. No one is in a position to speculate whether this, in fact, would be the case.

CHAPTER 8
SOBER REFLECTION

This chapter looks at the Citizens' Assembly approach to electoral reform in British Columbia as a whole, and reflects on some of its features that were critical to the results it produced. The specific features of the Assembly approach discussed in this chapter include the following:

- The mandate of the Citizens' Assembly;
- Assembly composition and member-selection;
- Assembly process;
- Member contribution;
- The role of government; and
- Second referendum.

The purpose of this reflection is to recognize some special strengths and the shortcomings of the Assembly approach to electoral reform that should not go unnoticed. This would be of special help to those who may try to adopt the same or a similar approach to electoral reform in the future in British Columbia or any other democracy.

8.1   Assembly mandate

The mandate of the Citizens' Assembly had three major limitations. First, the Citizens' Assembly's role in electoral reform was limited to the manner in which voters' ballots were translated into seats in the Legislative Assembly. This was not necessarily a futile strategy, especially going by the failures of past Canadian electoral reform exercises, such as the Meech Lake (1991) and Charlottetown (1992) Accords. They tried to look at too many issues in a single electoral reform exercise. The Citizens' Assembly would not have had enough time to deal with other issues given its limited time frame.

Second, if the Citizens Assembly wanted a change in the manner of translating votes into seats, it could recommend to the public only one alternative model for that purpose. In its Leaning Phase, the Assembly learnt a number of electoral systems that would meet the needs of British Columbians better when compared to the existing FPTP system. The Assembly also heard the preferences expressed by the public for such alternative systems during its Public Hearing Phase. In the end, the Assembly considered all what it learnt and heard and designed in some detail two electoral systems, MMP and STV, which they thought were the best of those superior to the existing FPTP system. Having done this, it appeared illogical to ask the public to make a choice between one of the best alternative systems and the existing FPTP system. Instead, the public should have been given a choice between the two best alternative systems, MMP and STV, as they both were considered superior to the existing system. It could have been easy to achieve this by asking two separate questions at a referendum. One of the questions could have been framed to determine the extent of support among voters for changing the existing electoral system. The other could have been framed to determine the extent of support among voters for each of the two best alternative systems. Such an approach would also give an opportunity to the public to demonstrate that they needed change but not to any of the proposed alternative systems. This would have generated highly sensational debates on electoral reform, as witnessed during the Assembly public hearings, between those who support and oppose change, and between those who support and oppose each of the two alternative systems recommended by the Assembly. In contrast, the referendum held managed to spark debates only on the fronts of those who resisted change and those who supported one of the best two alternative systems, BC-STV, giving the voter a restricted choice between the existing FPTP system and BC-STV.

Third, the mandate of the Citizens' Assembly was short of a public funded program for communicating the Assembly final recommendation to the public, even if it were for change. In traditional approaches to electoral reform, the role of Royal Commissions or Legislative Select Committees appointed to recommend electoral changes end with the submission of their final recommendations. The recommendations then become a subject of discussion at the Legislative Assembly. It is the Legislative Assembly that decides whether or not the recommended changes should be implemented. The citizens at large do not play any role in making the final decision in this process.

The Citizens' Assembly approach was created to make electoral reform decisions differently. In this approach, the citizens at large were to make the final decision through a referendum on a recommendation made by the Citizens' Assembly that consisted of 160 randomly selected British Columbians. For effective implementation of this approach, there was a need for communicating the recommendation made by the Citizens' Assembly to the entire citizenry and educating them on its merits. This could have been achieved through a properly planned program of action with public funds and other resources it needed. The Citizens' Assembly mandate should have been extended to cover the implementation of such a public communication and education program through the Assembly members, who knew best how and why they arrived at their final recommendation. The lack of such a program certainly defeated the very purpose of choosing this approach to electoral reform.

The members of the Citizens' Assembly viewed this as a major flaw in the Assembly approach from the very beginning. When all their efforts failed to convince the government to have such a publicly funded program, some of them even discussed the possibility of Assembly members running as candidates under a new political party of their own to draw public attention to their final recommendation. Many other concerned citizens, including some well-known journalists, also expressed their concerns on this issue both before and after the May 17, 2005, referendum. For example, in his Vancouver Sun column of June 2, 2005, Craig McInnes wrote:

> If there was a flaw in the (Citizens' Assembly) process, it was that, having launched the assembly, the provincial government was unwilling to support its findings even to the extent of funding a substantial educational campaign. As a result, many voters rendered their judgment without really understanding what it was they were voting for or against (McInnes, 2005b).

8.2 Assembly composition and member selection

The composition and the member selection process of the Citizens' Assembly had a number of interesting and unique features. The Assembly had 161 members, including its chair, Dr. Blaney. Two different processes were used to select them, a random process for the members and a legislative approval process for the Chair. Attorney General Plant first nominated Dr. Jack Blaney as the Chair of the Assembly at the time the all-party Special Committee on the Citizens' Assembly on Electoral Reform of the Legislature was established. Later, the Government formally appointed Dr. Blaney to the position of the Chair of the Citizens' Assembly after the Special Committee reviewed and unanimously approved his nomination. This process of selecting the Chair of the Citizens' Assembly was strategic in nature in two ways. First, the Attorney General had the opportunity to nominate a person with adequate qualifications and experience to steer the Assembly process as planned by the Government. Second, only a nonpartisan person of integrity would finally become the Chair of the Assembly with the support of all political parties in the Legislature. This ensured immediate acceptance of the Chair by the Assembly members and professional leadership to staff and office support functions.

Terms of Reference and the Duties of the Chair laid out some guidelines for the random selection of the other 160 members. The Assembly followed these guidelines and first selected 158 members representing the adult population of British Columbia. This member selection process ended up with a unique Citizens' Assembly consisting of 79 men and 79 women, with one man and one woman from each electoral district. These 79 men and 79 women came from all walks of life and from all ethnic groups in British Columbia, except its aboriginal community. The names of these 79 men and 79 women had been drawn at all the three random draws held in the member-selection process.

The selection of the 158 members by these three random draws had two distinct advantages. First, it helped to clearly demonstrate the randomness in the

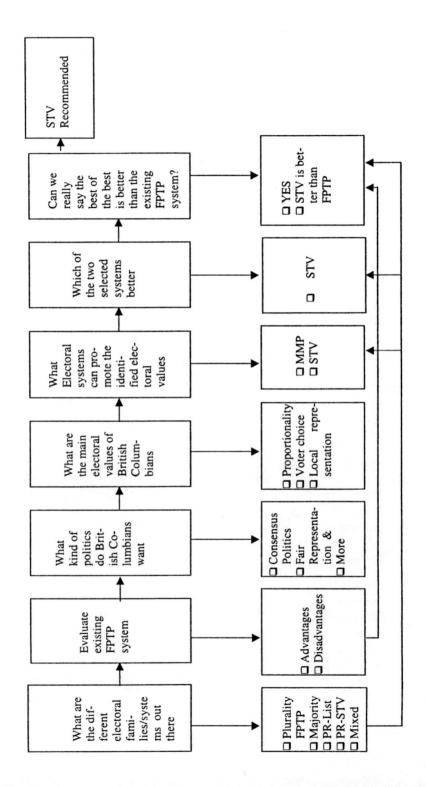

Figure 8.1: Citizens' Assembly Decision-Making Process

member-selection process. Second, it helped to select 158 members who met all the eligibility requirements and were both able and willing to be part of the proposed electoral reform process. In the first instance, only those who met the eligibility qualifications and were able to make a commitment to the Assembly process accepted the initial invitation. Then, at the final selection meetings, those who were present were again asked to declare, this time publicly, if they met the eligibility requirements and were still interested in becoming an Assembly member. Only those who did so qualified to be candidates for the last round of random selection. Thus, the random selection process had an interesting built-in feature that could check out those who did not meet the eligibility requirements or were not able or willing to participate in the Assembly process.

After selecting the 158 members, the Chair of the Assembly noticed that none of them may have come from the aboriginal community of BC. Therefore, the Chair took some steps to correct the situation. He first verified whether any of the 158 members selected through the three-step random process had any aboriginal roots. Upon the realization that none of them could be considered as aboriginals, the Chair initiated another round of random selection as described in Chapter 3 and selected two members from the aboriginal community to be part of the Assembly. This increased the total number of Assembly members selected on random basis to 160. Figure 8.1 diagrammatically demonstrates the complete random selection process used.

The extra efforts so made by the Assembly Chair to ensure aboriginal representation in the Citizens' Assembly were strikingly significant from a historic perspective. The Native population of British Columbia have been ignored and excluded from the political process for a good part of BC's history; they were disenfranchised for a good portion of the first century, and underrepresented for the rest of BC's political life. If the Assembly were to represent all British Columbians, then First Nations would need to have a voice in the process. A random sampling of voting lists in particular ridings would not necessarily bring First Nation's people into the reform process. Selecting two additional members to include aboriginal representation was a way to address some of the historic inequities that remain problematic in the exercise of democracy within Canada.

The very nature of the random-selection process ensured that all the 160 Assembly members were both nonpartisan and representative of the adult population of British Columbia by age, gender, and geographic distribution. In addition, it ensured that they were able and committed to follow the Assembly course. These 160 members were given the power to make a recommendation on electoral reform and take it directly to the rest of their fellow citizens for a final decision. By all these indicators, the Citizens' Assembly became a unique and historical instrument for making an important decision on electoral reform. This is the first time that such a process was established in any modern democracy for making an important decision crucial to the practice of democracy. Thus, the Citizens' Assembly approach in British Columbia has set the tone for future democratic processes in all democracies.

8.3   Assembly process

The overall Assembly process had a number of interesting features. It was first separated into three main Phases: Learning Phase, Public Hearings Phase and Deliberation Phase. The order followed by the three phases was logical and meaningful. During the three-month long Learning Phase (January to March) of the Assembly the Assembly members could learn together about the BC's existing electoral system and those of other democracies around the world. The political education the Assembly members received during this period was an essential prerequisite to their effective participation in the rest of the Assembly process. This educational phase of the Assembly helped to bring all its members to a level field in terms of knowledgeability in matters of electoral reform, before the Public Hearings and Deliberation phases.

In addition to their learning about electoral systems, the Assembly members made use of the training opportunities given to them to sharpen their skills in a number of key areas critical to the Assembly business. The specific areas of training offered to the Assembly members include Internet browsing, media interaction, conflict resolution, and consensus building. With the training in these areas and political education they received, the Assembly members were given an opportunity to become an extraordinary group of British Columbians uniquely qualified to do the job expected of them.

The break between the Learning Phase and the Public Hearings Phase (April) gave the Assembly members some time to publicize the Assembly and generate interest in the upcoming public hearings in their local communities. The Assembly members did this in a number of ways, including one-on-one and group discussions, public presentations, and media interviews. They made their public presentations at local schools, churches, service clubs, chambers of commerce, and the like. All these activities of the Assembly members resulted in a notable upsurge of written presentations and heavily crowded public hearings with an unprecedented number of presenters and other attendees.

The carefully crafted format of the public hearings helped to produce desired results. The presenters as well as other attendees of the public hearings were pleased with the way the Assembly conducted them throughout BC. The special plenary sessions of the Assembly, held soon after the public hearings (50 hearings in all) in Prince George over the last weekend of June 2004, were critical to the Assembly process. They gave an opportunity for the Assembly members to review together what they heard at the public hearings and the written submissions made to the Assembly. It was a time to consolidate ideas, with a view to building consensus on the best electoral options for British Columbia. The review of the written submissions was done with the help of their summaries prepared by the Assembly research officers. Only a very few Assembly members had read in full all the written presentations made by that time. The Assembly members realized that it would be difficult to expect every one of them to find time to read all the written submissions before the Deliberation Phase. For this, they first compared their notes on what they had already read, and agreed to recommend to each other written presentations that were found particularly important to read in full. This special weekend plenary sessions also helped the Assembly members to start planning a workable decision-making process for the Deliberation Phase that lay ahead. With a potential list of selective readings and an initial plan for their decision-making process, the Assembly members left Prince George, hoping to spend the next two months (July and August) in preparing for the final (Deliberation) phase of the Assembly.

The plan for the decision-making process of the Deliberation Phase appeared both strategic and results-oriented. It had identified all the tasks needed to be done in reaching a final decision to retain or change the existing electoral system in BC and formulated a critical path to complete the entire decision-making process on time and budget. The critical path formulated consisted of ten important interim decisions leading to a final decision of the Assembly, and showed their dependency levels and targeted completion dates. In essence, the critical path required the Assembly members to revisit and confirm their electoral values (Decision 1), choose (alternative) electoral options that could secure and consolidate those values (Decision 2), work out details of the selected electoral options (Decisions 3 & 4), choose the best out of the selected alternative options (Decision 5), reassess and reconfirm the merits of the existing FPTP system (Decision 6), and, finally make a choice between the existing system and the best alternative system (Decisions 7, 8, 9 & 10).

Revisiting and confirming the electoral values of Assembly members was a logical place to begin the Deliberation Phase. Choosing and working out details of electoral options that could secure those values helped to narrow down the possible electoral system options to two: MMP and STV. All the ten working groups of the Assembly had determined that the existing FPTP system was least important in that regard. Going by the logic so far, a choice between MMP and STV should have brought the decision-making process to an end, as FPTP system was also given due consideration at the time of selecting electoral options that could best reflect the reaffirmed electoral values. The critical path required the Assembly to revisit and reconfirm the merits of the existing FPTP system, and compare it with the one selected as the best of all systems. This extra step of looking at the existing FPTP system at this stage was planned to further strengthen the Assembly's relationship with the public and the political class. This extra step was, however, both unnecessary and illogical. The time allocated for this extra step should have been more productively used in areas that needed more time and were essential for making a final decision. For example, the Assembly failed to find adequate time to complete building the basic features of MMP, one of the two electoral system alternatives considered for final selection. This resulted in a vote in the Assembly to make a choice between the two systems MMP and STV, without the advantage of looking at MMP in a thorough manner. Some members had even interpreted the Assembly's failure to work out the basic details of the MMP system within its allocated time period as a sign of complexity and peculiarity that may be associated with it. One could argue, if the MMP system was equally laid out as the STV system, the chances of more Assembly members opting for MMP in preference to STV would have been much greater. This was evidenced from the type of questions some members raised and the related discussions that followed during the MMP-STV debate based on their own assumptions on undecided MMP features, such as ballot forms, formula for allocating PR seats, and possible overhang seats. Even the questions and discussions on the MMP features already built were not totally valid, as at least some of them could have been revisited and changed in completing a MMP model for BC.

The plenary sessions of the Citizens' Assembly held in Prince George helped the Assembly to raise its image as a public institution that truly represented and cared for both rural and urban areas of British Columbia. Furthermore, they gave an opportunity to Assembly members who came from the southern areas of the province to get first-hand information about the issues and concerns of British Columbians living in the North. It would have been better if the Assembly held its plenary sessions in several other outside communities as well.

Despite the extra efforts of the Citizens' Assembly to ensure aboriginal representation, there was no significant contribution to the Assembly process by the aboriginal community. The two Assembly members of aboriginal roots did share their experiences and concerns with other members of the Assembly throughout its process. There was no significant contribution in the form of written presentations to the Assembly or verbal presentations at its public hearings by the aboriginal community of the province. Many view this as an important omission in the Assembly process.

Meanwhile, some critics believe that the research officers of the Assembly and other experts who made presentations to its plenary sessions influenced the Assembly decisions in a biased manner. According to the critics, both the Assembly research officers and the outside experts on electoral matters who addressed the Assembly were academics, who lacked practical experience in the political field. This, the critics say, led to Assembly decisions that were theoretically biased. According to the critics, this situation could have been avoided if the Assembly had the advantage of having some input from practicing politicians during the deliberation phase, especially after choosing the best two alternative electoral options, MMP and STV. For this the Citizens' Assembly could have invited at least two practicing politicians from a country practicing each of these electoral systems, one in favour and the other not in favour of their existing electoral system, to come and share their practical experiences and concerns with the Citizens' Assembly members. This, in turn, could have enabled the Assembly members to weigh both the theoretical and practical aspects of the two best alternative electoral systems in making a choice between them. Not having any practicing politicians involved in the Assembly process was a serious drawback, especially considering that only two of the 160 Assembly members had some practical experience in the political field. As a result, the practical aspects of the different political systems were not in the radar of a vast majority of the Assembly members. For example, how increased electoral district size could influence women's role in politics was never discussed in the Assembly. Christy Clark, a former Deputy Premier of BC, later said:

> The proposal that's come out of the Citizens' Assembly will, in my opinion, make it much harder for women to actually be represented....The reason that's

the case is that because the Citizens' Assembly, while it's made up half of women, is not made up of people who have actual active experience in politics (Tieleman, 2005).

At the same time, the Assembly research officers and outside academic experts who addressed the Assembly were expected to remain objective and noncommittal to any particular electoral choice for British Columbia. This was an unwritten and unspoken rule that all the academic experts should have strictly obeyed. The rule applied to the Chair of the Assembly as well, except at a time of casting a deciding vote in the event of a tie. Any suggestion as to which electoral system was best for British Columbia by any of the experts or the Chair of the Assembly could significantly influence the decisions made by its members.

Unfortunately, this rule was broken by Dr. David Farrell, who came from the United Kingdom to address the Assembly. He was also the author of *Electoral Systems: A Comparative Introduction*, copies of which had been distributed to the members of the Assembly as a basic reference source. In response to a question raised by the Assembly member F. W. Zens, Dr. Farrell first replied that it was not appropriate for him to suggest any particular electoral system to the Assembly members and that British Columbians should decide what was best for them. When the question was repeated by the same member, three times Dr. Farrell maintained the same answer. However, when the same question was asked one more time, he simply said, "STV." Later, Zens became one of the biggest advocates for STV, and even tried to distribute specially prepared STV buttons to Assembly members to be worn on their jackets. The Assembly Chair stopped him from distributing the STV buttons and asked all the Assembly members to abstain from exhibiting anything showing their personal electoral system preferences.

The Assembly conducted its Learning Phase through a series of formal presentations (lectures) on electoral systems conducted by the Assembly research officers and the invited outside experts. The Assembly members listened to these presentations and tried to learn as much as they could from them. Although the Assembly members gathered more information about electoral systems from additional sources, the primary focus of most of them, if not all, was on what was learnt from the Assembly sessions. This means that any critical information that was missed by the research officers and the guest speakers to the Assembly could have affected the important decisions made on the floor of the Assembly. For example, the critics of the BC-STV system later questioned the wisdom of the Assembly experts for not exposing the Assembly members to the negative or not so good experiences with the STV system in other countries, especially in Malta,[3] before they were asked to make a choice between the MMP and STV systems. At the same time, the expert presentation on possible consequences of change to a MMP system focused only on the experiences of New

---

[3] According to a column in the Georgia Strait of October 16, 2005, written by one of the critics, Bill Tieleman, in Malta, where the STV system has been used since 1921, women make up just 9.2 percent of the legislators. It also had no independent candidate since 1950.

Zealand, which was still going through an electoral transition period. The MMP countries, such as Germany, where the MMP system has been well established, do not experience the problems and difficulties New Zealand is still going through. For example, having two types (constituency and PR) of elected representatives in the legislature is not problematic in countries like Germany where the MMP system has been in use for lengthy periods, while it can be viewed as a problem at the initial stage of transition from the FPTP system to MMP.

The member surveys conducted from time to time had a two-fold use. The member surveys conducted at the end of every weekend the Assembly met helped to make improvements to the way how its plenary sessions and group discussions were conducted, on an ongoing basis. Meanwhile, the three main member surveys conducted with the help of three questionnaires before, during and after the Assembly process gave critical information regarding the work and the process involved in a Citizens' Assembly. In these three surveys, the Assembly members were told in advance that their individual answers to the specific questions asked would be treated in strict confidence. This encouraged the Assembly members to express themselves freely in answering the questions asked. It also helped to produce a reliable pattern of thinking among the Assembly members on the issues in question.

8.4   Member contribution

The Assembly members always displayed a high level of enthusiasm and interest in what they did throughout the Assembly process. In the initial stage of the process, however, only a limited number of members took part in the discussions held in the Assembly plenary sessions. As weeks and months passed by, more and more members joined in the plenary discussions, making those of the Deliberation Phase most interesting with the participation of a good number of members. In group discussions held in between plenary sessions, all members freely participated throughout the Assembly process.

How the Assembly members conducted themselves at times of their decision-making was particularly interesting and noteworthy. All members always tried their best to build consensus among them on issues that were central to the key decisions expected of them as a group. They managed to make only some decisions by consensus. For others, they sought majority support through a vote. Once a decision was made by a vote, even those who voted against the decision gladly accepted it in the true spirit of democracy. For example, the author, who vociferously advocated the MMP system in the MMP-STV debate, made a statement on the floor of the Assembly soon after the debate accepting the Assembly majority decision for STV. In his statement on this occasion, the author also stressed the importance of making the final decision of the Assembly, between now chosen STV and the existing FPTP system, with undivided support for one electoral system. This, the author added, would make the final recommendation of the Assembly more acceptable to the general public. Every other Assembly member also generally accepted the Assembly decisions he or she may not have individually supported. By this way of their conduct, the Assembly members had demonstrated both their irrevocable commitment to the Assembly process and their ability to play their role in the practice of democracy in an exemplary manner.

Meanwhile, the members of the public that came in contact with the Assembly members showed complete trust in them. The flow of complimentary and congratulatory messages to the Assembly members during the Assembly process testified to this. As stated earlier, the presenters at the Assembly public hearings who proposed new (alternative) electoral systems also left their details to be worked out by the Assembly members. It is, thus, clear that the Assembly members had a remarkable record of successes in building public trust.

Despite the above successes and achievements on the part of the Assembly members, some critics had raised three main concerns about the manner in which they made the key Assembly decisions. First, in making their key decisions, the Assembly members overdepended on academic experts, and, as a result, the main decisions they made were academically biased. These critics point out that one of the main objectives of the Citizens' Assembly approach was to avoid dependence on experts (and politicians) in making electoral reform decisions. The critics, nevertheless, agree that there was an essential role for the academic experts to play in educating the Assembly members on different electoral systems and their applications in world democracies. The critics' concern was that many Assembly members looked to the academic experts for much more than that. For example, some members of the Assembly wanted its research officers to intervene in the Assembly's plenary discussions and debates on electoral choices even at the time they were about to make their final decision. The research officers declined to give advice on electoral choices at that late stage in the Assembly process. The very fact that some members tried to depend on the research officers so late in the Assembly process suggests that there was a degree of overdependency on academic experts in the Assembly decision-making process.

Second, some critics point out that the Assembly members made their choice between the two best alternative (to the existing system) systems, MMP and STV, prematurely, as one of them had not been adequately modeled for BC by the time of making that choice. This matter has been discussed in detail earlier.

Third, according to some critics, the Assembly members did not give adequate consideration to the suggestions and recommendations made to the Assembly by the public through their written and verbal (public hearings) presentations. The Terms of Reference for the Citizens' Assembly specifically stated that in its role in assessing electoral models and making a final recommendation as to whether the existing electoral system should be retained or changed, the Assembly "must consult with British Columbians and provide British Columbians with the opportunity to make submissions to the Citizens' Assembly in writing, and orally at public meetings." Accordingly, the Assembly did consult with British Columbians and provided them with the opportunity to make written and verbal submissions. On their part, British Columbians joined the Assembly process in record numbers, and did make an unprecedented number of written and verbal presentations. The Assembly members showed interest to review the presentations, but paid less attention to their recommendations at the time of their plenary discussions on electoral choices during the Assembly's Deliberation Phase. During these plenary discussions, some members, especially those who had a strong leniency towards the STV system, felt that they should not be "influenced" by the recommendations made in the public submissions in making electoral choices on the floor of the Assembly. This, in fact, constituted a negative approach to public presentations.

These critics point out that the unresponsiveness of the Assembly members to the overwhelming support for the MMP system among those who made verbal and written presentations to the Assembly, in particular, was both improper and questionable. There were two main reasons for the Assembly members' indifference to the MMP system. First, the mandate limitation ruling out any increase to the number of seats in the BC Legislature prohibited the potential adoption of a fully proportional MMP system. A fully proportional MMP system would require some flexibility to increase the number of seats in the Legislature temporarily under certain conditions. The need for such flexibility depends on the percentage of PR seats in a given MMP model; the higher the percentage of PR seats, the lesser the need for such flexibility. A MMP model could have been designed for BC with enough PR seats to meet full proportionality without any increase to the number of seats in the Legislature. Despite this, the strict limitation of the Citizens' Assembly mandate to the translation of votes to seats in the Legislature was seen as a negative connotation to any new electoral models where the number of seats in the Legislature may have to increase, temporarily or permanently.

Second, there was a bias against the MMP system among many members of the Citizens' Assembly all along the Assembly process. There were three main factors that caused this bias. One factor was the strong anti-party premonition developed by many Assembly members from the very beginning of the Assembly process. These members viewed the MMP system as a party-friendly system, and were somewhat indifferent to its potential strengths and benefits. Another factor that led to the bias was the strong position taken by the BC Green Party and its leader Adriane Carr for adopting a MMP model in BC. This negatively impacted the discussions of the Assembly members on the MMP model both within and outside their plenary sessions. In their discussions on the subject, many Assembly members interpreted the strong support for MMP by the BC Green Party and its Leader as an indication that any MMP model would meet the best interests of small parties and minorities, but not the province as a whole. At the same time, these Assembly members also viewed a vast majority, if not all, of those who made verbal and written presentations to the Assembly in support of MMP as one single lobby group of British Columbians, who were politically linked to the BC Green Party and its Leader's earlier initiative for a MMP model in BC. The Assembly members who had this view also argued that the overwhelming support for MMP among the presenters to the Assembly gave a false impression of the wants and dislikes of British Columbians. The third factor was Adriane Carr's physical presence at most of the Assembly plenary sessions as an observer. Many members interpreted her physical presence at the Assembly plenary sessions as yet another act of influencing them to support MMP. All the above factors together constituted a significant bias among many Assembly members in their review of the overwhelming support for MMP in public presentations to the Assembly.

8.5   Role of government

The BC Government received both praise and criticism for its role in the 2004/05 electoral reform efforts it initiated. There was widespread praise for the Government for creating a unique electoral reform process, giving the power to make decisions on electoral reform to the voter. It was a truly democratic process that allowed the people to decide for themselves whether they should retain or change the existing electoral system, and, if a change were necessary, what sort of a new system they would prefer. Unlike in the traditional approaches to electoral reform, the legislature was kept out of the decision-making process. Because of its uniqueness, this new approach to electoral reform became a subject of interest throughout the democratic world. Many of those who came to know about the unique approach praised the BC Government for conducting a new experiment in the practice of democracy.

At the same time, the BC Government also came under heavy criticism for not having a carefully planned publicly funded program to adequately educate the voter on the final recommendation of the Citizens' Assembly before the referendum that followed. This, the critics say, did not help the voter to make a well-informed decision on the referendum question based on the final decision of the Citizens' Assembly. According to the critics, this was a serious omission in the well-intended electoral reform process. The critics also argue that if the government was serious about the electoral reform process it had initiated, such an omission should not have occurred. Immediately after the Citizens' Assembly prepared its Final Report, the Government decided not to "promote" the new electoral system it recommended. What was needed was not a government program to 'promote' the new electoral system proposed by the Assembly, but an adequately funded province-wide program to 'educate' the voter on the proposed new system through discussions and debates in an unbiased manner. Through such a program of discussions and debates on the subject all British Columbians should have had the advantage of looking at pros and cons of the new electoral system proposed by the Citizens Assembly before the referendum. For this, the Government depended only on a centralized information office in Victoria that could provide the details of the new electoral system proposed by the Citizens' Assembly on request. This was far from what was really needed to educate the BC voter on the newly proposed electoral system.

Meanwhile, both the major political parties of the province that had grass-root level support decided to remain neutral on the referendum issue. As a result, those who actively engaged in educational debates and discussions on the refer-

endum issue were limited to two minor political parties and a few other groups
and individuals. The groups that took part in the referendum debates and discussions include the Citizens' Assembly Alumni group, Fair Voting BC, Fair Vote
Canada, "Know STV," and "Yes to STV." All these and other groups and individuals who actively took part in educating the public on the referendum issue
had to work within very limited budgets. As a result, until the media increased
its coverage on election issues after the official announcement of the upcoming
provincial election (April 19, 2005), the referendum ballot on the Election Day
was mostly left to chance, rather than to well-informed decisions of BC voters.
Critics put the blame for this situation squarely on the part of the BC Government, and, in particular, on the part of Premier Campbell, who initiated the electoral reform process. For example in his April 29, 2005, Vancouver Sun column,
Norman Spector, a well-known BC journalist, wrote:

> Campbell who promises a golden decade, won't say whether he thinks STV
> would benefit our province. Worse, he's refused to fund an informed debate be-
> tween advocates and opponents. In effect, he's invited British Columbians to
> go into a dark room filled with their children and throw darts (Spector, 2005).

Most of the critics agree that the new electoral system the Citizens' Assembly had recommended, BC-STV, was too complicated to understand. At the
same time the minimum level of support it needed—60 percent province-wide
and more than 50 percent in at least 48 electoral districts—to be validated at the
referendum was too high. These were good enough reasons for the government
to plan and implement a publicly funded program to adequately educate the public on the new electoral system proposed by the Citizens' Assembly. The Government chose not to do so, and was complacent with the establishment of a centralized information office to provide details of the newly proposed system on
request. If not for the perseverance of those who volunteered to spend their time
and energy in educating the public on the referendum issue and the media coverage it received, especially after April 19, 2005, the referendum question may
have been an insignificant factor at the May 17, 2005, BC election.

8.6   Second Referendum

The new Liberal government is planning to hold a second referendum on the
recommendations of the Citizens' Assembly as a way of responding to the majority vote for BC-STV that failed to pass at the May 17th referendum. The government's plan for the second referendum addresses some of the main concerns
expressed by many about the way how the first referendum was conducted. Such
concerns addressed in the plan for the second referendum include not enough information to adequately understand the proposed new electoral system (BC-
STV) and lack of funding for active information campaigns.

The concerns not addressed in the plan for the second referendum could remain contentious in the months and years ahead. The biggest concern not addressed in the plan for the second referendum is the omission of the MMP sys-

tem from possible options for electoral change. It is a more traditional voting system (than STV) used by most proportional representation countries in the world. Carol James, the Leader of Opposition, has publicly shown her preference for MMP. The Law Commission of Canada has recommended it for Canada. An overwhelming majority of the presenters at the public hearings of the Citizens' assembly advocated it as the best electoral system for British Columbia. The Citizens' Assembly members also considered it, along with STV, as a system much better than the existing FPTP system. The Assembly members, however, could not recommend to the public both MMP and STV as possible alternative systems due to strict limitations imposed by the Assembly mandate; the mandate allowed only one alternative system to be recommended to the public. As a result, the Assembly members had to choose one from MMP and STV to be finally recommended to the public. In making this choice they showed preference for STV over MMP. But this does not rule out the legitimacy of their arguments preferring MMP to the existing FPTP system. Furthermore, the whole purpose of the Citizens' Assembly approach is to give power to the people, meaning all British Columbians, to make a final decision on electoral change. For this, it is important to present to the public both STV and MMP systems that have been identified by the Citizens' assembly as superior to the existing FPTP system. In this situation, a mere choice between the present FPTP system and BC-STV at a referendum, ignoring MMP altogether, may not 'take the challenge of electoral reform in BC to its ultimate conclusion' as expected by the new government. It is very likely that MMP would remain as an alternative electoral system of interest to British Columbians both before and after the second referendum, irrespective of its results.

CHAPTER 9
CONCLUSION

9.1 Ongoing need

Elections are an essential tool in the practice of democracy in the modern world. Through elections, modern democracies choose a manageable number of citizens to represent the entire citizenry for participation in their governing institutions. This facilitates democratic rule through elected representatives. This also implies that the degree of democracy in a country or any other political unit depends on the extent of representation of its citizenry in those governing institutions. Different democracies have developed different electoral systems for choosing representatives of the people. Over the years, many democracies have also taken time to review and reform the electoral systems they have developed, hoping to reach higher rates of inclusion in democratic rule through elected representatives. As more countries turn to democracy as a form of sustainable government, developing and reforming electoral systems will be more prevalent in the world.

As described in Chapter 1, the issues of franchise and fair representation in the legislature have primarily driven the wheels of electoral reform. Universal franchise has now become the norm throughout the democratic world. Fair representation in the legislature mirroring the range of opinion in the electorate continues to remain a dominant issue of electoral reform. The ongoing discussions on fair representation in modern democracies focus on many issues. These issues include nonrepresentation or underrepresentation of minorities, disparity in gender, age, rural-urban representation, inequality of votes, the lack of accountability, the cynical behaviour of elected representatives and their parties, and votes-to-seats party imbalances. Conflicts around these issues, at times, manifest themselves into major political crises. Such crises appear in many forms. The most common indicators of such crises include elected governments with too much power, rampant corruption of governments and other elected officials, failure of existing government system to function, high level of voter apathy, yo-yo type politics and policy-making, and increased skepticism about political parties and politics. People generally look for electoral reform at times of such political crises.

9.2   No perfect electoral system

The immediate aim of electoral reform is an electoral system that would engage citizens in government through a fair representative system. This, in turn, is expected to meet the end results of good democratic governance. There is, however, no perfect electoral system. Every electoral system has its own strengths and weaknesses, which positively or negatively influence the practice of democracy in any given country. For example, as stated before the FPTP system promotes broad-based inclusive parties, produces stable governments, holds elected representatives and governments accountable, and provides effective local representation. These are significant strengths of the FPTP system. At the same time, by its very nature, the FPTP system can often produce disproportional election results with votes-to-seats imbalances, promotes an overly adversarial type of politics, produces wrong winners through artificial majorities, underrepresents women and minorities, and establishes "friendly dictatorships." These are significant weaknesses of the FPTP system.

As a result, the choice of any particular electoral system is more a trade-off among the strengths and weaknesses of the different electoral systems, rather than an identification of one of strongest democratic features. The specific trade-offs made by one community in choosing an electoral system may differ from those made by another. The trade-offs made by any particular community or country is based on its own electoral and democratic values and priority considerations among them. The specific electoral and democratic values that are most important to a community and its priority considerations are based on a number of factors uniquely applicable to it. These factors include one's own history, existing political structure and social composition. No two communities or countries are identical with regard to any of these factors. As a result, an electoral system best suited for one particular community or country may not be equally good for another. For example, the proportional electoral systems in Israel and Italy have produced very unstable coalition governments, while similar systems in a number of other countries, including Switzerland, Austria, Sweden, and Norway, have produced regular coalition governments with a very high degree of stability. In fact, Switzerland ranks first in government longevity among democratic countries of both proportional and nonproportional systems; the average government duration of Switzerland is 8.59 years (Farrell, 2001, p.195). This clearly shows that each community or country should find time to develop an electoral system that serves its best interests based on its own circumstances. There is no one perfect electoral system that is equally good for every community or country.

9.3   Superiority of the Citizens' Assembly approach

The traditional approaches to electoral reform based on recommendations of either a select legislative committee or special commission appointed for that purpose have had two main disadvantages. First, the number of people at the decision-making table is too small to adequately represent the citizenry. For example, as described earlier in the book, the decision-making bodies in the Meech Lake Accord and Charlottetown Accord in Canada were limited to the premiers of its provinces and 12 appointed prominent Canadians, respectively. Second, those who take part in the decision-making process come to the table representing particular interests; they are there to get something for those whom they represent. These and other disadvantages of the traditional approaches to electoral reform translate to decisions that lack the desired degree of objectivity. Once a select legislative committee or special commission makes a decision in the form of a recommendation, the legislature has the power to approve it for its implementation. The general public have very little or no part to play in the whole reform process; the extent of public consultation by select legislative committees and special commissions appointed on electoral matters has been minimal, if it occurs at all.

The Citizens' Assembly approach to electoral reform used in British Columbia was uniquely designed to meet two main objectives. One objective was to overcome the shortcomings of the traditional approaches to electoral reform through select legislative committees and special commissions. The other was to relegate power to the people, instead of politicians or experts, to decide on the type of electoral system that would best serve the entire citizenry. In implementing the new approach in BC, an electoral reform recommendation made by the Citizens' Assembly was put directly to the citizenry, bypassing the legislature, for a final decision. As stated before, this was the first time citizens have been directly entrusted with the power to reshape the electoral process or any other major aspect of the political process in any democracy.

The first time application of this new approach to electoral reform in BC (2004/05) demonstrated its special strengths in five main areas. First, the new approach received an unprecedented level of public support and confidence. This was evidenced by the stream of letters of appreciation received by the Citizens' Assembly and the congratulatory remarks made by the presenters at the Assembly public hearings. The primary reason for such public support appears to be the deliberate controls the Assembly had in place to exclude past and present politicians and political party officials from the Citizens' Assembly member-selection process. This has brought instant credibility to both the process and the final recommendation of the Citizens' Assembly. Due to this, some critics argue, many British Columbians even voted for BC-STV at the referendum without knowing enough about it. Second, the membership of the Citizens' Assembly consisted of a man and woman from each electoral district and two aboriginal representatives. Together they represented all regions and communities of British Columbia. This, in turn, enabled the Assembly to give equal consideration to concerns and interests of all the regions and communities of British Columbia. Third, although the Citizens' Assembly members were chosen on an electoral district or community basis, every member was expected to represent British Columbia as a whole. Every Citizen's Assembly member lived up to this expectation throughout the Assembly process, and even beyond, to the time of the referendum.

Fourth, the three-phase process used in the new approach was both strategic and results-oriented. It helped the Assembly members to complete many tasks within a comparatively short period of time of eleven months. During these eleven months, they joined the Assembly with an open mind, acquired adequate knowledge on electoral systems, researched together how the different systems worked in world democracies, listened to their fellow British Columbians on what they had to say on electoral reform, and selected one electoral system as the best system for British Columbia. Some of the features of the Assembly process were both historic and unique. These features include the random selection of the Assembly members, educational programs for the members, special training in conflict resolution and consensus building, one-on-one and group discussions of the Assembly members with the public, public hearings across the province, a critical path approach for decision-making and public debates on the related referendum question. With these features, the Citizens' Assembly process in BC provides a transferable template for other democracies, while considering cultural and political flexibility within the host body politics. Fifth, at the end of the Citizens' assembly process, the Assembly members became a ready-made team of volunteers spread out throughout BC anxiously waiting to educate the public on the final recommendation of the Assembly. This was primarily due to the sense of ownership to the Assembly final decision they shared. A properly funded government program facilitating their effective participation in educating the public on the Assembly final decision could have resulted in a more meaningful and conclusive referendum.

The above shows that the Citizens' Assembly approach to electoral reform is not only unique; it is also superior to the traditional approaches to electoral reform used by democracies all over the world. The Citizens' Assembly approach has shown a new way for arriving at difficult public policy decisions in a democracy with the full involvement of its adult citizens.

9.4   Lessons for the future

The drawbacks and shortcomings that may be experienced in the application of any approach to electoral reform offer valuable lessons for the future. The earlier chapter discussed a number of shortcomings experienced in the first time application of the Citizens' Assembly approach to electoral reform in British Columbia. The lessons that can be learnt for the future from these shortcomings are discussed below under five separate subheadings: mandate restrictions, code of conduct for participants, electoral system comparison, input from practicing politicians, and dual voting on the Election Day.

9.4.1 Mandate restrictions

The mandate given to the Citizens' Assembly should facilitate a free and open process where the role of the assembly members is not restricted in the following areas:

1. Ability to consider all possible electoral systems;
2. Ability to recommend more than one electoral system to the public for their final decision at the follow-up referendum; and
3. Ability to educate the public on the Assembly's final recommendation, preparing them for the follow-up referendum.

In the experiment of electoral reform in British Columbia, the need to limit the number of seats in the legislature to 79 significantly influenced the Citizens' Assembly decision on the MMP system, as explained earlier. The mandate given to a Citizens' Assembly should not include such limitations, directly or indirectly influencing its decisions on any electoral system in any manner. The seat restriction was a measure to ensure that there would be no additional costs associated with any new electoral system recommended by the Citizens' Assembly. It is meaningful to have such a restriction to avoid new electoral systems that would be associated with unaffordable costs. The seat restriction introduced, however, discouraged the Citizens' Assembly from considering alternative electoral systems of additional costs, both affordable and unaffordable.

The British Columbia's experiment also showed that its reform process could have been more meaningful and conclusive if both the alternative electoral systems the Citizens' Assembly identified as superior to FPTP were presented to the public for a final decision. This chapter does not go into more details on this matter, as it has been extensively covered in the previous chapter.

Further, the British Columbia's experiment showed that its Citizens' Assembly members were the best suited to educate the public on their final recommendation for the following four reasons:

1. The Assembly members were the ones who were directly involved in making the final recommendation;
2. The Assembly members were fully equipped with the presentation material required to articulate and defend the final recommendation;
3. The Assembly members constituted a network of British Columbians strategically located throughout British Columbia; and
4. The Assembly members were more than willing to engage in a province wide educational program to the best of their ability.

All what was required to facilitate their full and effective participation in the much-needed public education was to extend their role to include public education and provide them with the additional resources they needed for it. This did not happen. Instead, the public education on the final recommendation of the Citizens' Assembly was left to those who took part in the discussions and debates on the referendum question on voluntary basis. If the Government was serious about the new approach to electoral reform, it should have planned and implemented an education program for the public, enabling them to fully understand the Citizens' Assembly's final recommendation before the referendum.

There is no need for public education in a traditional approach to electoral reform, where the members of the legislature make a final decision based on a recommendation made by a select legislative committee or a special commission. For this, the legislature would provide every one of its members with the details of the recommendation and conduct formal debates and discussions on the subject, enabling the body to make a well-informed final decision. Thus, in a traditional approach to electoral reform there is a built-in, organized process to adequately educate all those who take part in making the final decision. In the new approach to electoral reform it is prudent to include public education on the final recommendation of the Citizens' Assembly in its mandate.

9.4.2 Code of conduct for participants

The rules for the conduct of the Assembly business adopted in the first plenary session on January 10, 2004, helped the Assembly to generally carry out its tasks in an orderly manner. These rules, however, did not cover some of the situations that arose during the Assembly process. Such situations include the following:

1. Inadequate consideration of public input;
2. Some Assembly members assuming the role of experts;
3. Overdependence of some Citizens' Assembly members on experts; and
4. Public expressions of personal preferences of electoral choices by experts invited to address the Assembly.

Earlier chapters described when and how such situations arose during the Assembly process. The Assembly could have avoided them if the rules for the conduct of its business included a specific Code of Conduct applicable to such eventualities for the Assembly members and the invited experts.

9.4.3 Electoral systems comparison

The comparison of the effects of two or more electoral systems in a democracy can be made with the help of their electoral models especially developed for it. Every one of these electoral models must exhibit all its basic comparable features that are essential for the intended comparison. The comparison becomes less dependable if any of the models is short of its comparable features. This is what really occurred in the comparison of the MMP and STV systems as applicable to British Columbia during the first time application of the Citizens' Assembly approach.

In this first time experience, the BC Citizens' Assembly went ahead and conducted a MMP-STV debate without having both systems adequately modeled for BC; only a STV model had been developed for BC to the required extent by then, as explained earlier in the book. The BC Citizens' Assembly should have first completed its MMP model for BC to a comparable level of details as in the case of the BC-STV model before making any comparison between them. Overlooking the need for that was a serious error in judgment on the part of the BC Citizens' Assembly, especially considering that the one chosen between them was going to be tested with the existing FPTP model in BC for a final decision.

9.4.4 Input from practicing politicians

The selection of an electoral system for a democracy needs to take into account both the theoretical and practical aspects of the different electoral systems. The theories behind electoral systems are universally acceptable. This cannot be said about the practical aspects of the different electoral systems; as discussed before, any one system can produce different results in two different democracies. For this reason, it is prudent to include direct input from at least a few practicing politicians in the Citizens' Assembly process. Complete dependence on academics for practical aspects of the different electoral systems as well by the members of a Citizens' Assembly could lead to academic biased decisions.

Some BC Citizens' Assembly members believed that the lack of input into the BC Citizens' Assembly process from practicing politicians had negative influence on the Assembly Members' judgment on electoral systems, especially at times of their comparisons. As stated earlier, only two of the 160 Assembly members had some practical experience in the political field. The involvement of the rest of the Assembly members at times of elections was mostly limited to voting for a candidate of their choice under the existing FPTP system. As a result, the Assembly members generally depended on the Assembly research officers and other academics that took part in the Assembly discussions for both theoretical and practical aspects of the different electoral systems. The research officers and the other academics that joined in Assembly discussions, however, did not have any practical experience in the political field. This over-dependency on academics on the part of the Assembly Members, especially at times of comparisons among different electoral systems, was not productive. This was a deficiency inherent in the Assembly process as planned and implemented in British Columbia. As a solution to this situation, the Assembly should have invited few practicing politicians from countries already using the alternative electoral systems under consideration to come and share their experiences with the Assembly Members, as suggested in the earlier chapter.

9.4.5 Dual voting on the Election Day

The setting up of the electoral referendum on the day of the general election had two main advantages and one disadvantage. One advantage was that it helped to complete the referendum at minimum cost. In British Columbia, the Government has not quantified the exact cost associated with the referendum on the dual election of May 17, 2005, at the time of this book. It is reasonable to assume that the cost associated with the referendum on May 17, 2005, was only a portion of what it would have cost if held separately. The other advantage of having the referendum and the general election together was that more voters would vote on the referendum question than in a separate referendum voting. This became evident by the fact that some voters had made up their minds to vote on the referendum question only after entering a polling station; these voters were either uninformed or not adequately informed about the issues around the referendum question up to the time of voting. Some of these voters did take time to read the copy of the Final Report of the Citizens' Assembly kept at the polling station before voting. The rest of these voters either returned the referendum ballot unmarked or cast their vote on the referendum question on the spur of the moment. The final count of the ballots showed that, on the whole, only three percent fewer voters participated in the referendum than in the general election, as already stated elsewhere in the book.

The major disadvantage of having both an electoral referendum and a general election at the same time is the overshadowing of the public interest in the referendum by the general election. For example in the dual-election in British Columbia, the referendum failed to draw the same level of public attention as for the general election. The political parties and their candidates dominated the center stage of the political arena of the province during the election period. Major parties and their candidates, in particular, spent millions of dollars, including public funds they had secured under existing election laws, in their election campaigns. They battered the province with public meetings, rallies, protests, and demonstrations in every one of the 79 electoral districts. At no time, did any of them talk about the issues around the referendum during this period. The leaders of the major political parties crisscrossed the province in jets with a number of stops a day to meet as many British Columbians as possible before the Election Day. In the midst of all this, the work done by voluntary groups and individuals on the referendum front during the same period failed to get the public attention it deserved. There was insufficient media coverage for the work they managed to accomplish in educating the general public on the referendum issues. The media coverage on the referendum issue during this period was only a minute fraction of that given to the general election.

The above lessons from the first time application of the new approach to electoral reform should be taken into consideration in future applications of the same or a similar approach in any democracy.

9.5   Scope of applicability of the new approach

The Citizens' Assembly approach can be used for a variety of purposes in many countries. These purposes can be categorized into two main areas: changes to existing political systems through electoral and constitutional amendments, and resolution of major conflicts within democracies.

The purpose of the Citizens' Assembly approach in British Columbia was to make a decision on electoral reform. The specific mandate given to the BC Citizens' Assembly restricted this electoral reform exercise to the way votes were translated into seats in the legislature. Any proposal for electoral change had to be consistent with both the Constitution of Canada and the Westminster Parliamentary System of Government. The Citizens' Assembly approach is, however, not limited to this stricture; it can be used to make decisions on any number of other electoral issues or constitutional amendments in a democracy.

The Citizens' Assembly approach can also be an effective tool to resolve major internal conflicts, including those that remain seemingly unsolvable by traditional means, within democracies. Such conflicts have been generally caused by ethnic or religious divides, and have turned into civil wars in a number of democracies. In trying to resolve such major conflicts, politicians tend to take divisive stands based on the views of their support bases. This has often worsened the conflicts they are trying to resolve. Once a civil war has begun, politicians and governments have managed to bring about occasional cease-fires and peace-talks among conflicting parties, but not necessarily permanent solutions to their ongoing tensions. This indicates that permanent solutions to major conflicts do not lie solely with the traditional approaches to problem-solving by politicians and government directed mandates.

The ordinary citizens of a democracy can play a positive role in bringing about lasting solutions to such conflicts. There are two main reasons for this. First, the ordinary citizens are the ones that suffer most as a result of such conflicts. In consequence, they have an unquestionable desire and feel the urgency to end them. Second, ordinary citizens continue to live within their communities; it is a social necessity that they build bridges across their ethnic, religious, or other differences in their daily life, even during conflicts. This gives them the special ability to look at conflicts in a much more objective manner, free from any form of divisive politics. This approach, with a non-political and nonpartisan citizens' assembly, could give power to ordinary citizens to resolve major conflicts within their communities. In their deliberations for a workable solution to major conflicts, a nonpartisan citizens' assembly would represent the interests of the entire community, and not take sides on the conflicts they are trying to resolve. This would make the solutions they arrive at more credible and legitimate, than the ones framed by a group of partisan politicians of undisclosed or questionable self-interests.

Before his own experience with the BC Citizens' Assembly, as one of its members, the author spent many years in researching a long-standing political (and ethnic) crisis in Sri Lanka. Sri Lanka adopted Westminster-style democracy in 1948. Sri Lankan Government's failure to solve the crisis by traditional means for more than two decades has turned it to a civil war by the early eighties. The government and the rebel leaders who staged the civil war spent the last twenty years trying to find a political solution to the crisis through discussions and negotiations—so far without success. The Sri Lankan Government also tried to introduce some corrective measures based on its secret negotiations with the rebel leaders on a number of occasions. Strong protests from the politicians in the opposition and some segments of the population prevented the implementation of these corrective measures. Two major political parties in Sri Lanka have alternated in government since the commencement of the civil war. The conflict, however, continues without a permanent solution, regardless of who forms the government.

The ongoing crisis in Sri Lanka is further compounded by the requirement of two-thirds majority in the legislature for any significant change to the country's constitution. Under the existing proportional representation system in the country, the chances for any one political party to enjoy that much of a numerical majority in the legislature are slim. At the same time, the dynamics of party politics in Sri Lanka indicate that the chances of its major political parties to unite on a common strategy to solve the crisis are also slim. Indications are that Sri Lanka is in a political deadlock with no apparent permanent solution to the crisis through traditional democratic means. The Sri Lankan government and the rebel leaders have entered into a ceasefire agreement in 2002, but as of the writing of this work (2006), the truce has crumbled with renewed violence on both sides. In his *Sri Lankan Ethnic Crisis: Towards a Resolution* (Herath, 2002), the author recommended that any new approach to solve the crisis democratically should encourage and facilitate open and direct participation of the public in the corrective process. The argument follows that if the people of Sri Lanka get an opportunity to look at the crisis in a nonpartisan and impartial manner and decide on a solution, their politicians would be compelled to implement it. This is very much in line with the Citizens' Assembly approach used to make a decision on electoral reform in BC. There is also consensus among those who have studied the Sri Lankan crisis that any proposal made by non-partisan citizens of Sri Lanka to end its present crisis would likely be acceptable to the parties in conflict in that country. For example, Siri Gamage of the University of New England, Australia, says, "A proposal emerging from a civilian, nonpartisan forum .... can have much more credibility in the eyes of the parties to the conflict" (Gamage, 2006).

The author's previous work, *Sri Lankan Ethnic Crisis: Towards a Resolution* (Herath, 2002), also made a number of suggestions as to how to involve the public in an open and direct dialogue in resolving the Sri Lankan crisis. With the author's involvement with the Citizens' Assembly on electoral Reform in BC, he feels that, given the right climate, the Citizens' Assembly approach can be used to meet the same ends in a comparatively shorter period of time. Many features of the Citizens' Assembly approach, including the mode of selection of Assembly members, three-phase Assembly process and public education through presentations of Assembly members in their local communities, are particularly important in the Sri Lankan context.

The Citizens' assembly approach can be equally applied to find a lasting solution to the ongoing political crisis in Northern Ireland. It is a crisis that has grown over several generations between Protestants and Catholics living in Northern Ireland. Its current population is approximately 55 percent Protestant and 45 percent Catholic. At the time of formation of the new state of Northern Ireland in 1921, roughly 65 percent of the population were protestant. It is a state within the United Kingdom, and its sovereignty is retained in Westminster. From the inception of the new state there has been political tension between the majority Protestants and minority Catholics, a continuation of the old problems, but with the majority now focused on the Protestant population. During the 1960s a civil rights movement began to campaign for more equitable access to political and economic power and social provision for the minority Catholics. This met with resistance, turning politics to violent confrontations between the two groups. These confrontations grew by the year; the Northern Irish State establishment failed to contain the violence. In 1969, the London government deployed the British Army to restore order. In retaliation, the most powerful militant movement of the Catholic minority, Provisional Irish Republican Army (PIRA/IRA), started its campaign against the British Army in the following year. For the militants, removing the British presence from the Irish soil and unifying with the rest of Ireland was more important than finding a solution to the ongoing crisis through internal reforms.

Since IRA staged war against the British Army, the British government has made numerous efforts to bring lasting peace to Northern Ireland. In these efforts, the British government worked with politicians at local (Belfast-based), national (London based) and international (including The Republic of Ireland and the USA) levels. The British government also had numerous face-to-face discussions with the IRA leaders. As a result of all these, the IRA has announced several ceasefires since 1994. It has also announced arms decommissioning plans on three occasions: 2001, 2002, and 2003. By these measures, IRA has shown its preparedness to find a political solution to the ongoing crisis. On July 28, 2005, IRA issued a statement, ordering its members to dump arms and end their armed struggle against the British government. It is time now to look for a process to work out a lasting political solution to the ongoing crisis in a manner acceptable to all the concerned parties. The Citizens' Assembly approach is best suited for this purpose. Sri Lanka and Northern Ireland have been discussed here only as examples. The Citizens' Assembly approach equally applies to other democracies of similar political crises. It has the power to solve difficult problems created by conventional politics in modern democracies.

In the application of the Citizens' Assembly approach to outer jurisdictions, one must, however, first consider the preconditions that are essential for the conduct of the Assembly process. The members of a Citizens' Assembly need to operate in an open and direct manner. This means that they would need to speak openly and have the ability to express their views, even if they are in opposition to those of the political elite. This is simply not possible in some countries. In those countries, where citizens do not have the ability to openly express themselves, the Citizens' Assembly process would become meaningless.

At the same time, in their deliberations, Citizens' Assembly members should be able to treat each other on a politically equal basis. If not, they would not be able to engage in meaningful discussions and arrive at decisions benefiting the entire citizenry. In addition, societies where freedom to assemble or personal security is an issue, overriding security needs would also have a detrimental effect on the Citizens' Assembly process. In order to bring average citizens together one needs to be free to gather in a safe and public manner. In some places, domestic violence or civil wars create an environment where public assembly or the personal security of individuals is logistically impossible. In some situations, elements within the society make participation in a public process for change impossible; the participants become targets for people unwilling to peacefully accept the changes that the reform process would bring. This shows that personal freedom (thought, speech and assembly), political equality, and respect for human life are three preconditions that are essential for the conduct of the Citizens' Assembly process. These preconditions exist in established democracies, except at times of civil wars. New and emerging democracies take time to establish the needed preconditions in them. Sri Lanka and Northern Ireland have had established democratic institutions, and have implemented political reforms through democratic means before. They can, however, benefit from this approach with a Citizens' Assembly only during the times of effective ceasefires among their warring parties.

People living in all established democracies have experienced changes to their political systems through democratic means. With this long drawn experience, they will be able to immediately identify the BC approach to electoral reform as a next logical step in furthering democracy in their future endeavours. The decision taken by the Governments of Ontario and the Netherlands to adopt the BC approach even before the end of the BC Citizens' Assembly process clearly testifies to this reality.

Thus, the BC Citizens' Assembly approach is similarly applicable to other established democracies both within and outside Canada. Some established democracies might face new challenges in replicating the BC Citizens' Assembly process due to the enormity of their jurisdictions. These challenges are primarily logistic in nature. For example, it may not be practicable for the members of a Citizens' Assembly for Canada to meet at a central location during alternate weekends as BC Citizens' Assembly members did, due to its large land mass. These members would find very difficult, if not impossible, to find enough time to travel to and from the meeting place while still being active in their normal jobs. Such logistic challenges can be effectively addressed through modern technology. For example, meetings by way of electronic means are now common. Despite such technological solutions to the challenges of democracies of large geographic areas, the smaller the geographic area of a democracy, the easier it becomes for a citizens' assembly to function in it.

There are three main factors that can stand in the way of implementation of the citizens' assembly approach in new and emerging democracies. First, they may not have the preconditions that are necessary to conduct the Citizens' Assembly process. New and emerging democracies generally take many years, if not decades, for the necessary preconditions to come to fruition. Second, new and emerging democracies have limited or no history of political changes by democratic means. Their citizens and politicians need to learn from the experiences of established democracies in shaping and reshaping their own democratic systems and institutions. Third, the political leaders may not be committed to democracy to the same extent as in the case of established democracies. The political leaders of at least some new democracies appear to be busy in building "dynasties" to ensure that ruling power remains in their family lineages, as is the case of several former Soviet Republics. If the citizens of such countries do not exert enough pressure on their governments for democratic reforms, their leaders would not take any initiative to improve on their democratic institutions and practices. The citizens of these countries will eventually be politically educated to learn and understand the practices of democracy in established democracies, and take initiatives to follow suit.

9.6 Summary

The Citizens' Assembly approach to electoral reform in British Columbia was both historic and unique. It had a number of striking, extraordinary features. It entrusted the people with the power to control the entire decision-making process of electoral reform. The Citizens' Assembly, the body that studied the different electoral options and made a recommendation to the public for a final decision, consisted of 160 randomly selected nonpartisan ordinary citizens. They uniquely represented the adult population of British Columbia, particularly respecting age, gender and geographic distribution. In their Assembly deliberations, they represented the interests of the entire citizenry, disregarding the specific areas or communities they came from. This enabled them to look at the issues in question in a much more objective manner, than in a traditional legislative committee or special commission of persons of partisan interests. At the beginning of the Assembly process, there was a carefully crafted educational program to bring all the 160 Assembly members to a level field in terms of knowledgeability on electoral matters. This was done with the help of a number of national and international experts on the subject.

The applicability of this new approach is not limited to electoral reform. It can be equally used to effect changes to many other aspects of a political system or to find solutions to long, drawn out conflicts within communities where traditional approaches to resolve them have not been successful. The same approach can be effectively used for making changes to an existing constitution. This approach has the power to bring about fundamental changes to the character of a nation's government through democratic means.

The Citizens' Assembly approach can be effectively utilized in any jurisdiction where some basic preconditions exist. One of these preconditions is the freedom of thought, speech and assembly. The other basic preconditions include political equality and respect for human life. Political education and democratic maturity among the public can be particularly advantageous. These preconditions generally exist in established democracies. They can start using the Citizens' Assembly approach immediately to bring about political changes or to solve any internal crises among their communities with the involvement of the citizenry.

With its extraordinary features and extent of potential applicability, the Citizens' Assembly approach is not only historic and unique, but also superior to the traditional approaches to political reform. It shows the world a higher active participatory democracy, which truly empowers the people to take control of their own destiny.

The first time application of the Citizens' Assembly approach was extremely challenging and groundbreaking. No one expected an experiment with any new approach of that magnitude and complexity to be flawless. There were shortcomings in the application of the Citizens' Assembly approach, and they can be summed up in five main areas: mandate restrictions, external influence, inadequate funding for public education, incomplete system modeling, academic bias, and dual voting on the Election Day. These drawbacks present new challenges to be overcome in the future applications of the Citizens' Assembly model in British Columbia or any other democracy in the world. Despite these shortcomings, all those who took part in the Citizens' Assembly approach in British Columbia should be congratulated for the manner in which they accomplished their historic mission. They have left a template for a new, revolutionary approach to the practice of democracy.

THE END

APPENDIX

1 Special Committee on the Citizens' Assembly

MEMBERS

John Les, MLA, Chair	Chilliwack-Sumas
Jeff Bray, MLA, Deputy Chair	Victoria-Beacon Hill
Ida Chong, MLA	Oak Bay-Gordon Head
Kevin Krueger, MLA	Kamloops-North Thompson
Blair Lekstrom, MLA	Peace River South
Joy MacPhail, MLA	Vancouver-Hastings
Rob Nijjar, MLA	Vancouver-Kingsway

CLERK TO THE COMMITTEE

Craig James, Clerk Assistant and Clerk of Committees

COMMITTEE RESEARCHER

Jonathan Fershau, Committee Researcher

Source: Citizens' Assembly (2004n)

---

2 Staff of the Citizens' Assembly

Policy and Procedures:
Dr. Leo Perra, Chief Operating Officer

Research and Education:
Professor Ken Carty, Chief Research Officer
Professor Campbell Sharman, Associate Research Officer

Media and Communication:
Marilyn Jacobson, Director of Communication
Don MacLachlan, Associate Director of Communication
Paul Harris, Media Expert

Administration:
Cathy Stooshnov, Office Manager
Christina Wong, Assistant to the Chair
Susanna Hass, Project Coordinator
Carol Fleming, Database Coordinator
Christine Cheung, Administrative Assistant

Discussion Group Facilitators:
Amanda Bittner
Cameron Broten
Greg Clarke
Terri Evans
Michelle Garvey
Catherine Hirbour
Royce Koop
Julia Lockhart
Cara McGregor
Hilary Pearse
Mark Pickup
Kashi Tanaka
Russel Williams

Source: Citizens' Assembly (2004o)

---

3   Members of the Citizens' Assembly

1   *Beverly Huseby,* Abbotsford-Clayburn: Lived in BC since 1974. Human resources supervisor for Monterey Mushrooms. Enjoys gardening and riding her motorcycle.
2   **John Zall,** Abbotsford-Clayburn: Lived entire life in BC, & has been always interested in politics. Owns a distribution firm for forest products. Enjoys tennis, swimming & hockey.
3   **Dave Callaghan,** Abbotsford-Mt. Lehmen: Born in Vancouver. A teacher and student counsellor at Langley Christian Middle/High School. Enjoys squash, coaching soccer, reading & biking.
4   *Manjit Dhaliwal,* Abbotsford-Mount Lehmen: Born in Ambala, India. Lived in BC since 1978. Worked for Canada Trust until 1989, & opened an auto service business with husband. Enjoys reading.
5   *F.W. (Fritz) Zenns,* Alberni-Qualicum: Full-time dentist and a part-time farmer. Born in Germany. Came to BC in 1964. Big interests in farming and politics.
6   *Susan Wood,* Alberni-Qualicum: Lived in BC all her life. She now lives outside Qualicum Beach & is married with two children, 21 and 24. Enjoys gardening & traveling.
7   *Micheal Pritchard,* Bulkey Valley-Stikine: Forest technologist. Lives in Burns Lake with wife Kim & daughter Kaelyn. Enjoys kayaking, climbing, mountain biking & other outdoor sports.
8   *Joanne Vander Meulen,* Bulkey Valley-Stikine: Born & lived in Smithers. Widowed with two boys, 11 and 15. Receptionist at a car dealership. Enjoys volunteering (fundraiser), camping, fishing, reading, stained-glass handicraft & sewing.

9 *Mo Asim,* Burnaby-Edmonds: Born in Guyana & lived in BC since 1974. Courier driver for DHL. Married with three 2 teenage children. "Hockey fanatic" & a big Canucks fan.

10 *Gerry Hurst,* Burnaby-Edmonds: Retired fund-raising assistant. Married with 3 grown children & 6 grandchildren. Lived in BC since she was 4 months. Enjoys reading, music, walking & yoga.

11 *Craig Henschel,* Burnaby-Willingdon: Intern architect. Volunteers at the BC Architectural Institute. Born in Toronto & lived in BC since 1986. Single. Enjoys designing, drawing, pottery & furniture building.

12 *Adina Irimescu,* Burnaby-Willingdon: 3rd-year commerce student at UBC, majoring in marketing & logistics. Born in Bucharest, Romania, & lived in BC since 1993. Single. Lives in Burnaby & enjoys skiing.

13 *Mary Drew,* Burnaby North: Born in Davidson, Saskatchewan, & lived in BC for 50 years. Worked as a day care centre operator & Kentucky Fried Chicken Outlet manager. Enjoys gardening, cooking, reading, & walking.

14 *John Mak,* Burnaby North: Tax auditor with the BC government. Lives in Burnaby. Born in Hong Kong & lived in BC for 27 years. He is single & enjoys golf.

15 *Nancy McAskill,* Burquitlam: Office manager in a home-based manufacturing business. Married with 2 daughters. Treasurer of Cliff Avenue United Church & Girl Guides of Canada administrator. Enjoys quilting.

16 *Sam Todd,* Burquitlam: Born in Kingston, Ontario, & lived in BC since 1997. Married with a 3-year daughter. Manages a branch of Pacific West, a construction supplies company. Enjoys playing the guitar.

17 *Bob Monk,* Cariboo North: Born in Saskatchewan, & lived in BC since 1962. Pulp mill worker. Member of the Quesnel Rod & Gun Club & a CORE examiner. Enjoys target shooting, hockey, fishing and boating.

18 *Anna Rankin,* Cariboo North: Married with 2 children, 7 & 10. Born in England & lived in BC since 1967. Environmental technologist at Quesnel River Pulp Co. Enjoys skiing, hiking & camping.

19 *Deborah Young,* Cariboo South: Born in Ontario & lived in BC for 14 years, presently at Lone Butte, near 100 Mile House. Married. Self-employed in the tourism industry, promoting the "Fishing Highway."

20 *Tony Naccarato,* Cariboo South: Born in Italy & lived in BC since 1952. Married with 3 children. Member of the Williams Lake Rotary Club & Chamber of Commerce. Enjoys skiing & traveling abroad.

21 *Ingrid Carmichael,* Chilliwack-Kent: Born in Vancouver & lived in BC all her life. Married w. 2 children, 7 & 10. Kindergarten teacher at Yarrow Elem. School. Enjoys playing baseball & watching her children play sports.

22 *Will Kilsby,* Chilliwack-Kent: Born in New Westminster & lived in BC all his life. 3 children. Letter carrier. Coordinated the United Way campaign for Canada Post for 10 yrs. Asst. district Commissioner for Scouts Canada in Chilliwack for 8 years. Enjoys camping.

23 *Sharon Taylor,* Chilliwack-Sumas: Born in Yukon & lived in BC since 1980. Tax consultant & bookkeeper. Member of Beta Sigma Phi Sorority & enjoys reading & bowling.

24 *C.J. (Cory Jay) Thiessen,* Chilliwack-Sumas: Born in Saskatchewan & lived in BC since 1996. Single. Works in the office of Friesen Floor & Window Fashions. Enjoys playing soccer & reading.

25 *Michele Miller,* Columbia River-Revelstoke: Born in Alberta & lived in BC since 1980. Secondary school teacher. Three daughters, 8, 10 and 12. Works with the Girl Guides & Brownies. Enjoys art classes & writing.

26 *Paul Galbraith,* Columbia River-Revelstoke: Retired manager of intergovernmental relations for Parks Canada. Runs his cattle ranch. Married with 2 grown sons. Enjoys fly fishing and canoeing.

27 *Rev. Richard Hall,* Comox Valley: Retired United Church clergyman. Lived in BC all his life, except for 3 years. Married with 3 children, 4 grandchildren & 2 step-grandchildren. Enjoys community dev works.

28 *Heidemarie (Heide) Riemann,* Comox Valley: Born in East Germany. Lived in BC since 1980, except for 5 yrs. Wal-Mart pharmacy sales associate. Married with 3 grown children. Lions Club & United Mennonite Church member.

29 *Linda Dorey,* Coquitlam-Maillardville: Born in England & lived in BC since 1957. Preschool program coordinator. Marred with 2 daughters, 17 &19. Enjoys reading, gardening, decorating, cooking & sewing.

30 *Robert Westfall,* Coquitlam-Maillardville: Born in Vancouver & lived in BC all his life. Married with 2 grown children. Retired teacher, most recently at Templeton Sec. Sch. Vancouver. Enjoys woodworking, golf & t. tennis.

31 *Jean Ensminger,* Cowichan-Ladysmith: Born in France & lived in Winnipeg since 1979 & moved to BC in 1992. Married with a 14--year daughter. Substitute high school teacher. Also farms organic blueberries & chickens.

32 *Thea Melvin,* Cowichan-Ladysmith: Born & lived in Ladysmith. 5 yrs in Greece. Married with 2 boys, 6 & 8. Worked at Canada Trust and Island Savings Credit Union. Enjoys reading, singing, camping, biking & walking.

33 *Edith Davidson,* Delta North: Born in Ontario & lived in BC since 1965. Married with one daughter. Tech. supervisor at St. Paul's Hospital. Volunteers at the George Derby Centre. Enjoys reading & skiing.

34 *Peter Indyk,* Delta North: Born in Saskatchewan & lived in BC for 14 years. Works with City of Surrey. Married with a son & a daughter. Enjoys swimming, skating, camping & sporting events with family.

35 *Marijke Merrick,* Delta South: Recent empty nester and the Career Development Coordinator for the Delta School District. Enjoys needlepoint, gardening &getting together with her 3 children.

36 *Jakob Skovgaard,* Delta South: Born in Denmark & lived in Canada since 1964 & in BC since 1974. Married with 2 children 19 & 21. A lead hand in a precast concrete plant. Interested in politics & sports.

37 *Allan McKinnon,* East Kootenay: Born in UK & moved to BC as a child. Married with 3 children. Employed by UBC as a Drug Information Pharmacist with BC Drug & Poison Inf. Centre. Enjoys outdoor activities, yoga & others.

38 *Sharon Arola,* East Kootenay: Born in Ontario & lived in BC since 1973. Widow with 3 grown children. Retired govt. agent for Sparwood & Fernie. On the board of Lilac Terrace, an assisted-living seniors' complex.

39 *Lana Donnelly,* Esquimalt-Metchosin: Born in Ontario & lived in BC since 1986. Married with a daughter & a son. Mail services courier & coordinator for Canada Post's United Way campaign. Enjoys nature walks, skiing, & camping.

40 *Art Beaumont,* Esquimalt-Metchosin: Born in Quebec & lived in BC for 35 yrs. Married with 2 grown children. Retired ship's officer on towboats on BC Coast & along US west coast. Enjoys helping kids, woodwork, watching TV.

41 *Ron Walberg,* First Nations, Abbotsford: Member of the Nisga'a Nation. Born in Prince Rupert. Married with 4 sons, 17–22. A lead hand & charge hand at Kal Tire's retread shop in Coquitlam. Enjoys golf, tennis & woodworking.

42 *Jacki Tait,* First Nations, Gitwinksihlkw: Born in Terrace. Payroll and benefits clerk with Nisga's Valley Health Board. Married with 2 children. Was busy with local Lions Club Yuletide Com. Enjoys kids' sports & basketball.

43 *Ian Hay,* Fort Langley-Aldergrove: Born in Terrace & lived in BC all his life, now in Aldergrove. Single. Corporate tax consultant. Enjoys interpretative literature, music & independent film.

44 *Janet Loewen,* Fort Langley-Aldergrove: Born in Queen Charlotte & lived in BC all her life. Married with 2 boys, 2 & 4. Home daycare provider. Murrayville Com. Church member. Enjoys tennis, reading, gardening & swimming.

45 *Katie Cavaletto,* Kamloops: Born & lived in Kamloops. Married. New graduate in human geography. Waitressing at the moment & waiting for a fabulous job. Volunteers with SPCA on data entry & fostering.

46 *Ray Jones,* Kamloops: Born in Montreal & lived in BC since 1971. Works in the construction industry. Married with 2 children. Enjoys reading (mostly war and adventure stories) & photography.

47 *Lee Harris,* Kamloops-North Thompson: Born in Prince George and now lives in Kamloops. Married with 3 children. Spends most of his free time with kids. Hobbies include boating with his family in the summer.

48 *Ilene Zurowski,* Kamloops-North Thompson: Born in Saskatchewan & lived in BC since 1970. Widow with 3 children. Former Sask. Govt. employee. In family business. Enjoys golf, Walking & making quilts for premature babies.

49 *Tanya McDonnell,* Kelowna-Lake Country: Born in Vernon & lived in BC all her life. Child and youth worker with the Okanagan Boys & Girls Clubs. Enjoys reading, badminton, beach volleyball & socializing with friends.

50 *Norm Womacks,* Kelowna-Lake Country: Born in Vancouver & lived in BC all his life. Married with 2 children, 3 & 7. Worked as a Laser programmer for Northside Steel. Trinity Baptist Church member. Enjoys hiking, skiing and fishing.

51 *Sheri Keller,* Kelowna-Mission: Born in Kelowna & lived all her life in BC. Married with one daughter. Administrator of a property management firm. Hobbies include hiking, walking, golf & tennis.

52 *Harley Nyen,* Kelowna-Mission: Born in Penticton & lived in BC for all but 5 years in Alberta and Ontario. Married with 2 boys, 11 & 13. Managing Kelowna Wal-Mart sporting goods dept. Enjoys golfing, fishing, camping.

53 *Ian Fleming,* Langley: Born in Ontario & lived in BC for 10-1/2 years. Married with 2 sons, 3 & 5. Manager of Langley Sony Store. Enjoys photography & sailing.

54 *Sylvia Williams,* Langley: Born in India, moved to England in 1946 & to BC in 1974. Married with 2 grown sons. Retired adult education instructor. Garden Club member. Does volunteering, painting & reading.

55 *Darryl Hawkins,* Malahat-Juan De Fuca: Born in Manitoba & lived in BC since 1975. Retired govt. employee. Manages computer systems. Small business owner. Enjoys home & garden care, camping & listening to his music.

56 *Barbara Kohne,* Malahat-Juan De Fuca: Lived in BC all her life. Retired sales coordinator. Married with 3 grown children & 4 grandchildren. President of the now defunct Rural Ass. of East Sooke. Enjoys gardening, the arts & reading.

57 *Don Phillips,* Maple Ridge-Mission: Born in Quebec & lived in BC for 33 years. Married with grown children. Sr. tech. specialist in computer software. Enjoys photography, classic cars, home renovation & wildlife appreciation.

58 *Lynelle Ridewood,* Maple Ridge-Mission: Born in Victoria & lived in BC her entire life. Married. Grade 7 teacher at Golden Ears Elementary School in Maple Ridge. Enjoys reading, hiking & cooking.

59 *Fred Beyer,* Maple Ridge-Pitt Meadows: Born in Manitoba & lived in BC since 1945. Married w 4 grown children & 8 grandchildren. Retired Sales Manager. Visually impaired. Enjoys curling, golfing, woodworking & five-pin blowing.

60 *Angela Hsu,* Maple Ridge-Pitt Meadows: Born in China & lived in BC for 27 years. Married with 3grown children. Accounting assistant. Enjoys cooking, gardening, knitting, music & reading.

61 *John Chapman,* Nanaimo: Born in Hungary. Shot thrice by Hungarian & Russian Communists as he fled Hungary in 1956. 1st moved to UK & later to BC. 6 languages. Retired govt. financial officer. 3 children & 3 grandchildren. Enjoys chess & gardening.

62 *Linda Nicolaisen,* Nanaimo: Born in Toronto & lived in BC since 1952. Married with 5 grown children and 8 grandchildren. Member of the Nanaimo Evangelistic Tabernacle & the After Five Club. Enjoys spending time with family & reading.

63 *Tanis Dagert,* Nanaimo-Parksville: Born in Alberta & lived in BC 23 years. Executive director of the Nanaimo Food Share Society, a nonprofit organization. Teaches yoga. Runs a small organic farm.

64 *Glen Mackinnon,* Nanaimo-Parksville: Born in Manitoba & lived in BC for 35 years. Ret. building contractor. 4 children., 9 grandchildren & 1 great-grandson. In Canadian military during the 2nd World War. Royal Can. Legion Branch President & Queen's Jubilee Medal recipient.

65 *Ken Gosling,* Nelson-Creston: Born in Alberta & lived in BC for 15 yrs. Has 2 grown children & 2 grandchildren. Retired from Canadian Armed Forces. Has computer business. Enjoys flying planes, photography & writing poetry.

66 *Vickie Gowing,* Nelson-Creston: Born in Nelson & lived in BC her entire life. Stay-at-home mom. Once ran her own restaurant. Two children, 7 & 10. Enjoys riding her motorcycle, acting & horseback riding.

67 *Diana Cochran,* New Westminster: Born in England & lived in BC since the 1970s. Married. Human resources business partner in BC Hydro. Volunteered with St. James Anglican Church. Enjoys swimming.

68 *Allan Flemons,* New Westminster: Born in Vancouver & lived in BC all his life. Married with 2 daughters, 10 & 12. Teacher at D.W. Poppy Secondary School. Soccer coach. Enjoys with family sports, hiking, biking & swimming.

69 *Margaret Anderson,* North Coast: Grew up in Michigan & moved to Canada in 1973 & to BC in 1992. Prof. of First Nations Studies at University of Northern BC. Hobbies: weaving, reading, baking, gardening & travel.

70 *Dan Green,* North Coast: Lived in BC most of his life. Single. Fire suppression technician. 5 yrs. With Canadian military. Dart league member. Enjoys hiking, backpacking, canoeing, camping & snowshoeing.

71 *Robert Jones,* North Island: Born in Ontario & lived in BC for 10 years. Married with 2 grown children & a grandchild. Owner-operator of a truck & works for Purolator Courier. Enjoys history, hockey & baseball.

72 *Linda Fantillo,* North Island: Born in Victoria & lives in Campbell River. Secondary School Secretary. Married with 2 grown children. Helped food bank, parish council & immigrants. Enjoys walking, reading, cooking, & more.

73 *Ralph Smith,* North Vancouver-Lonsdale: Lived all his life in BC. Married. He & his wife own Dash-Hound Pet Services & have two puppies of their own—a dachshund & a border collie.

74 *Cherie Mostrovich,* North Vancouver-Lonsdale: Lived in BC her entire life. Single. 2nd Yr. business admin. Student at Capilano College. Works part-time in a restaurant. Enjoys traveling, the outdoors, swimming & yoga.

75 *Lynn Hill,* North Vancouver-Seymour: Born in Germany & lived in BC for 25 years. Married with 2 grown sons. Post-Secondary teacher & educator in computer programming. Enjoys reading, gardening & walking.

76 *Cliff Garbutt,* North Vancouver-Seymour: Born in Vancouver & now lives in N. Vancouver. Married with one daughter. Animation director. Won an Emmy for graphic design in 1990. Enjoys painting on canvas, scuba diving & hiking.

77 *Janet Hewsick,* Oak Bay-Gordon Head: Born in Prince Rupert & now lives in Victoria. Operates her own cleaning, gardening, pet care & companion business. Interested in Buddhism, meditation, reading & traveling.

78 *Jack MacDonald,* Oak Bay-Gordon Head: Born in Victoria & lives there now. Lived some years in US & Ottawa. Retired assistant deputy minister. Now doing consultant work. Enjoys golfing, traveling, reading, painting & drawing.

79 *Georges Boucher,* Okanagan-Vernon: Born in France & lived in BC since 19 years. Married with 2 daughters & 5 grandchildren. Owner of a Fishing Resort. Lumby Chamber of Commerce member. Enjoys flying, fly fishing & camping.

80 *Ann Davis,* Okanagan-Vernon: Born in England & lived in BC since 1960. Retired govt. employee. Vice president/Film Society. Volunteer with Performing Arts Centre. Member of a book club & a naturalists' club.

81 *Darin Follestad,* Okanagan-Westside: Born in Kelowna & lived there all his life. Runs a gas station at Westbank. Darin see the Citizen's Assembly as a unique process.

82 *Wendy Gonsalves,* Okanagan-Westside: Born in England & lived in BC since 1981. Retired. Four grandchildren. Member of Westbank Rotary Club, Central Okanagan Naturalists Club & Kelowna Garden Club. Loves to travel.

83 *Sheila MacDermott,* Okanagan Valley: Born in Saskatchewan & lived in BC since 1973. Widow with 2 grown children. Physiotherapist. Member of the United Church & Naramata Choir. Enjoys knitting, reading, gardening, classical music.

84 *John Stinson,* Okanagan Valley: Born in Vancouver & lived in BC all his life. Retired RCMP officer. Worked w. Can. Air Force before. Now a member of the Penticton Golf and Country Club. Also enjoys skiing & gardening.

85 *Wilf Chelle,* Peace River North: Born in a Saskatchewan & lived in Buick since 1967. Rancher. Member of Canadian Legion, Buick Friendship Soc., Peace River Woodlot Ass.& Peace River Cattlemen's Ass.

86 *Darleen Dixon,* Peace River North: Born in Sasatchewan & lived in BC since 1991. Married with 2 grown children & 7 grandchildren. Retired nurse. Owns a fabric store. Involved in Fort Nelson Cham. of Comm., Garden Club Sewing, quilting & other needlecrafts.

87 *Bill Jackson,* Peace River South: Born in Regina & lived in BC for 12 years. Married with 3 children. Prosecutor. Founding member of Peace Energy Cooperative. Involved in women's & elder abuse issues.

88 *Amanda Medley,* Peace River South: Born in Jasper & lived all her life in BC. Married with 2 children, 4-1/2 and 1-1/2. Teacher on call. Interested in photography & music. Teaching her daughter to play the piano.

89 *Jerry Stanger,* Port Coquitlam-Burke Mountain: Born in Alberta & lived in BC since 1976. A Fraser Health Authority director. Working on his masters UBC. Enjoys gardening, golfing & playing music w. Fraser Valley Bluegrass Soc.

90 *Betty Walters,* Port Coquitlam-Burke Mountain: Born is Ontario & lived in BC for 9-1/2 years. Married with 2 children, 4 stepchildren & 9 grandchildren. Retired nurse. Enjoys gardening, reading, gym & yoga classes.

91 *Deb Beuk,* Port Moody-Westwood : Born in New Westminster & lived in BC all her life. Married with 3 daughters. Sears Collection Rep. Involved in sports organizations & Parent Adv. Council. Enjoys softball & Crafts.

92 *Brad Yee,* Port Moody-Westwood: Born in Vancouver & lived in BC all his life. Married with 3 children. Past President of Sports Medicine Council of BC & BC College of Chiropractors &. Enjoys basketball & running.

93 *Rick Dignard,* Powell River-Sunshine Coast: Born in Richmond & lived in BC his entire life. Married with 2children, 5 & 9. BC Ferries shipwright. Helps out at Beaver Cubs. Enjoys sports, hiking, woodworking, hunting, & fishing.

94 *Anne Whitelaw Dykes,* Powell River-Sunshine Coast: Born in Ontario & lived in BC since 2002. Lived in UK for 13 yrs. Married. Works with *The Coast Reporter.* Member of Conservation Asso. & Eco. Dev. Partn. Ass. Administrator. Enjoys walking, reading, interior design.

95 *Mary Jarbek,* Prince George-Mount Robson: Born in Nova Scotia & lived in BC since 1969. Restaurateur. President of BC Restaurant Ass., Director of Special events & Child Dev. Centre. Past president of Lions Club. Enjoys painting & playing guitar.

96 *Jim McConaghy,* Prince George-Mount Robson: Born in PG & lived there all his life. Single. Farms, mostly in cattle and hay. Also operates a pet cemetery. Enjoys skiing & quading, which he describes as riding a 4-wheel motorcycle in the bush.

97 *Tina Ouellette,* Prince George-Omineca: Born in Alberta & lived in BC since one year. 4 children. Bookkeeper for her family business. Works at Lakeshore Remax Realty. Actively involved in Minor Hockey Ass. Enjoys skiing.

98 *Steve Sage,* Prince George-Omineca: Born in Victoria & lived in BC all his life. Calls himself "house husband." Has been building the family home "for years." Member of East Francois Lake Comm. Ass. Also enjoys fishing.

99 *Evelin Morison,* Prince George North: Lived in PG all her life. 3 children & 1 g-child. Former BC TEL traffic Operator. Watercolours finalist in the Western Canada Art Fest. Extensively traveled. Twin Rivers Art Gallery volunteer.

100 *Douglas Waller,* Prince George North: Born in Vancouver & lived all his life in BC. Married w. 3 children. Sch. teacher. Announcer. WESCAR Pub. Relations person. P/president, PG Radio-Controlled Car Club. Enjoys fishing & bird hunting.

101 *Brooke Bannister,* Richmond-Steveston: Lived in BC for 10 yrs. Married with 2 daughters. Copywriter & partner for Marketing Den advertising agency, Saskatoon. Retired on disability (post-polio syndrome). Enjoys sports & movies.

102 *Evelyn Krenz,* Richmond-Steveston: Born in Alberta & lived in BC since 1968. Married w. 3 grown children & 1 grandchild. Food preparer and cashier. Trinity Lutheran Church member. Enjoys fishing, camping, traveling, gardening.

103 *Jack Zhang,* Richmond Centre: Medical doctor from China. Lived in BC 14 years. Married with 2 children. Practicing acupuncturist. Mental Health Association of Canada member & a Tai Chi instructor. Enjoys basketball & swimming.

104 *Paola Barakat,* Richmond Centre: Born in Italy & lived in BC since 1966. Married with 2 grown children & a grandson. Travel agent for an airline. Enjoys drawing, sewing & traveling.

105 *Caroline Fader,* Richmond East: Born in England & lived in BC for 38 yrs. Widow w. 3 grown children & 6 grandchildren. P/president of Variety Women of BC & b. member of Jewish Family Ser. Agency & Historical Soc.

106 *Craig Peterson,* Richmond East: Born in Richmond & lives there today. Married with 2 children. Mechanical Engineer. Enjoys gourmet cooking, reading, researching green energy alternatives & playing racquet sports.

107 *Cary Laing,* Saanich North and the Islands: Born in Vancouver & lived in BC all his life. Married with 2 grown children. Sales manager. Volunteered with soccer and baseball minor sports. Enjoys walking, hiking & reading.

108 *Diana Byford*, Saanich North and the Islands: Born in England & lived in BC since 1969. Married with 3 grown sons & 2 granddaughters. Hobby is sewing; especially husband's choir concerts theatre costumes. She also sews replica dolls.

109 *Rosemary Vanderbilt*, Saanich South: Born in Winnipeg and has lived in BC for 12 years. Married. A new mother. Chartered accountant & controller with PRT. Both she & her husband enjoy camping & the outdoors.

110 *C. Chris Andersen*, Saanich South: Born in Denmark & lived in Canada since 1958 & in BC since 1965. Married with 2 daughters. Elem. school teacher. Semiretired carpenter. Enjoys camping, woodwork & a good novel.

111 *Claude Armstrong*, Shuswap: Born in Manitoba & lived in BC since late 1980s. Married w. 8 children & 12 grandchildren. Retired architectural drafting, interior design & const. Tech. teacher. Enjoys building & `renovating.

112 *Clara Munro*, Shuswap: Born in Salmon Arm & lived her entire life in BC. Student at Okanagan University College. Enjoys writing fiction & poetry, drawing & swimming.

113 *Wolf Scholz*, Skeena: Born in Germany & lived in BC 50 yrs. Married w. 2 adopted daughters & 5 grandchildren. Former Maintenance equipment clerk & Lions Club member. Ran a German CFTK radio program.

114 *Sandra Hart*, Skeena: Born in Montreal & lived in BC 14 yrs. 4 daughters & 6 grandchildren. Retired Ele. School teacher, researcher, settlement counsellor & program coordinator. Enjoys sewing, reading & porcelain dolls.

115 *Cheryl Blaschuk*, Surrey-Cloverdale: Born in Winnipeg & moved to BC 11 yrs ago. ICBC Claims adjuster & a computer programmer-analyst. Worked for Canadian Wheat Board before. Enjoys walking her German shepherd.

116 *Aaron Schallie*, Surrey-Cloverdale: Born in Surrey. Manager of a com. that runs events & supplies audio and video equipment. Public relations & corporate events consultant & audio eng. before. Enjoys sailing & other outdoor activities.

117 *Jay Konkin*, Surrey-Green Timbers: Lives in Surrey & bicycles to work. Software programmer. Married with 3 children, 5, 9 & 13. Likes to play with her kids, hike and walk the family's black Labrador.

118 *Charles (Chuck) Walker*, Surrey-Green Timbers: Born in Ontario & lived in BC 28 yrs. Married. Artist, writer, cartoonist & music teacher. Was P/T actor. Written 6 books & produced 3 CDs. Hosted BC Int. Cartoon Festivals 1989–1991. Once ran for New West city council. Enjoys playing tennis.

119 *Lill Brulhart*, Surrey-Newton: Born in Alberta & lived in BC since 1974. 4 grown daughters & 4 g-children. Registered nurse. Member of Van. Metro Theatre Board. Enjoys music, theatre, sewing, gardening & travel.

120 *R.B. (Bob) Herath*, Surrey-Newton: Born in Sri Lanka & lived in Canada since 1990 & in BC since 1992. Married with 3 grown daughters. Engineer, author, poet and dramatist. Led a new democratic political party in Sri Lanka. Enjoys tennis, swimming and writing.

121 *Dalbir (Dal) Sidhu*, Surrey-Panorama Ridge: Born in Vancouver & lived in BC all his life. Married. Govt. correctional officer. Enjoys playing hockey, practicing karate, watching movies & spending time with his family & friends.

122 *Priya Singh*, Surrey-Panorama Ridge: Born in Richmond & lived in BC all her life. Single. Child & youth counselor & an F/T student at University College of the Fraser Valley. Enjoys traveling & spending time with family & friends.

123 *Susan Johnson*, Surrey-Tynehead: Born in New Westminster & lived in BC all her life. Married. May be BC's first female drywaller. Ran own d/w company before retiring in 1996. Enjoys reading, woodworking, & gardening.

124 *Colin Redekop,* Surrey-Tynehead: Born in Langley & lived in BC all his life. Married with a baby son. Mechanical engineer with Works with Ballard Power Systems. Enjoys playing hockey & woodworking.

125 *Derrick Harder,* Surrey-Whalley: Born in Richmond & lived all his life in BC. 3rd-year student at SFU. Previous experience in polling station duties. Simon Fraser Student Society board member. Enjoys playing guitar & reading.

126 *Kimberlee MacGregor,* Surrey-Whalley: Born in Montreal & has lived in BC since 1977. Two daughters, 11 & 13. Liquor Distribution Branch store clerk. Loves to read, paint, cook & do crafts.

127 *Barbara Carter,* Surrey-White Rock: Born in Ontario & lived in BC since 1963. 1 son. Mid. Sch. fine arts teacher. Prof. musician before. Directs musicals & dramas. Owns her own business. A director of Kiwanis Club, White Rock.

128 *Sandeep (Shawn) Rai,* Surrey-White Rock: Born in Richmond & lived his entire life in BC, except for 4 years in US. Married. Chiropractor. Volunteer supervisor at Fraserview Boys & Girls Club. Enjoys squash, hockey & playing.

129 *Lianne Ashley,* Vancouver-Burrard: Born in Alberta & lived in BC 10 yrs. Manager of a cigar store. She's an avid reader, a moviegoer & a rabid Canucks fan. She loves saxophone music & plays the sax a little as well.

130 *Neall Ireland,* Vancouver-Burrard: Born in Sechelt & lived in BC most of his life. With long-term partner. Long-term care aide, P/T make up artist, strata council president, West End Citizens' Action Network member.

131 *Frederick Shum,* Vancouver-Fairview: Born in Hong Kong & lived in BC for 26 yrs. Coastal Health Auth. case mgr. Christ Church of China member, Soccer coach. Member of BC Reg. Nurses Ass.& Psychiatric Nurses. Enjoys tennis, cycling,

132 *Arlene Tully,* Vancouver-Fairview: Born in Ontario & lived in BC since 2000. Looking after her young son. Worked in office administration and make up artistry before. Enjoys reading, playing piano & singing, animal welfare.

133 *Jyoti Gill,* Vancouver-Fraserview: Born in India & lived in BC for 14 yrs. Married with 2 children. Sales associate at The Bay. Her hobbies include cooking "all kinds of foods, not just Indian," & the outdoors.

134 *Wayne Wong,* Vancouver-Fraserview: Second-year business student at UBC. Enjoys the critical thinking of chess, rush of speed when skiing, & music as a relaxing escape from the world.

135 *Nicholas (Nick) Boudin,* Vancouver-Hastings: Born in Florida & lived in BC for 23 yrs. Single. 2nd year at SFU. Aiming for graduate studies in education. Cook for 6 yrs. Enjoys literature, Tai Chi, music composition, photography, swimming.

136 *Shoni Field,* Vancouver-Hastings: Born in England & lived in BC since three. Married with 1 child. Fundraiser for the Sierra Legal Defence Fund. Enjoys reading, writing & cooking.

137 *Frankie Kirby,* Vancouver-Kensington: Born in England & lived in BC since 1972. Daughter of 15. Key account officer for Translink. Enjoys playing violin, tennis, reading & walking.

138 *Tom Townrow,* Vancouver-Kensington: Born in Prince George & lived in BC all his life. Single. Student at Langara College. Bridge Baptist Church member. Arranges children's sports camps & parties. Enjoys soccer and hockey.

139 *Firmin Hung,* Vancouver-Kingsway: Single. Student at SFU in Professional Development Program. Also works in a pharmaceutical warehouse. Enjoys biking, snowboarding, rollerblading, tennis & collecting Japanese anime DVDs.

140 *Sally De Luna,* Vancouver-Kingsway: Born in Philippines & came to BC in 1981. Widow with 2 grown sons & 4 grandchildren. Life skills inst. Worked for a law firm earlier. First Filipino Baptist Church member. Enjoys reading & dancing.

141 *Nancy Bednard,* Vancouver-Langara: Born in New Westminster & lived in BC all her life. Married. 3 children & 6 grandchildren. Retired medical lab bacteriologist. Lawn Bowling Club member. Enjoys walking, reading, theatre & traveling.

142 *Andrei Popa,* Vancouver-Langara: Born in Romania & has been in BC since 1997. Single. Software engineer with Mobile Data Solutions Inc., Sports fan, works out at the gym & likes to play basketball during the summer.

143 *Donna Dew,* Vancouver-Mount Pleasant: Born in Saskatchewan & lived in BC for 14 years. Married with 2 grown children & 3 grandchildren. Care aide for 20 years before. Now on disability pension. She is an avid bingo player.

144 *Ken Nielsen,* Vancouver-Mount Pleasant: Born in Denmark & lived in BC for 32 yrs. Owns a furniture and design shop. Member of Whistler Merchants Ass. Enjoys billiards, marathons, baseball, golf, racquetball, filming & writing.

145 *Jill Reilly,* Vancouver-Point Grey: Born in Winnipeg & lived in BC since 1991. Married w. 2 boys. P/T graduate student at SFU. Also works. On parent advisory council. Enjoys cycling, hiking, travel, music & reading.

146 *David Wills,* Vancouver-Point Grey: Born in England & lived in BC since 1974. Married with a grown son. Computer systems consultant. Whistler Mountain Ski Club member. Officiates at ski races. Enjoys fitness.

147 *Stephen Paetkau,* Vancouver-Quilchena: Born in Alberta & lived in BC since 1993. Married with 1 child. Occupational diver: boat inspections, underwater photography for insurance purposes & minor boat repairs. Enjoys running & reading.

148 *Ann Rushlow,* Vancouver-Quilchena: Born in Ottawa & lived in BC since 1999. Teacher of English as a Second Language. Volunteer accountant for the Tilopa Buddhist Centre. Avid skier, rollerblader. Enjoys biking & hiking.

149 *Jeremy Young,* Victoria-Beacon Hill: Lived most of his life in BC. Married. Marine Consultant/ship's captain. Fairfield Comm. Ass. Past president, Mem. of Comp. of Master Mariners of Canada & Royal Victoria Yacht Club.

150 *Dorothy Coombes,* Victoria-Beacon Hill: Born in England & lived in BC since 1977. Retired govt. employee. Mem. of BC Land Conservancy, Habitat Acquisition Trust & Victoria Natural History Society. Historical garments & walking.

151 *Darren van Reyen,* Victoria-Hillside: Born in Alberta & lived in BC for 15 yrs. Single. Seamanship training officer at the Canadian Forces Fleet School in Esquimalt. Enjoys scuba diving, motorcycling.

152 *Wendy Bergerud,* Victoria-Hillside: Born in New Jersey & lived in BC since 1966. Married with 2 children, 11 & 16. Statistician for the BC Ministry of Forest. Hobbies include genealogy & reading (science & science fiction).

153 *Russ Miller,* West Kootenay-Boundary: Born in Chilliwack. Married with 2 grown children & 5 grandchildren. Farm labourer. Member of Grand Forks Gyro Club, Boundary Hospital Board & Chamber of Commerce.

154 *Gladys Brown,* West Kootenay-Boundary: Born in Alberta & lived in BC since 1970. Widow w. 2 grown children & 2 grandchildren. Retired paramedic. Mem. of Midway Seniors & BC Naturalists Fed. Develops a sp. variety of orchard.

155 *Linda Crawford,* West Vancouver-Capilano: Born in Sault Ste. Marie, & lived in BC since 1996. Married. Computer programmer analyst. Member of a running club. Enjoys the outdoors, skiing, hiking, gardening, & travel.

156 *Ray Spaxman,* West Vancouver-Capilano: Born in England & came to Canada in 1966. Four grown children & three grandchildren. President of Spaxman Consulting Group. Enjoys music, art, reading. golf & walking.

157 *Jule Boehmer,* West Vancouver-Garibaldi: Born in Ontario & lived in BC since 1989. Mother of 2. Self-employed int. eng. consultant. Travelled in Europe, Indonesia, US & Canada. Enjoys gardening, carpentry, reading & travel.

158 *Gene Quan,* West Vancouver-Garibaldi: Born in Victoria & lived in BC his entire life. Married with 2 adult sons. Retired banker. Volunteers in the community. Active in his parish. Enjoys the outdoors, camping & hiking.

159 *Susan Patry,* Yale-Lillooet: Born in Ohio & lived in BC for 20 yrs. Reg. clinical counsellor & psycho-educational consultant. Drug & Alcohol Society. Enjoys horseback riding & reading.

160 *Stan Pietras,* Yale-Lillooet: Born in Saskatchewan & lived in BC since 1981. Married with 2 grown children. Was head nurse at Princeton Gen. Hospital. Playing slow pitch softball & curling with "the seniors."

Source: Citizens' Assembly (2004p)

---

4 Policies & Procedures

That the following policies and procedures have been adopted, recognizing that, as we learn to work together, these policies and procedures may be amended or amplified.

1. On matters of meeting procedure, that is, how we conduct meetings, common sense and reasonableness will prevail. A list of shared values will be developed and adopted by the Assembly during the first weekend of meetings. These shared values will act as a guideline for how the group will work together. These guidelines can be revisited for clarification or amendment.

2. The conduct of the Citizens' Assembly meetings normally will be informal and, where feasible, most decisions will be reached by consensus.

3. When formality is required, the Citizens' Assembly will be guided by the Terms of Reference and policies and procedures of the Assembly. Where the Terms of Reference, and policies and procedures are silent, the Chair will make decisions regarding procedure for the meetings of the Assembly. Such decisions may include referring a matter to the Assembly. The spirit and aim of the Assembly's
procedures should be to develop our own way of working as we learn to work together, rather than having to resort to a formal meeting system such as "Roberts Rules of Order."

4. A quorum will be fifty percent of the membership of the Citizens' Assembly. A quorum is the number of members required to be in attendance in order to make decisions and conduct Assembly business.

5. The Chair may summarize a consensus position and that consensus position will be deemed equivalent to a vote unless a vote is requested by several members of the Citizens' Assembly.

6. Consensus means that in the opinion of the Chair a very clear majority of the members support or can "live with the decision."

7. Where a formal decision is required, such as those noted in the Terms of Reference and Duties of the Chair, the decision will be made by a vote of the majority (50% plus one) of the Citizens' Assembly members present.

8. Voting will be by a show of hands, or by the electronic motion button in the *Asia Pacific Hall*, or by secret ballot as determined by the Chair in consultation with members.

9. The Chair does not have a vote, but may cast a deciding vote in the event of a tie on a resolution.

10. The Chair will ensure that all decisions of the Assembly are recorded and provided to Assembly members.

11. A daily question period, on all matters of interest to Assembly members, will begin each morning session of the Assembly. The question period normally will continue for 15 minutes, but may be extended if required.

12. Discussion groups will be composed of similar numbers and their membership will be changed each weekend. A facilitator will support the work of these discussion groups.

13. Normally, any motions to the Assembly to address or decide on an issue will first be put forward as a notice of motion.

14. The activities of the Citizens' Assembly will be open to the public and media.
(a) Members of the public and media shall not disrupt the proceedings of the Assembly and will be accommodated on an "as-space-is-available" basis.
(b) Access to discussion groups, however, will be constrained by the limited available space and will be subject to review by the Assembly.

15. Submissions to the Citizens' Assembly are considered to be in the public domain and may be posted on the web site. Submissions also will be available to members and the public during weekend meetings and at the Assembly office during regular office hours.

Source: Citizens' Assembly (2004q)

----

5 List of Citizens' Assembly Public Hearings

#	Location	Date	Venue	Time (pm)
1	Vancouver (first of three)	May 3rd	Wosk Centre, 580 W. Hastings Street	6:30–9:30
2	Richmond	May 4th	Vancouver Airport Marriott 7571 Westminster Hwy.	6:30–9:30
3	Burnaby	May 5th	Holiday Inn Metrotown, 4405 Central Blvd.	6:30–9:30
4	New Westminster	May 6th	Inn at Westminster Quay, 900 Quayside Drive	6:30–9:30
5	Surrey (first of two)	May 8th	Aston Pacific Inn, 1160 King George Hwy.	1:30–4:30
6	Valemount	May 8th	Holiday Inn Valemount, 1950 Highway 5 South	1:30–4:30
7	Grand Forks	May 10th	Selkirk College, 486 72nd Avenue	6:30–9:30
8	Prince George	May 10th	PG Civic Centre, 808 Civic Plaza	6:30–9:30
9	Quesnel	May 11th	Sandman Inn, 940 Chew Avenue	6:30–9:30
10	Fort Nelson	May 11th	Woodlands Inn, 3995 50th Avenue	7:00–10:00
11	Nelson	May 11th	Prestige Lakeside Resort, 701 Lakeside Drive	6:30–9:30
12	Fort St John	May 12th	Quality Inn N. Grand, 9830 100th Avenue	7:00–10:00
13	Dawson Creek	May 13th	Northern Lights College, 11501 8th Street	7:00–10:00
14	Powell River	May 15th	Powell River Rec Complex, 5001 Joyce Avenue	1:00–4:00
15	Sidney/Victoria	May 15th	Holiday Inn Victoria, 3020 Blanshard Street	1:30–4:30
16	Ucluelet	May 15th	Seaplane Base Rec. Hall, 160 Seaplane Base Road	1:30–4:30
17	Chilliwack	May 18th	Rhombus Hotel, 45920 First Avenue	6:30–9:30

18	Maple Ridge	Thomas Haney School, 23000 116th Avenue	6:30–9:30
19	Langley	Hampton Inn, 19500 Langley Bypass	6:30–9:30
20	Port McNeill	Haida Way Motor Inn, 1817 Campbell Way	6:30–9:30
21	Courtenay/Comox	Coast Westerly Hotel, 1590 Cliffe Avenue	6:30–9:30
22	Nanaimo	Coast Bastion Inn, 11 Bastion Street	6:30–9:30
23	Vancouver(second of three)	Van. Convention Centre, (at Canada Place)	1:30–4:30
24	Surrey (second of two)	Sheraton Guildford Hotel, 15269 104th Avenue	6:30–9:30
25	Coquitlam	Executive Plaza Hotel, 405 North Road	6:30–9:30
26	North Vancouver	Lonsdale Quay Hotel, 123 Carrie Cates Court	6:30–9:30
27	Whistler	Convention Centre, 4010 Whistler Way	6:30–9:30
28	Abbotsford	Ramada Inn, 36035 North Parallel Rd.	1:30–4:30
29	Sechelt	Driftwood Motor Inn, 5454 Trail Avenue	1:30–4:30
30	Smithers	Hudson Bay Lodge, 3251 East Highway 16	6:30–9:30
31	Duncan	Travelodge Silver Bridge, 140 Trans Canada Hwy.	6:30–9:30
32	Terrace	Coast Inn of the West, 4620 Lakelse Avenue	6:30–9:30
33	Port Alberni	Hansen Hall, 3940 Johnston Road	6:30–9:30
34	Prince Rupert	Crest Hotel, 222 West First Avenue	6:30–9:30
35	Victoria	Harbour Towers Hotel, 345 Quebec Street	4:00–9:30
36	Vancouver (third of three)	Marriott Pinnacle Hotel, 1128 W. Hastings	1:30–4:30
37	Queen Charlottes/Haida Gwaii	Skidegate Comm. Hall, Skidegate	1:30–4:30

Appendix 5 (Continued)

#	Location	Date	Venue	Time (pm)
38	Princeton	June 14th	Community Skills Centre, 206 Vermillion Avenue	6:30–9:30
39	Merritt	June 15th	Days Inn, 3350 Voght Street	6:30–9:30
40	Lillooet	June 16th	Recreation Centre, Mezzanine	6:30–9:30
41	Kamloops	June 17th	Coast Canadian Inn, 339 St. Paul Street	6:30–9:30
42	Salt Spring	June 19th	Lions Hall, 103 Bonnet Avenue	12:00–3:00
43	Williams Lake	June 19th	Overlander Hotel, 1118 Lakeview Crescent	1:30–4:30
44	Cranbrook	June 21th	Prestige Inn, 209 Van Horne St. South	6:30–9:30
45	Vernon	June 21th	Prestige inn, 4411 32nd Street	6:30–9:30
46	Radium	June 22th	Community Hall, 4863 Stanley Street	6:30–9:30
47	Revelstoke	June 22th	Coast Hillcrest Hotel, 2100 Oak Drive	6:30–9:30
48	Penticton	June 23th	Pent. Lakeside Resort, 21 Lakeshore Drive W.	6:30–9:30
49	Sparwood	June 23th	Rec. Centre Hall, 367 Pine Avenue	6:30–9:30
50	Kelowna	June 24th	Coast Capri Hotel, 1171 Harvey Avenue	6:30–9:30

Source: Citizens' Assembly (2004r)

6 Contents of the Final Report

Making every vote count
THE CASE FOR ELECTORAL REFORM IN BRITISH COLUMBIA
BRITISH COLUMBIA CITIZENS' ASSEMBLY ON ELECTORAL REFORM

CONTENTS

Making every vote count

THE FINAL REPORT OF THE BRITISH COLUMBIA CITIZENS' ASSEMBLY ON ELECTORAL REFORM

"We are here to invent a new way to engage citizens in the practice of democracy...."

To the Honourable Geoff Plant, Attorney General, and
To the people of British Columbia

The members of the Citizens' Assembly on Electoral Reform feel exceptionally honoured to have been given this historic opportunity to serve British Columbians on a matter so central to our democracy.

Our mandate was to assess different models for electing members of the Legislative Assembly and to recommend whether our current system for provincial elections should be retained or whether a new model should be adopted. Elsewhere, such a task has been given to politicians or to electoral experts. Instead, British Columbia chose to make history and to give this task to the voters.

For eleven months we have studied voting systems, we have listened to thousands of British Columbians in 50 public hearings and received and read 1,603 written submissions. What we most wanted to learn was what values, hopes and desires should underlie our electoral system and which principles should direct our decisions and recommendation. This work has led us to the following recommendation:

The Citizens' Assembly on Electoral Reform recommends our province adopt a new voting system, which we call "BC-STV." This single transferable vote system is customized for this province. It is fair and easy to use, and it gives more power to voters.

BC-STV is easy to use. Voters rank candidates according to their preferences.

BC-STV gives fair results. The object is to make every vote count so that each party's share of seats in the legislature reflects its share of voter support.

BC-STV gives more power to voters. Voters decide which candidates within a party, or across all parties are elected. All candidates must work hard to earn every vote, thereby strengthening effective local representation.

BC-STV gives greater voter choice. Choosing more than one member from a riding means that voters will select members of the Legislative Assembly from a greater range of possible candidates.

On May 17, 2005 the referendum question placed before all voters will be this:

Should British Columbia change to the BC-STV electoral system as recommended by the Citizens' Assembly on Electoral Reform? Yes/No

We know that a new voting system will take time to become a smooth working part of our political life and we believe that it should be reviewed after it has been used for three provincial elections and that citizens should be involved in the review. In the rest of this report we compare our current voting system with BC-STV. We outline how BC-STV will work and why we believe this system will best serve this diverse province. A second volume, the Technical Report, addresses all aspects of our work and deliberations in detail. Information on how to get a copy of the Technical Report can be found on the last page of this report. Together these two reports complete our work. The next decision belongs to all British Columbians.

Basic values

Through our work and by listening to British Columbians, we have identified three basic values which we believe should form the basis of our electoral system. These are:

Fair election results through proportionality

Democracy is "rule by the people," therefore, the results of an election—the number of seats won by each party—should reflect the number of votes each party has earned from the voters. The results—votes to seats—should be "proportional." No electoral system does this perfectly, but that does not reduce the importance of proportionality. Proportional election results are the fairest election results. The preference of voters should determine who sits in our legislature. That is fair.

Effective local representation

Each community has a distinct personality; each makes its own unique contribution to our provincial life. To be effectively represented, each community needs the opportunity to choose the people who speak for it in the legislature, and to hold them accountable in democratic elections. Effective local representation has long been a principle of our democratic tradition. It is central to our electoral politics. Strengthening local representation should be a test of any electoral reform.

Greater voter choice

As citizens, we all are responsible for the health of our democracy, and therefore we must have the fullest possible opportunity to choose the candidates that best represent our interests. Our choice in elections should include choosing among party candidates, as well as across all parties. To give voters a stronger voice, greater voter choice should be part of our voting system. In addition to these values, two issues were consistently highlighted in our discussions on choosing an electoral system.

The voter and political parties

There is a groundswell of opposition in this province to the current imbalance of power between voters and parties. Indeed, some of the submissions we received called for banning parties on the grounds that they so dominate electoral politics that local representation is undermined by party discipline and practices, and voter choice is stifled. While concerned about this imbalance, we recognize that parliamentary government depends on parties to conduct elections, organize the work of the legislature and carry out the business of government. We believe that the solution lies in adopting an electoral system that encourages voters and politicians to work together in a balanced partnership.

The voter and majority, coalition and minority governments

Most often in Canada—both provincially and federally—parties that form majority governments earn much less than half of the vote, but take well over half of the seats. These are called "artificial majorities." Nonetheless, Canadians are so familiar with single-party majority governments that we easily assume they are the natural outcome of elections.

A majority government, real or artificial, will claim a mandate and act on it. And it can easily be held accountable at the next election. However, we are convinced that the simple nature of majority governments should not override the basic values of fair election results, effective local representation, and greater voter choice. Most other successful western democracies do not depend on majorities, yet have stable and effective governments, governments that often are both inclusive of different interests and consensual in making decisions.

We have all seen ineffective or divisive majority governments, and we have seen progressive and successful minority governments that work through legislative coalitions, particularly the federal governments of the 1960s. We believe that our electoral system should not override fairness and choice in favour of producing artificial single-party majority governments.

The current system of voting in BC

The case for majority government

For most of our history this province has used a "single member plurality" electoral system, popularly referred to as "First-Past-the-Post" (FPTP). The first candidate to cross the finish line—the one with the most votes—wins the seat and represents the local district in the legislature. Governments are formed by the party with the most seats. It is a simple system.

Supporters of FPTP typically argue for its ability to produce majority governments, often cautioning against the unequal power small parties might exercise in coalition or minority governments. Governments with a legislative majority may claim a mandate for action. They do not have to bargain with other parties to act on their policies, but can plan and take the administrative and financial decisions necessary to implement their program. Similarly, at election time, voters know who is responsible for the government's successes or failures and can clearly indicate which party they wish to govern the province.

This tendency toward majority government is FPTP's most important feature: without it, British Columbia would not have had majority governments throughout much of its recent history. In fact, British Columbians have only rarely given one party a majority of their votes.

Does FPTP meet the needs of British Columbia?

A basic principle of FPTP is local representation—every corner of the province is represented in the legislature. Voters directly choose who they wish to represent them and their community, with every area of the province choosing one representative.

We believe local representation must be a fundamental objective of any British Columbian electoral system. However, although local representation based on the FPTP system has worked in the past, it is now seen as too easily compromised in at least two ways.

1.   Citizens wishing to support a particular party must vote for the single candidate the party offers and not necessarily for the local candidate they may prefer. This often means that the real competition is for a party's nomination and not for the voters' support on election day.

2.   Party discipline quickly turns members of the Legislative Assembly into party advocates rather than local advocates. Many British Columbians now see MLAs as providing "Victoria's" voice to the people, rather than the people's voice to Victoria.

FPTP is a simple system—voters need only place an "X" beside the name of an individual. However, FPTP does not promise or provide fair election results. There is no logical or systematic relationship between a party's total share of the votes cast and its seats in the legislature. Local candidates do not have to win a majority in their district to win a seat. In exceptional cases—for example, in British Columbia in 1996—this meant that the party with the most votes lost the election. Governments elected with fewer votes than their opponents are not legitimate in a modern democracy.

The FPTP system can produce other undesirable outcomes. In the 2001 election, the opposition was reduced to two of 79 seats in the legislature, despite winning 42% of the popular vote. Not only is this obviously unfair, it weakens the opposition so greatly that the legislature cannot hold Government to account. The very principle of responsible government, the heart of our constitution, is thrown into question. Many citizens understand that the current system is responsible for these results and believe that they are neither fair nor acceptable.

great many British Columbians told us that political parties too easily dominate this system, that it produces a style of local representation that is easily stifled by party discipline, that it fails to connect voters' decisions with election results, and that it offers minimal choices to voters. We agree.

BC-STV: a new way of voting in BC

BC-STV is a "single transferable vote" (STV) system. The main feature of these systems is that, rather than marking an "X" beside one name, voters number candidates from most favourite to least favourite (i.e., 1, 2, 3, 4, etc.). If a voter's favourite candidate (#1) is not elected, or has more votes than are needed to be elected, then the voter's vote is "moved" to his or her next most favourite candidate (#2). The vote is transferred rather than wasted. The aim of this system is to make all votes count.

We are recommending that British Columbians adopt BC-STV as their voting system. We are convinced that this system best incorporates the values of fair election results, effective local representation, and greater voter choice.

Fair election results

Proportionality—ensuring that each party's share of seats in the legislature reflects its actual share of votes—is the basis of fair election results. A proportional system needs multimember districts so that the share of seats in the legislature can reflect the votes cast by British Columbians and that voters can elect candidates that represent their true preferences.

Proportionality is not possible in our current single-member districts, so electoral districts will be amalgamated to provide between two and seven members for each new district. To provide for the fairest results, districts will be designed to have as many members as possible. The number of MLAs in the legislature will not necessarily change; nor will the number of MLAs for any particular region change.

[SAMPLE BALLOT]

BC-STV will produce fair results but not the kind of extreme fragmentation that different proportional systems have promoted in countries such as Israel.

Effective local representation

There are two road blocks to effective local representation in British Columbia. The first is geographic, the second political. BC-STV removes both of these.

Geographic: MLAs are expected to represent their local communities. In British Columbia this can mean providing effective representation for citizens that live in relatively small, densely populated urban areas, or in large, thinly populated rural areas of the province. Those of us from the rural and more remote corners of the province understand the problems that long distances create for participating in public meetings or contacting an MLA.

BC-STV will adapt to different regional needs. Electoral districts in our new system will be organized to reduce these difficulties while ensuring proportionality. In the north and southeast this means adopting districts of two to three members. In the south-central and southwest of the province this means new districts of between four and seven members. The number of members for each region will remain the same; no region will lose representation, but each will contribute to better proportionality.

HOW BC-STV WORKS*

- o   Electoral districts have more than just one MLA.
- o   Voters rank the candidates in the order of their preference—1, 2, 3, 4 etc.
- o   The number of votes needed for election (called the quota) is calculated.
- o   Everyone's first preference vote is counted.

o Any candidates that reach the quota are elected.

o If a candidate has more votes than necessary those votes are not wasted but transferred to the voter's second choice.

o If no one is elected the person with the fewest votes is dropped and their votes transferred to the voter's next preference.

o The process continues until a district has elected all its MLAs.

o Few votes are wasted so most voters make a difference to getting someone elected.

o Because this is a proportional system the number of seats a party wins matches their share of the popular vote.

*A full description of the technical aspects of the proposed system can be found in the section entitled "The Recommended BC-STV Electoral System" in the *Technical Report.*

Political: In our current electoral systems, political parties, not voters, control the way MLAs represent their communities. BC-STV corrects this imbalance by being voter-centred and candidate-focused: to be elected, candidates will need to put communities first.

Greater voter choice

BC-STV increases choices, allowing voters a much greater say in determining who will be their local representatives. It allows voters to choose between candidates and parties, it lets voters show which candidates they prefer and in what order, and it ensures that their preferences count. This will provide increased opportunities for candidates from underrepresented groups.

BC-STV is also the only proportional system that allows independent candidates a real chance to be elected. Although increasingly rare, we believe that independents must have opportunities to participate in our provincial elections equal to candidates who work through political parties.

BC-STV responds to British Columbia's basic values. It provides for fair election results, effective local representation, and greater voter choice, and it best balances these three values of electoral politics. Similar systems have been used successfully—in some cases for decades—to elect members to various positions in Australia, the United Kingdom, and the Republic of Ireland, countries that share our Westminster parliamentary tradition. The Irish government has twice tried to use referendums to abolish STV, but the voters said "No." This is a system designed by voters for voters.

Ballots and by-elections

Ballots in multimember districts can be organized in a number of ways. Because we know that parties play an important role in our parliamentary system, and because some British Columbians will want to vote for a party, we are recommending that candidates be grouped by party on the ballot. However, in order to ensure that no candidate or party benefits from the order that names appear on the ballot, we recommend that both be randomly ordered on individual ballots.

We further recommend that when a legislative seat becomes vacant, the by-election to fill the seat should use the same ballots. Where there is only one seat to be filled, the winning candidate will need to get 50% + one of the votes cast to be elected.

What happens if we adopt BC-STV in BC?

If British Columbians vote to accept the BC-STV electoral system on May 17, 2005, the politics and governance of our province will change.

For some British Columbians it is clear that the greatest change—and the greatest regret—will be the loss of easily achieved majority governments. BC-STV can produce a majority government if a majority of voters vote for one party. While this is possible, the province's history suggests that governments under the new system will likely be a minority or a coalition of two or more parties. This will mean a change in party organization and practices; parties will need to be more responsive to the voters and less adversarial with their opponents and partners.

Our electoral districts will grow geographically under BC-STV, but the number of voters per MLA will not change. Voters will have more than one MLA representing them in Victoria, more than one person to turn to for help. Because each district is likely to elect members from different parties in proportion to the votes cast, voters may well be able to go to an MLA who shares their political views. This will help provide more effective local representation.

Perhaps the most significant change for voters and candidates will strike closer to home. There will be no more "safe seats" that a party can win no matter who it runs as its candidate.

Changes for voters

Voters will have more power. This means voters will make more and different kinds of choices.

For example, voters will be able to consider candidates and parties, rather than simply putting an "X" beside one person's name. Staunch party supporters will be able to rank their party's candidates. Both of these changes will mean that candidates will have to work hard to earn voters' first preference support.

Changes for candidates and MLAs

With the loss of safe seats, no candidate, including sitting MLAs, will be able to count on winning election. Under BC-STV, voters will decide which of a party's several candidates are elected in each district. A party's candidates will compete not only against those in other parties for first preference support, they will also compete against candidates from their own party. Recognizing that they may not be "first preference" on enough ballots to win a seat, candidates will need to encourage supporters of other candidates to mark them as their second or third preference. This need to appeal to a greater number of voters should lower the adversarial tone of election contests: voters are unlikely to respond positively to someone who aggressively insults their first choice.

In order to stand out from other candidates, MLAs will need to clearly represent their districts. This will reinforce effective local representation and encourage MLAs to resist party discipline when it is not in the community's interests. MLAs will have to work harder to ensure that their party's positions reflect their constituents' views.

Changes for parties

Parties will run several candidates in the new multimember electoral districts. This should encourage parties to nominate a diversity of candidates within a district so that they can appeal to the groups and interests that have been underrepresented or ignored in our current "winner-take-all" FPTP system.

Because the voter will have real power in determining who is elected, parties will have a reason to involve more citizens in their organizations and to make their nominating processes more open and accessible. Because legislative caucuses will include MLAs whose continuing electoral success will depend on representing their local communities, regardless of party policies, the pressures of party discipline will decrease. Our politicians will be better able to represent faithfully the interests of our communities, as well as the province as a whole.

And finally, a party's strength in the legislature will reflect its actual support among voters—not more, not less. Having lost the ability to win artificial majorities, parties will have to learn to work together. This will not reduce the competitive character of British Columbia's politics, but it may engender a more consensual style of decision-making in which broad agreement is sought for major policy changes.

Changes for the Legislative Assembly

The most immediate and dramatic change to the Legislative Assembly will be that its power to choose and effectively supervise governments will be restored. The basic theory of our parliamentary system is that governments are chosen by, and are responsible to, the legislature. However, the presence of strictly disciplined parties, enlarged by artificial majorities, has reversed this principle, making the legislature a creature of the government.

BC-STV will end artificial majorities. Governments will need to depend on winning the support of a majority of the legislature and will be able to pass only those laws that a majority of MLAs support.

The Legislative Assembly will adapt to these new realities. MLAs will be more sensitive to local interests, and the concerns and hopes of voters will be more commonly heard in the legislature. At the same time, legislative committees will take on a more important role in debating and deciding important public policy issues.

Changes for provincial governments

The BC-STV system will end majority governments built on a minority of votes. No single party will be able to implement a platform without meaningful public debate in the legislature.

Unless a majority of voters support candidates from one party, future governments will likely be minorities or coalitions of more than one party. Some coalitions will form before elections in the hope of attracting enough votes to gain a majority; others will form when the elected members find out how much support the voters have given them.

Coalition governments, and the more consensual decision-making they require, are normal in most western democracies. The experience of coalition governments in other successful parliamentary systems has been positive and we expect no less from our elected representatives and parties. Governments will depend on members from different parties deciding to work together and making agreements that command broad public support. With BC-STV, the people will get the government they vote for.

[PIE CHART SHOWING THE CHANGE IF BC-STV HAD BEEN IN PLACE IN THE LAST (2001) ELECTION]

In conclusion

We are convinced that British Columbia will improve its practice of democracy by adopting BC-STV. Election results will be fairer, reflecting a balance between votes and seats, voters will have more choice and candidates will work harder to earn their support. Political parties will remain at the centre of the electoral process, but they will give up some of the excesses of party discipline and the adversarial style that alienates many voters. The Legislative Assembly will be strengthened in its ability to hold governments accountable.

No one in the Assembly is so naive as to think that BC-STV will answer every call for change or correct every inequality or inefficiency in our province's political system. We have come to believe, however, that by changing the electoral system we can build a political climate that is more faithful to the values that most British Columbians want as the foundations of our political life.

British Columbians have an unprecedented opportunity to take control of some of the most important rules of democracy. After considering all of the options—including doing nothing—we are convinced that by adopting the BC-STV electoral system the voters will create a system where they, the voters themselves, are closer to the centre of the system. In a democracy, that is what "fair" is about.

Signed (Jack Blaney)
ON BEHALF OF THE 160 MEMBERS OF THE CITIZENS' ASSEMBLY ON ELECTORAL REFORM

Other issues raised by British Columbians

Our mandate as a Citizens' Assembly was focused and clear. This helped us complete the task we were given on time and on budget, and led us to our decision to recommend the BC-STV electoral system.

A number of other issues were also raised by the thousands of British Columbians who spoke to us at public hearings, community meetings and through their formal presentations and submissions. As these issues are beyond our mandate, we deliberately did not engage in sustained debate on them, nor do we presume to make any recommendations or discuss them in detail here. However, the fact that they speak to the deep concern many citizens have for the health of our democracy gives them a place in our second volume, the *Technical Report*. In brief, the nonmandate issues raised in this process were:

- **Enthusiasm for citizen involvement in electoral reform.**
  This discussion reflects both the wide public approval of the government's decision to create a Citizens' Assembly and the importance of encouraging public debate and involvement on issues important to our democracy.

- **Facilities for access to local MLAs.** British Columbians attach a great deal of importance to strong local representation and the need for MLAs to stay in touch with their districts. This is of particular concern in Northern and rural ridings.

- **The role and operation of political parties.** British Columbians recognize the central role of political parties in the democratic process, but believe that more openness and responsiveness —particularly in the nomination process and issues related to parliamentary reform—would help reduce what are often referred to as gaps in the democratic process.

- **Public participation in BC's democracy.** British Columbians are concerned with declining voter turnout and increased public cynicism, believing that we need to build a more participatory political process. A system that fully involves women, First Nations peoples and minorities would make a major contribution to strengthening our province's democracy.

Note from the chair

Never before in modern history has a democratic government given to unelected, ordinary" citizens the power to review an important public policy, then seek from all citizens approval of any proposed changes to that policy. The British Columbia Citizens' Assembly on Electoral Reform has had this power and responsibility and, throughout its life, complete independence from government.

I want to acknowledge this unique gift by first thanking Premier Gordon Campbell for creating the Assembly. While several community leaders promoted the idea, it was the premier, in collaboration with Attorney General Geoff Plant, who took the steps necessary to create and secure the Assembly.

I also want to recognize the role of the provincial legislature. The Terms of Reference, as well as the conditions governing any referendum, were approved by the Legislative Assembly in unanimous votes. Members of our Legislative Assembly united in making history.

The members of the Citizens' Assembly—British Columbians who unstintingly gave their time and energy—demonstrated how extraordinary ordinary citizens are when given an important task and the resources and independence to do it right. Over the eleven-month course of the Assembly, only one of 161 members withdrew and attendance was close to perfect. Their great and lasting achievement is the birth of a new tool for democratic governance.

With an impressive commitment to learning so many new concepts and skills, and with a grace and respect for one another in their discussions that was truly remarkable, the Assembly members demonstrated a quality of citizenship that inspired us all. My deepest thanks and regard go to each and every one of them.

The idea of a citizens' assembly—its unique authority and its importance as a democratic process—clearly exerted a powerful force, attracting highly talented staff, researchers and administrators to its cause. Their work enriched the Assembly's work, and all staff members performed their tasks with exceptional professionalism and integrity. Twelve-hour days, seven days a week were common: they willingly provided anything that the Assembly needed to get the job done and done right. In each session's evaluation Assembly members consistently gave to staff their highest marks.

The facilitators—graduate students in political science from Simon Fraser University and the University of British Columbia—were also exceptional. These outstanding, exemplary colleagues deserve enormous credit for the Assembly's achievements. All Assembly members and staff are indebted to Gordon Gibson. At the government's request, he prepared the Constitution of the Citizens' Assembly on Electoral Reform.

With few variations, we followed Mr. Gibson's clear and sensible plan. And, during the Assembly's tenure, I often consulted Mr. Gibson for his wise, helpful and objective advice.

I also want to thank and recognize the contributions of Harry Neufeld, Chief Electoral Officer, and Linda Johnson, Deputy Chief Electoral Officer, of Elections BC who were essential and very helpful partners throughout the Assembly's work; Neil Reimer, David Winkler and Carol Anne Rolf of the Attorney General's ministry who helped us use government services in ways that supported our independence; members of the Research Advisory Committee from the University of BC, Simon Fraser University and the University of Victoria; community leaders who helped to promote the idea of a citizens' assembly; and the staff of the Delta Vancouver Suites and Morris J. Wosk Centre for Dialogue, who adopted us as a special family.

And the heartiest of thanks to those citizens who attended hearings and made presentations and submissions, and to all British Columbians—your support made possible this wonderful invention in the practice of democracy.

Signed (Jack Nlaney)
JACK BLANEY, CHAIR

[Sections 8, 9, and 11 of the Final Report not included)

Source: Citizens' Assembly (20041)

---

7 Former Premier Bill Bennett's Open Letter

By BILL BENNETT

Open letter to BC Citizens:

On May 17, 2005 British Columbians will be asked to vote twice. Once in the provincial general election. Secondly, on a referendum on electoral reform. It is the second issue that causes me great concern and prompted me to write.

First let me acknowledge the hard work and dedication of the members of the Citizens Assembly in carrying out their duties. Their recommendations on electoral reform will ask British Columbians if they want to change how they elect their Members of the Legislature. With the greatest respect for their effort, I must disagree with their recommendation.

My view is based on both appreciation of our history and hope for our future. Our parliamentary tradition is seated in the tradition of one person equals one vote. A citizen selects a candidate or a party to represent them and votes accordingly. In this proposed system you end up with partial votes determining the outcome because of the complicated counting formula. It allows a few to manipulate the outcome of the majority in favour of biased minorities.

hen you vote on May 17, 2005 think hard about switching to a system that will hobble our Province's bright future. I urge you to VOTE NO!

Yours truly,

Bill Bennett
Premier of BC, 1975-1986

218   *Appendix*

Source: Downtown Eastside (2005)

---

8 Former Premier Dave Barrett's open letter

By DAVE BARRETT

Open letter to BC Citizens:

On May 17, 2005 British Columbians will be asked to vote twice. Once in the provincial general election. Secondly, on a referendum to change our voting system. It is the second issue that causes me great concern and prompts me to write.

The vote on electoral reform will ask British Columbians if they want to change how they elect their Members of the Legislature.

My opinion is based on both appreciation of our history and hope for our future. In BC for over a hundred years we have followed the British Parliamentary system. It is based upon responsibility and accountability. One person—one vote. The citizen is responsible to cast their vote wisely. The person elected is accountable to all the citizens irrespective of their vote.

The proposed system loses this principle because the complicated counting formula replaces clear voter choice with academic theory. Most importantly voters will lose accountability because they will have between two and seven MLA's representing them in huge ridings. On every difficult issue buck passing and finger pointing would replace true representation.

For those reasons when you vote on May 17, 2005 think hard about switching to a system that will hobble our Province's bright future. I urge you to VOTE NO!

Yours truly,

Dave Barrett
Premier of BC, 1972-1975

Source: Downtown Eastside (2005)

SELECT BIBLIOGRAPHY

Amy, D. (2000). *Behind the Ballot Box: A Citizen's Guide to Voting Systems.* New York: Praeger Publishing.

BC Stats. (2005). *2001 Census Profile: British Columbia.* Retrieved August 31, 2006, from http://www.bcstats.gov.bc.ca/data/cen01/profiles/csd_txt.asp

Blais, A. (1991). The Debate over Electoral Systems. *International Political Science Review,* 12(3), pp. 239–260.

Blais, A. & Massicotte, L. (1996). *Comparing Democracies: Elections and Voting in Global Perspective.* Thousand Oaks: Sage Publications.

Blaney, J. (2004). *Introductory Comments.* Paper presented at the January 10, 2004, meeting of the Citizens' Assembly on Electoral Reform, Vancouver, BC.

Boei, W. (2005, April 30). Only a miracle will save STV, Vancouver Sun poll suggests. *The Vancouver Sun,* p. A4.

Brulhart, L. (2004, January 23). Citizens' Assembly is a first for democracy. *Surrey/North Delta Leader,* p. A11.

Butler, C.T.& Rothstein, A. (1991). *On Conflict and Consensus: a handbook on Formal Consensus Decisionmaking .* Portland: Food Not Bombs Publishing.

Carty, K. (2004a). *Political Parties and Party Competition.* In J. Blaney (Chair), Symposium conducted at the meeting of the Citizens' Assembly on Electoral Reform, Vancouver, BC.

Carty, K. (2004b). *What we heard at the public hearings.* In J. Blaney (Chair), Symposium conducted at the meeting of the Citizens' Assembly on Electoral Reform, Prince George, BC.

Citizens' Assembly on Electoral Reform. (2004a). *Shared Values Developed by Assembly, January 10, 2004.* Paper presented at the January 10, 2004, meeting of the Citizens' Assembly on Electoral Reform, Vancouver, BC.

Citizens' Assembly on Electoral Reform. (2004b). *Political Parties and Party Competition.* Paper presented at the January 24, 2004, meeting of the Citizens' Assembly on Electoral Reform, Vancouver, BC.

Citizens' Assembly on Electoral Reform. (2004c). *Proportional Representation (PR-List) Systems.* Paper presented at the February 21, 2004, meeting of the Citizens' Assembly on Electoral Reform, Vancouver, BC.

Citizens' Assembly on Electoral Reform. (2004d). *Electoral Thresholds.* Paper presented at the March 20, 2004, meeting of the Citizens' Assembly on Electoral Reform, Vancouver, BC.

Citizens' Assembly on Electoral Reform. (2004e, March 21). *A preliminary Statement to the People of British Columbia, Spring 2004.* Vancouver: Author.

Citizens' Assembly on Electoral Reform. (2004h, October 22). *STV vs. MMP.* Retrieved October 22, 2004, from http:/www.myassembly.ca/member/phpbb/ viewtopic.php

Citizens' Assembly on Electoral Reform. (2004j). *Record of Proceedings of the Citizens' Assembly on Electoral Reform October 23–24, 2004.* Paper presented at the November 13, 2004, meeting of the Citizens' Assembly on Electoral Reform, Vancouver, BC.

Citizens' Assembly on Electoral Reform. (2004i). *Record of Proceedings of the Citizens' Assembly on Electoral Reform November 13–14, 2004.* Paper presented at the November 27, 2004, meeting of the Citizens' Assembly on Electoral Reform, Vancouver, BC.

Citizens' Assembly on Electoral Reform. (2004l, December). *Making every vote count: the case for electoral reform in British Columbia: Final Report.* Vancouver, BC: Author.

Citizens' Assembly on Electoral Reform. (2004m, December). *Make every vote Count: the case for electoral reform in British Columbia: Technical Report.* Vancouver, BC: Author

Citizens' Assembly on Electoral Reform. (2004n). *CA in Action: Legislative Committee.* Retrieved December 11, 2004, from the Citizens' Assembly website: http://www. Citizensassembly.bc.ca

Citizens' Assembly on Electoral Reform. (2004o). *CA in Action: CA Staff.* Retrieved December 11, 2004, from the Citizens' Assembly website: http://www. Citizensassembly.bc.ca

Citizens' Assembly on Electoral Reform. (2004p). *CA in Action: Assembly Members.* Retrieved December 11, 2004, from the Citizens' Assembly website: http://www. Citizensassembly.bc.ca

Citizens' Assembly on Electoral Reform. (2004q). *History of CA: Assembly Policies and Procedures.* Retrieved December 11, 2004, from the Citizens' Assembly website: http://www. Citizensassembly.bc.ca

Citizens' Assembly on Electoral Reform. (2004r). *Get Involved: Important Dates.* Retrieved December 11, 2004, from the Citizens' Assembly website: http://www. Citizensassembly.bc.ca

Colley, T. (2005, May 25). STV is for losers, so I'm glad the vote failed. *The Now,* p. 8.

Downtown Eastside. (2005, May 6). *C'mon Elder Statesmaen Write Your Own Letters.* Retrived January 8, 2006, from http://downtowneastside. blogspot. com/2005_05 _06 _ downtowneastside_archive.html

Elections British Columbia. (1988). *Electoral History of British Columbia* (Elections BC Publication No. C88-092145-5). Victoria, BC: Chief Electoral Officer of British Columbia

Elections British Columbia. (2002). *Electoral History of British Columbia Supplement, 1987–2001* (Elections BC Publication No. C2002-960118-5). Victoria, BC: Chief Electoral Officer of British Columbia.

Elections Canada. (2001). *Canada's Electoral System* (Elections Canada Publication No. C00-980456-OE). Ottawa, ON: Chief Electoral Officer of Canada.

Elections Canada. (2002). *Representation in the House of Commons of Canada* (Elections Canada Publication No. C2002-9800002-IE). Ottawa, ON: Chief Electoral Officer of Canada.

Electoral Reform Referendum Act, SBC2004, CHAPTER 74 (2004).

Fair Voting BC. (2005). Update. *Fair Voting BC Newsletter, May 21, 2005.* Unpublished.

Farrell, D. M. (2001). *Electoral Systems: A comparative Introduction.* New York: Palgrave

Field, S. (2004, April 21). Electoral reformers will have open minds. *The Vancouver Sun,* p. A19.

Gamage, S. (2006, August 17). Role of Civil Society and a Joint Forum for Durable Peace in Sri Lanka. *Asian Tribune*. Retrieved October 1, 2006, from http:/www.asiantribune.com/index.php?q=node/1600

Great Gift to BC. (2004, December 3). *Citizens' Assembly on Electoral Reform Newsletter*, 1.

Hall, N. (2004, May 1). West Vancouver students juggle election ideas. *The Vancouver Sun*, p. C2.

Hamilton, G. (2005, May 19). B. C. should revisit electoral reform, James says. *The Vancouver Sun*, p. A4.

Herath, R. B. (2002). *Sri Lankan Ethnic Crisis: Towards a Resolution*. Victoria, BC: Trafford Publishing

Hodgson, A. (2005, May 11). Take STV for a test drive. *The Surrey/North Delta Leader*, p. 7.

Interparliamentary Union. (1986). *Parliaments of the World*. New York: Facts on File Publications.

Jackson, R. & Doreen. (1990). *Politics in Canada: Culture, Institutions, Behavior and Public Policy*. Scarborough, ON: Prentice-Hall Canada.

Kaner, S., Lind, L., Toldi, C., Fisk, S., & Berger, D. (1996). *Facilitator's Guide to Participatory Decision-Making*. Philadelphia: New Society Publishers.

Lee, J. (2005, May 19). Voters delivered a message, premier says. *The Vancouver Sun*, p. A4.

Leonard, D. & Natkiel, R. (1986). *World Atlas of Elections: Voting Patterns in 39 Democracies*. London: The Economist Publications.

Lijphart, A. (1999). *Patterns of Democracy: Government Forms and Performance in Thirty-six Countries*. New Haven and London: Yale University Press.

Loenen, N. (1997). *Citizenship and Democracy: A Case for Proportional Representation*. Toronto: Dundurn.

Loenen, N. (2004). *[British Columbia's Citizens' Assembly on Electoral Reform: Its Origin.]* Unpublished raw data.

Mackie, T. T. & Rose, R. (1997). *The International Almanac of Electoral History*. Glasgow, Scotland: Center for the Study of Public Policy, University of Strathclyde.

McInnes, C. (2005a, May 12). If STV fails, it will be years before we get change. *The Vancouver Sun*, p. A15.

McInnes, C. (2005b, June 2). Voters want electoral reform: Campbell and James should just do that. *The Vancouver Sun*, p. A13.

Mickleburgh, R. (2005a, April 18). New voting formula elicits little passion. *Toronto Globe and Mail*, p. S1.

Mickleburgh, R. (2005b, May 13). STV question still baffles most voters. *The Globe and Mail*, p. S1.

Ministry of Attorney General: BC. (2003a, May 12). *Terms of reference of the Citizens' Assembly on Electoral Reform* (OIC 0495-646/2003/13). Victoria, BC: Author.

Ministry of Attorney General: BC. (2003b, May 12). *Duties of the Chair of the Citizens' Assembly* (OIC 0496-645/2003/13). Victoria, BC: Author.

Nagel, J. (2005, May 20). Electoral Reform vote misses mark. *The Surrey/North Delta Leader*, p. 13.

Neiman, G. (2004, April 26). BC gets recognition. *The Nanaimo Daily News*, p. A8.

New Zealand Electoral Referendum Panel. (1992). *The Guide to the Electoral Referendum*. Wellington: New Zealand.

Nordic Research Group (2005). *Over half of British Columbians don't know if BC should change to a Single Transferable Vote (STV) electoral system*. Retrieved July 11, 2005, from http://www.nordicresearch.net/2005-04-15.html

Norris, P. (2004). *Electoral Engineering: Voting Rules and Political Behavior.* Boston: Cambridge University Press.

"Ordinary People' set to reform B. C. elections." (2004, January 12). *The Globe and Mail,* p. A4.

Palmer, V. (2005a, February 22). 'Yes' side looking for millions to promote voting change. *The Vancouver Sun,* p. A3.

Palmer, V. (2005b, April 6). May 17 vote on electoral reform not necessarily the last word, James says. *The Vancouver Sun,* p. A3.

Palmer, V. (2005c, May 20). An overwhelming vote in favour of STV; politicians, now what?. *The Vancouver Sun,* p. A3.

Palmer, V. (2005d, June 18). Electoral Reform? It may not be coming soon, but it's not going away. *The Vancouver Sun,* p. A3.

Reynolds, A. & Reilly, B. (1997). *The International IDEA Handbook of Electoral System Design.* Stockholm, Sweden: International Institute for Democracy and Electoral Assistance.

Sauder School of Business, University of British Columbia (2005). *British Columbia Provincial Election 2005, Opinion Polls.* Retrieved July 11, 2005, from http://esm.ubc.ca/BC05/polls.php

Sept. 11 – Saturday session. (2004, September 15). *Citizens' Assembly on Electoral Reform Newsletter,* 2–3.

Smyth, M. (2005, May 1). Why I support the STV. *The Province,* p. A14.

Spector, N. (2005, April 29). The real danger is that voters just might go for the STV. *The Vancouver Sun,* p. A19.

Statistics Canada. (2005). *Study: Canada's visible minority population in 2017. (The Daily of March 22, 2005).* Retrieved June 22, 2005, from http:// dissemination.statcan.ca/ Daily/English/050322/d050322b.htm

Tieleman, B. (2005, February 10). Democracy Denied with STV Propaganda. *Georgia Straight,* p. 12.

The Newspaper's View: With so many flaws in the current system, it's time to try BC-STV. (2005, May 7). *The Vancouver Sun,* p. C6.

With so many flaws in the current system, it's time to try BC-STV. (2005, May 7). *The Vancouver Sun,* p. C6.

Veldhuis, N. & Clemens, J. (2004, May 6). Limits on government spending should be tied to electoral reform. *The Vancouver Sun.* p. A11.

Website milestone. (2004, October 5). *Citizens' Assembly Electoral Reform Newsletter,* 1.

Wikipedia (2005). *British Columbia electoral reform referendum, 2005.* Retrieved July 11, 2005, from http://en.wikipedia.org/wiki/British_Columbia_electoral_reform _referendum,_2005

Willcocks, P. (2005, May 14). Don't let chance to make politics work better slip away. *The Vancouver Sun,* p. C7.

INDEX

About the author

R.B. HERATH is a professional engineer, author, poet and a dramatist, who holds a Ph.D. in organizational behaviour. As an adult, he has always fought for the democratic rights of the people. He did this first as a student leader in his high school and university days, and later as an active participant in the national politics of his country of origin, Sri Lanka; once he cofounded and led a political party in that country by the name Podujana Party (meaning Peoples' Party). It was a nonviolent, centrist party that stood for democracy and consensus among all ethnic groups in Sri Lanka under a theme of *'One Lanka–One Nation, One Nation–One Family.'* After the ongoing ethnic crisis of Sri Lanka turned to a separatist war, taking control of its democratic political process, he left the country in 1984. He is well traveled, and has lived in many countries in Asia, Europe, Africa and North America. He has an excellent knowledge of the international scene. Presently, he lives in Canada.

In 1989, while he was in Zambia he wrote and directed a stage drama, *Angulimala*, depicting a story from Buddhist literature. Later he wrote and directed three other stage dramas based on historical political events of Sri Lanka: *Hoisting the British Flag, Keppetipola Heroism, and Independence Struggle*. These dramas were presented at the 50th Sri Lankan Independence anniversary celebrations held at Michael J. Fox Theatre in Burnaby, British Columbia, on March 7, 1998.

His earlier writings include four books, two in English and two in a Sri Lankan vernacular language, Sinhalese. One of the books in Sinhalese, *Sri Lanka Desapalanaya, Ayanna, Aayanna, Eyanna, Eeyanna* (translation reads as A, B, C, D of Sri Lankan Politics), analyses the contemporary political system of Sri Lanka. The other book he wrote in Sinhalese, *Desappremayen Odavadiwa Darudariyanta Kavivalinma Liyu Lipiyak* (translation reads A Letter to Our Children in Poems Written through Patriotism) is a book of poems. It conveys a message of love, mutual respect and unity to the children of Sri Lanka in a child's diction. The government of Sri Lanka purchased and distributed copies of this book to schools and municipal libraries.

The author's latest publication, *Sri Lankan Ethnic Crisis: Towards a Resolution* (Trafford, 2002), discusses the ongoing ethnic crisis in Sri Lanka and proposes a co-coordinated political solution to the crisis with a realistic plan of action for its implementation. The Honourable Bill Graham, Minister of Foreign Affairs, Canada, reviewed the book and forwarded it to others concerned, including the Canadian High Commissioner in Sri Lanka (www.rbherath.com).

In Canada, the author first served as a member of the Board of Directors of the South Asian Network for Secularism and Democracy (SANSAD) for a number of years. Later, he had the distinction of serving as a member of the historic Citizens' Assembly on Electoral Reform in British Columbia (BC). He believes that the BC Citizens' assembly has provided a template for a new, revolutionary approach to the practice of democracy throughout the world. He is married and has three grown daughters.